FORMING THE FUTURE

Jack O'Toole

This book is dedicated to my three sons, Curt, Sean, and Derek, who have been the true treasures in my life; to Nancy, for without her this book never would have been written; and to Miss Eleanor for all the editing and constant encouragement.

FORMING THE FUTURE

Lessons from the Saturn Corporation

Jack O'Toole

BLACKWELL
Publishers

The right of Jack O'Toole to be identified as author of this work has been asserted in accordance with the Copyright, Designs and Patents Act 1988.

First published 1996

Blackwell Publishers, Inc.
238 Main Street
Cambridge, Massachusetts 02142
USA

Blackwell Publishers, Ltd.
108 Cowley Road
Oxford OX4 1JF
UK

Library of Congress Cataloging–in–Publication Data

O'Toole, Jack, 1944-
    Forming the future: lessons from the Saturn Corporation / Jack O'Toole.
    p.   cm.
    ISBN 1-55786-836-0
    1. Industrial relations – United States – Case studies.
2. Automobile industry workers – United States – Case studies.
3. International Union, United Automobile, Aerospace, and Agricultural Implement Workers of America. 4. Saturn Corporation – Employees. I. Title.
HD6976.A82U556   1996
331'.04292222--dc20   96-7504
                                                              CIP

British Library Cataloguing in Publication Data

A CIP catalogue record for this book is available from the British Library.

Composition by Megan H. Zuckerman.

Printed in the USA by BookCrafters.

This book is printed on acid-free paper.

TABLE OF CONTENTS

FOREWORD

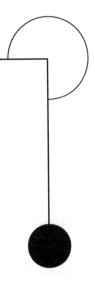

Saturn was conceived during one of the most difficult periods in the history of the American auto industry. All Big Three automobile companies had lost market share and employment was reduced by 30-60% from the 1979 levels. Many felt that American workers could not compete with the Japanese, particularly in manufacturing small cars. This book describes in detail the role the UAW workers themselves played in creating and building, not just a competitive product, but a high-quality winner in every way.

When General Motors advised the union in June 1983 that an engineering study was under way to design a new product to compete in this market as well as a new plant in which to build such a car, it was indeed encouraging news. Therefore, when Al Warren, vice president of General Motors, asked if the union would be interested in studying how to manage such a facility as well as the people systems, using the same "clean sheet of paper" approach, the response was a resounding, "Yes!" As union leaders we of the UAW had a great interest in saving jobs and becoming competitive without reducing the members' standard of living. This was the definition of competitiveness adopted by the Presidential Commission on Industrial Competitiveness, on which I served.

A committee of six was suggested to perform the huge task of studying how to manage such a plant. We knew we had talented people, knowledgeable in all phases of auto production, but we could not agree to allow a committee of only six to take on the full responsibility for so extensive a study. A committee of 99 resulted. The committee did exhaustive research both in the United States and abroad. Its report was a masterpiece and was completed in a relatively short time with the help of a very effective facilitator who worked in GM's Organization Development section, Keith Brooke. The manner in which this joint committee, from all across GM, performed its task was a great indicator of what could be accomplished by working together.

We had some experience with participation both at Ford and GM with our earlier efforts in Q.W.L. (quality of work life) and employee involvement but nothing like the massive undertaking at Saturn, which this book describes so well. Our faith in the membership was rewarded in dramatic fashion. There was also a enormous need for leadership in this tremendous undertaking. The author of this book, Jack O'Toole, describes the key role played by members of the UAW staff as well as GM managers.

During 1984 negotiations between the UAW and GM, Roger Smith agreed to ask the Board of Directors for the money to go forward with Saturn if the parties could translate the study committee report into a labor agreement. This was accomplished during the summer of 1985. As soon as the agreement was approved by GM and the Executive Board of the UAW, the decision to build the facility in Tennessee was announced. An immediate outcry opposed the agreement, coming from the "right to workers" and some critics in the union. It was amazing to see these two opposite groups making the same argument.

Because of cash flow problems along the way, the facility at Spring Hill was reduced in size, with plans to complete the Phase II portion later on. This has never been done and this failure severely strained the ability to be profitable, with only half the planned capacity and most of the overhead that would have been involved if the total 500,000 car capacity had been constructed.

The overwhelming success of this operation is a magnificent tribute to all the people involved at Saturn and the leadership of people like

Skip LeFauve, Bill Hoglund, the two presidents of Saturn, as well as UAW staff and local union leaders like Dick Hoalcraft and Mike Bennett and, in the earlier phases, staff like Joe Malotke and Jerry Mills.

Of course, many in the GM management thought and hoped Saturn would fail. They wanted the money for their own projects and were concerned that others would succeed in a competitive field where they had failed. Only the persistence of the chairman, Roger Smith, made it possible for Saturn to be completed.

This book is a remarkable history from an insider's perspective of the blood, sweat, and tears that made this unprecedented achievement a reality. Every member of the Committee of 99 would have a slightly different view of how things were accomplished. Jack O'Toole played a key role in the development and the operation of this different kind of company.

This is his story, told in a delightful fashion. I believe it is a valuable contribution to labor-management history as only a participant could tell it. This is not theory – this is history. Jack was not only involved from the earliest phases of the study committee but has played several different and challenging roles in the planning and implementation for starting production, in the production process, and in administering some of those highly unique people programs.

My only disappointment in Saturn is in what has not been done. With its great success, one would think others would have pioneered other, similarly new and exciting concepts. The only way we can preserve the American standard of living, as we know it, is to be daring and innovative. While I am extremely proud of Saturn, I would be delighted to see a Pluto or Uranus being built in America to further utilize the skill and talents of the American work force in yet another demonstration of the value of working together to achieve common goals rather than sharing an ever-shrinking economic pie.

Donald F. Ephlin
Vice President/Director
UAW/GM Department – Retired

PREFACE

O ver the last hundred years, very few people have helped build a car company from the ground up. Jack O'Toole, in my opinion, is one of them. The hopes and dreams of one of the ninety-nine men and women who helped create the Saturn Vision, would become America's hopes and dreams – hopes and dreams of helping General Motors return to its preeminent first class global competitive position – hopes and dreams of leading the American auto industry back to helping Americans capture their American dream through the distribution of wealth and good paying jobs. This Saturn story is a real story of those hopes and dreams and how difficult it is to overcome the inertia of mediocrity.

Michael E. Bennett
President, UAW Local 1853

The purpose of this book is to look at the forming and growth of a multibillion dollar corporation from a union person's perspective. This corporation was formed through a revolutionary partnership between union and management. During prosperous times, corporations are created by venture capitalists, structured under scientific management principles, and driven by Marquis de Sade managers who force working

men and women into unions – if these workers are to retain any sliver
of dignity or self-respect.

The project described here was undertaken in the early 1980s, when
times were bad, losses were nearing the billion dollar mark, and layoffs
were in the hundreds of thousands. Necessity being the mother of
invention, the largest corporation in the world, General Motors, finally turned inward in the hope of grasping back its former greatness. That
inward turn resulted in the most controversial decision made since Billy
Durant formed the corporation back at the turn of the century. The
decision was based on the vision of ordinary working people – not the
leaders of boardrooms. And, this decision showed the world that the
greatest vision of all is the insight that comes from allowing workers to
manage their own destiny. The decision resulted in the Saturn
Corporation.

THE GENESIS

> If you always do what you've
> always done – you'll always get
> what you've always gotten.
>
> Author Unknown

1

This is a very simplistic statement but very true. Unfortunately, too many leaders in American labor and management, including General Motors, believe that you can keep doing what you've always done, but you will get different results if only the other side will change.

The "other side" includes the union, where workers are organized, and the workers alone if they are unorganized; the government; the retailers or wholesalers; the suppliers; even the competition – but never ourselves. We're not the problem; the problem is over there, or there, or there! Alas, that very thought is the problem.

Through its years of grandeur, when "what was good for GM was good for the country" and every car GM built was sold, the only real costs of concern were the variables, and the largest variable cost of all was the employees. The managers who best controlled variable costs went swiftly up the corporate ladder – while the union leader who saved the most jobs went swiftly up the labor ladder. Tragically caught between these respective ascensions were the people I chose to join.

Ironically, I came from an all management family: father, mother, and five brothers and sisters – all were in the ranks of the ruling class. That was to be my calling, too. For my parents, like theirs, wanted a "better" life for their children than they had managed to eke out for themselves. But, alas, I heard a different drum, with a sound so low, at first, it could have been a heartbeat; but year by year it grew louder, as though beckoning me to a place and time I knew not where. It was akin to a quote from Freud: "The voice of the intellect is a soft one, but it does not rest until it has gained a hearing. Ultimately, after endless rebuffs, it succeeds. This is one of the few points by which one may be optimistic about the future of mankind." So, endlessly, it droned on, as I moved from plant to plant, learning the system of the adversaries. Yet, somehow I knew there had to be a better way! That never-ending cycle of winners and losers must have a chink somewhere that offered hope for "my children."

The early 1970s brought a single ray of light on a bleak and dark horizon – Q.W.L., but, this too, became just another tool in the arsenal of the adversaries. Quality of Work Life was the "legal" term in the UAW/GM national agreement when first introduced in 1973. However, it remained just "words" for several contracts. Then, when implementation was finally undertaken, Q.W.L. had two totally different meanings in the vocabularies and behaviors of the two adversaries!

To managers it became Quantity of Work Load and to the labor leaders it remained Quality of Work Life, but nothing ever materialized to improve the working person's life. It turned out to be just another attempt to increase how hard or fast one worked; that is, quantity of work load. The really ironic thing about Q.W.L. was that the people it really affected the most, the first-line foremen, were the last to know about it – and, even worse, they had to implement it. It eventually became another fine example of bureaucracy at its finest. "Take this program, that will eliminate your job, and make it work. By the way, we'll get your input if you can't make it work, but not until!" So it went, as it seemed, the newest program of the month.

The next phase of futility was the Employee Participation Group Intervention, or E.P.G. for short. Again, almost to the tune of "I'll walk with you again, darling," the E.P.G.s were supposed to further denigrate the first-line foreman's responsibility and authority. Yet, by this "grandiose design," they were to implement their own extinction and not reluctantly but with great vigor! To help the first line was the second line, the general foreman or G.F. In summary, the G.F.'s job under this new program was to help the foremen eliminate their jobs and hold onto the minute strand of hope that this stupid change movement would stop at all those generally ineffective foremen. For everyone knew that, if the foremen did their jobs, the G.F.'s job wouldn't be so difficult. How tragic! The general foremen didn't even realize that their own jobs were in greater jeopardy than those of the foremen they were dissolving with impunity!

Saturn Corporation's roots come from the premise that we can't keep doing what we've always done and get different results – for that is called insanity. So the quest began to explore ways to do things differently in building a world-class quality, competitively priced small car. We knew we had the technology needed, but we also, finally, realized that technology wasn't enough. The union and management had to work together if we really wanted to compete successfully over a sustained period of time.

On February 5, 1984, a bitterly cold Detroit night, 100 strangers from a cross section of GM and the UAW came together to undertake the most revolutionary study in the history of the auto industry. One of these 100 strangers said, "I don't like this" and went home, thereby creating the "committee of 99" that would ultimately present its radical "breakaway" recommendations to the corporation and the UAW International Union.

I could wax on in minute detail about all the events that led up to February 5, 1984, but that is not my purpose. I would rather explore the "breakaway thinking" approach that has been the cornerstone of Saturn's development. It all started with a mission and a philosophy. In retrospect, It really didn't seem at the time – a blinding flash of the obvious – but it since has become clear that the use of Professor Richard Walton's Bull's-Eye Model as the basic building block of how the "99" would study the best companies in the world was the catalyst that unleashed the greatest synergistic answer of the decade, if not the century, to union/management relationships.

3

FORMING THE FUTURE

That an organization should be founded on a mission (what would *not* happen if it didn't exist) "led" by its philosophy, or how it would achieve its mission, was not a new approach. Many organizations had been founded with a mission and philosophy prior to the "99" study and many since that cold and bleak February night in Detroit. However, it is almost ironic that this group of strangers from every strata of the world's largest and virtually leaderless corporation would be the Phoenix that would rise from the ashes with the solution for the transformation of labor and management relations in America.

For this diverse group of union and management representatives, the *why* was so strong that it made them *want* very much to do the work they were charged to do. The appropriate phrase to apply to this project is "No force is greater than an idea whose time has come." Could the answer have come from three or four individuals, who would then try to sell it to their respective organizations? Or was it an answer whose real meaning lay in "living" the quest? Of the three resources in any company – the physical, financial, and human – the last is the only one that can positively influence the other two. Let us explore these queries and many more as we unravel the Forming of the Future!

4

THE STUDY

Tell me, I'll forget;
show me, I might remember;
but involve me, and I'll understand.

Author Unknown

2

That first night in Detroit at the Renaissance Center was a precursor of events to come, but that fact remained obscure until much later in the fall of 1984. So there we were – 100 people – from all across General Motors and the United Automobile Workers. Only a handful of us had any idea of what we were there to do, and those who were supposed to know weren't sure of what was supposed to happen. A steering committee of three GM managers, three UAW officials, and one process consultant from the GM Organizational Research and Development staff was commissioned to orchestrate this study by Don Ephlin, director of the GM Department of the UAW and Al Warren, vice president of GM Industrial Relations. This committee was a direct result of an overture Al Warren made to Don Ephlin to ascertain his willingness to respond to an engineering study. The study pointed out to GM that, "technologically," the corporation could competitively build a small car in the United States, but from a labor relations perspective, GM was decidedly uncompetitive. Al's overture to Don was initially proposed somewhat like this, "Don, why don't you get three of your guys, and I'll get three of my guys, and we'll send them off to see

5

what they can find out?" To which Don – in one of his many, many examples of vision – replied, "Well Al, you don't have three guys that smart and neither do I, so let's open it up to the people who really understand what's wrong with our system!"

So we came together, 100 strangers, from 55 GM plants and 41 UAW locals, drinking cocktails and talking about our individual answers to the question, "Why are we here?" We didn't know who was management or who was union – initially. Speculation ran unbridled that cold February night. We talked; we laughed; we figured out who was who – labor or management – and then, as is typical, according to Morris Massey – "you are what you were when" – we separated into two distinct herds!

There was an occasional but very infrequent, foray into each other's territory, for our memories of distrust and opposition ruled the night. Our history is part of our memory and our potential is part of our imagination, but we didn't understand this yet. I don't know if it was premonition, wishful thinking, imagined potential, or just plain relief at getting away from the monotony of never-changing Flint Metal Fab that had my senses piqued, but I felt something that night – unlike anything I'd ever felt in my life. I knew deep inside me something special would come from this assembly of strangers in the night.

The study really began February 6, when we all converged on the Renaissance Center ballroom and the "clean sheet of paper" approach was explained to us. We were shown our mission – to explore ways to integrate people and technology to manufacture small cars in the United States as developed by the six-person steering committee. We were also given our philosophy: We believe that all people want to be involved in decisions that affect them, care about their jobs, take pride in their accomplishments, and want to share in the success of their efforts. No one in the crowd really understood the importance of these two statements that day. They would have a substantial impact on all our lives, down the road; but that day, they were just nice words.

We were oriented to how we must work over the next three months. Each of us was assigned to one of the seven teams, which were organized according to the engineering systems of an automobile. Each team was assigned a "process consultant," a skilled facilitator to help us

6

work the process we were being exposed to that week. At the conclusion of the orientation week, each of the subcommittees, ranging from 6 to 15 members, developed its own mission and philosophy using the process we were to live by for the entire study.

What a strange sound was the murmur of the herds! No voting! Consensus on all decisions! Conflict management where you shared *everything* you knew! No "designated" leader! This strange Bull's-Eye Model! A clean sheet of paper! Go wherever you want, and see whoever you want! Have a report ready to present the last week of the study! Did they really expect some order to come out of this apparent chaos by design? Well, yes, they did. For the "they" were the six-person steering committee. Three were from management: Ray McGarry, Neil DeKoker, and Dick Huber. Three were from labor: Joe Malotke, Buck Orvig, and Ed Raby. To support the committee was a simply brilliant consultant from the GM Organizational Development staff: Keith Brooke.

I think that cognitively they expected order, only because so many orderly people were in the study. But Keith felt deep in his soul that, if given unbridled freedom, the greatest human need – the need to be understood – would bring not only order but a new order of things. Keith really believed that, given the right environment, the right timing, the right opportunity, all the negative energy in both herds would blend into positive synergy that had no physical or spiritual boundaries. He shared this belief with the steering committee in such a way that, whether they saw it or not, they could say, "Why not?" After all, it's only a "study," but not everyone has to see the vision at the same time. they need only be willing to see the vision when it finally gets through the screens of their belief windows.

Keith knew that the greatest vision in the world is insight, not hindsight or foresight. For Keith himself started in one herd and ended up in the other, but he remembered what it was like when he started. He learned along the way that antagonism can be our ally. It will steel our nerves and sharpen our wits if we manage it and not allow it to manage us. He also knew that, if we put qualified people in charge of something and have the wisdom to stay out of their way, they will surprise us with their ingenuity. So then, who could be more qualified than the people from our plants – the artists of the auto industry. Our leaders

7

kept telling us they knew why it didn't work, but why then couldn't they correct it? The artists of the auto industry knew. As an artist, you don't see things as they "really" are. For if you do, you cease to be an artist. So let them paint the mural of the future, Keith convincingly told Don and Al and the steering committee. For after all, it was only a study!

So off they went, these 99 artists in seven subcommittees – armed with their mission and philosophy, a facilitator, a week of guidelines, 86 years of history, and imagination, fettered only by themselves. Each team went through Cog's Ladder, the stages of development that universally binds all teams. The first stage involved being polite. In this stage all are nice to each other; no one makes waves. I don't know about all the subcommittees; but mine, Metal Fabricating and Body Shop #2, stayed in this stage about an hour. Each subcommittee was at liberty to go anywhere and see anything, and the ability to do this was at their discretion, along with the responsibility that goes with it. So our first planning session went something like this: The general superintendent from Willow Run, Bob Moran, said, "Delbert, why don't you make travel arrangements; and "Jack, why don't you call these plants and why don't you do this and you do that..." Then, I said, "Wait a minute, who died and made you king?" At which, the other management guys said, "Wait a minute, Bob's just trying to get things organized!" To which my other union brothers replied, "Yeah, the way you guys organize everything – screwed up!" At this, our process consultant – the lovely, bright, and incredibly naive, Laurie Danko – replied, "Come on you guys, we've got to work together for the next couple of months!" Surprisingly, both herds responded almost simultaneously, "Butt out, Laurie!"

This process lasted several hours, during which our ancestry respectively was questioned – to the extent of whether our parents were married at the time of our births! So we progressed from the "polite" stage through the "what are we here for" stage. In a couple of hours, we were firmly ensconced in the "bid for power" stage, which lasted for the next several hours, where the herds were clearly identified and jockeyed for position. By the end of the day, we had progressed to the "performing" stage, where we became serious about accomplishing something. This was all rather remarkable when you consider I'd been on teams in the past that took weeks to progress from the first stage to the second, and months to move out of the third. We had successfully maneuvered our way to the fourth in one day, which could be interpreted several ways: (1) we had a large degree of talent in this team; (2) we were merely living out our expected roles; (3) we had an exceptional process consultant; (4) we were serious about doing something different; or, (5) all of the above.

As I look back, it was definitely number five, and I'm not sure if any of us really understood why at the time. But again, I think we somehow sensed that what we were doing was going to be special. We proceeded to choose roles to everyone's satisfaction: the travel arranger, the site selectors, the lead questioner, and so on. We had to leave the Renaissance Center the next day, Friday, to go back home; so we decided where we would set up shop the following Monday and took off.

When I got home that Friday evening, my wife asked me what I thought of this study. I'll never forget what I told her, "What we are doing will be historic." At which she responded, "That remains to be seen!" I didn't consider it unusual, at the time, but as I've progressed through these 10 years at Saturn, the same thought that she expressed has been repeated by others every step of the way. It seems to be almost an American thought through the 1980s and early 1990s – until I see, I won't believe!

The next Monday, we met at the Georgian Inn on the east side of Detroit, and we set out to organize ourselves for the quest : Gary Bloss, Bob Moran, Jack Glozier, Bill Green, Darryl Fraley, Delbert Person, Ron Leonard, Jeff Fraize, Laurie Danko, and I.

Gary Bloss was a career personnel type from Buick headquarters in Flint, Michigan. At first glimpse, you would think you had just met John Saxon – with light hair. Always impeccably dressed, Gary's dominant persona was one of aloofness and closely guarded emotion. Once you got past this gruff veneer though, you would find a caring, humorous person whose guarded style was but the result of the non-rep political environment he was in, as well as his career in the adversarial wars.

Bob Moran was a general superintendent from the Willow Run Assembly Plant in Michigan. He was young, bright, and upwardly mobile, being on a GM fast track program. He was very Irish, with the typical dancing eyes, disarming smile, and sharp wit. He, too, like all the non-reps was very guarded in what he revealed about himself, until you developed a rapport with him. Bob was very bright and opinionated but also would look openly at any possibility.

Jack Glozier was a skilled tradesman from my plant, Chevrolet Metal Fab in Flint, Michigan. His uncle was on the shop committee, and he came into the study a bit skeptical. He possessed the left-brained logical, analytical mind so prevalent in tradesmen and struggled initially with the right-brained creativity assignment we were charged with completing. He was a very honest, caring person who worked tirelessly toward our goals.

Bill Green was a long-term committeeman from Kansas City. He was inordinately quiet, but listened acutely. Many felt that his quiet demeanor was merely the outward manifestation of an internal lack of buy-in to our task. I talked with Bill a great deal, and that was not the case. He came from a very confrontational environment, and it took time for his trust to rise to a level where he felt comfortable to actively contribute.

Darryl Fraley was a non-rep planner from Hamilton, Ohio. With an engineering background, he came to our subcommittee garbed with a finely tuned left brain as well. He also was girded, like many of us, with an adversarial place of employment. As nonrevealing as Gary Bloss was initially, he warmed well to the task before us. He showed great insight into research – so critical in our quest.

Delbert Person was the youngest of our group and hailed from Oldsmobile in Lansing. Before being employed by GM, he had an extensive association with the UAW, as his mother was on the International UAW staff. Delbert, at first, was overly respectful of the experience in our group, but soon got by that and brought a wonderfully free-thinking mind, uncorrupted by years in the adversarial wars.

Ron Leonard was an engineer from the Delco Morraine Truck Plant in Dayton, Ohio. A truly decent, honest man, who really cared about people, as well as an accomplished engineer, he possessed the most remarkable, "trivia-loaded" mind any of us had ever encountered. No matter where we went during the study, he would tell everyone little known tidbits about the city, county, state, or company we were visiting. This trait would prove to be very stimulating during the long hours of our quest.

Jeff Fraize was from the Framingham Assembly Plant just outside of Boston, Massachusetts. He was a utility man in the body shop of a plant that had a long history of autocratic managers and militant labor leaders. Very aloof and mistrusting of the non-reps in our team, he and I almost immediately struck a bond. He brought insightful knowledge of how a plant should not be run and became an excellent contributor on what a plant could be.

Laurie Danko was the process consultant for our subcommittee during the study. She was from Pontiac Motors in Pontiac, Michigan, and worked on organizational development there. Not having grown up in the auto industry, Laurie brought a naiveté that was very refreshing, especially during our many brainstorming sessions on our vision development.

Bob M. suggested and we all agreed to the Chevrolet Pontiac Cadillac (C.P.C.) headquarters, where he knew we could get a war room to "brainstorm" our approach to this clean sheet of paper. We took dead aim on our Bull's-Eye Model and proceeded to list what everyone would ideally like to see if we took the roof off in this new order of things we were going to create. We used the mission and philosophy at the core and then systematically coursed our way out through the various rings being so cleverly creative, we thought! We were stretching so much, we thought, as we covered the walls with ideas for the future.

What a surprise we had when we made our first visit! We decided to take our futuristic ideas and build on them by examining close-up some real-world practices. We chose to look inside GM first. and then branch out to other industries, service organizations, academia, and government. So we went to our first learning opportunity, the Detroit assembly plant called Poletown. It received its name from being carved out of the Polish community of Hamtramck. Needless to say, selecting the site for this megaplant stirred up a lot of emotion, which we would later remember when we did the Saturn site search. Most of the emotion was negative, due to the displacement of many blocks of homes that had

11

been in families for generations. However, for the sake of jobs, taxes for the city, and especially for the good of the "General," this monolith to the future of the auto industry was constructed.

Into the bowels of this beast we went, armed with our futuristic pages of ideas so creatively and cleverly produced, only to find out that all of our ideas already were being implemented or planned to be implemented. What an "ah-ha" that was! This was the first of many instances in which we learned that we were too constricted in our thinking, too contained in our creativity, too locked into our ideas! Our thinking, molded by years of solid reductionist training and left-brain regimentation, had left us to replicate what we already knew; we just called it something different. This was our maiden voyage on the trip to systems thinking. We were genuinely demoralized by the time we got back to our war room at the GM Tech Center, which we endearingly called the Puzzle Palace. Where had we gone wrong? How had our collective minds been so restricted? We realized, when we set out to cover the walls with fresh ideas, that we had been conditioned by our schools and our companies to seek only what we thought we could get. After all, the system would allow you to go only so far. You might "fall off the end of the corporation."

This time we truly brainstormed – no evaluation, just throw out ideas and chart them, combine them, build off each other's ideas, and sort them out when we were done. What a difference that trip to Poletown had made! We had left the beaten path and were about to make our own trail!

Every trip after Poletown was viewed through the eyes of what could be, not what already was. Our "new-eyed" view forced us to take a fresh look at all aspects of automotive manufacturing. It brought us to the GM Truck and Bus Detroit Assembly Plant; Joseph Lamb, the designer and supplier of automotive automation systems; GMAD Janesville Assembly Plant; the Corvette Plant in Bowling Green, Kentucky; Packard Electric Wiring Harness Plant in Brookhaven, Mississippi; Rochester Products Carburetor Plant in Tuscaloosa, Alabama; Buick Plant 81 in Flint that produced torque converters; and Pontiac Fiero Assembly in Pontiac, Michigan. We did in-depth interviews and research on Japanese systems with Dr. Vladimir Pucik from the University of Michigan. We studied operations at the Volkswagen

Assembly in Westmoreland, Pennsylvania; Volvo Headquarters for Automated Carrier Systems in Troy, Michigan; the American Productivity Center in Houston, Texas; Hewlett-Packard in California; and the GM/Toyota joint venture NUMMI Assembly Plant in Fremont, California. We collectively read everything published about philosophy, goal setting, technology, job design and layout, building high-performance work units, organizational structures, changing roles, reward system development, information systems, symbols in an organization, recruitment and selection systems, orientation and training, and personnel guidelines. We talked with leaders from Saab, Kawasaki, and IBM. We viewed miles of videotape on Japanese manufacturing operations, human resource development, quality, marketing, and their complex *kieretsu* system. That last brainstorming session had given us such a boost in viewing everything we saw with a why-not approach.

Two leaders had emerged in our group, Bob Moran from the management side and me from the union side. We were informal leaders, for our guidelines of consensus prohibited use of power, or voting; so we had to rely on our respectively persuasive communication skills. Both of us, being of Irish descent, could tell people to go to hell in such a way they would look forward to taking the trip. We made them feel that they would be in heaven a half hour before the devil knew they were dead! There we were – from different sides of the tracks – steering a locomotive of change down the rails of the future. We both came to the same conclusion about a week into our study – after calling many, supposedly world class, organizations – all the subcommittees were pursuing the same organizations!

So the call from Bob and me went out to our illustrious steering committee. We need to send someone from each committee to meet periodically to coordinate who was going where and when, so we wouldn't appear to those we were courting as Keystone Cops. Bob and I, and not to our surprise, were designated to represent our group at the main committee meetings that were scheduled every two weeks for the duration of the quest. This main committee was a tremendous learning experience for both Bob and me, as well as those from other committees. As we looked at who was going where and why, some interesting patterns started to emerge. We were pursuing only those that were very visible; those that were in the press or were being popularized as duplicates of the "Pacific Rim innova-stealers!" At our first highly emotional, orally pontificated, severely verbally invective meetings, we came to the agreement that from this day forward, we would not approach the same individual facilities of these paragons of success but would, instead, seek out those that aligned the closest to our subcommittee's engineering system. That stroke of genius completed, we then undertook the task of coming up with the single most important decision of the study – the precursor of how Saturn Corporation would be built – the design of how our individual reports would be formatted: the rings of the "Bull's Eye." Little did we know that this decision would ultimately become the rings of Saturn!

"On the road again" – intuitive Willie unknowingly wrote this song for us – onward, under the beautiful spacious skies, across the amber waves of grain, over tops of purple mountain majesties, searching for that key to change. The main committee meetings became more valuable as the quest went on, until that day in March, when after thousands of hours of study and hundreds of thousands of miles of travel across North America, it became obvious to everyone, but the steering committee, that we needed to leave the continent. These seven semi-autonomous committees came to the same conclusion. We needed to see Europe and Japan firsthand. Innumerable articles, lectures, videotapes, and academic studies by the hundreds were created by those who had seen firsthand these territories of innovation; but we had come to understand that of true value in creating a vision is seeing it in the first person, smelling it separately and together, tasting it with the tongues of change, and feeling it in our empathetic hearts!

So the plea went out to the steering committee. If this were truly a clean sheet of paper, then we couldn't fill it up appropriately without a trek across the ponds of change. What a test of the commitment of the sanctioners! Was this truly a search for innovation or merely a boxed-in lesson in compliance to the status quo? Ah, but how this battle united those six steering committee members – all saying in unison that the cost was too great for the knowledge to be gained. "For after all, hadn't we watched the videotapes and read the beautiful and informative prose of those academics and managers who had been there already?" Herein lay the singular, most important decision of the entire quest! We persisted eloquently trying to convince the main committee, extolling the need to see it "together," and conversely the steering committee laid down many a pragmatic reason, including cost exceeding the value of such an endeavor. In the end, the decision was one born of synergy – the whole being greater than the sum of its parts. For, when the decision was ultimately reached, neither side had proposed what the correct answer turned out to be. Instead of each subcommittee traversing the Atlantic, we consensed on two from each subcommittee to take this "first step of a thousand mile journey."

Along about this time, Don E. and Al W. were asked by Roger S. and Owen B., "What are they doing?" "We don't know." "When will you find out?" "When they are ready to tell us!"

The site visits to Sweden and Germany were very educational, especially in light of their glaring differences. While both believed in automation, Volvo was automated but blended their automation with people in an optimal way. They looked for ways that people could be influential in making the process more effective and efficient. Volkswagen, on the other hand, in their Golf plant especially, had utilized automation in place of people. They had the lowest ratio of people to machinery anywhere in the world. The few technicians that were in the plant spent the majority of their time keeping all the equipment running, thereby allowing little time or incentive to make improvements. The contrast between the two that struck me the most was the glaring difference in their approaches to work. I believe it had a great deal to do with their national cultures, but it was blindingly obvious. Volvo spent untold hours and dollars in an attempt to make the assembly of an automobile as easy as it could make it for those who were building its product. VW chose to put its hours and dollars on repetitive tasks, seemingly ignoring all the data that give this method very low quality ratings, especially in a mass production mode. VW believed that compliance by workers would attain their goal, while Volvo believed that involvement of workers would lead to a better end.

A side benefit of this trip to Europe came in the bonding that took place. We all had experienced significant bonding in our respective subcommittees, but this was the first time a cross-committee team had worked in unison on research. Just like the relationships made in high school and college that last a lifetime no matter how far apart you are, so too would these relationships, formed with a common purpose, become a lifetime bond. They lacked the years spent together, but more than made up for the years with the learning, the emotional attachment to the task at hand, and living it together.

Japan was where we really wanted to go, but the process to enter the Land of the Emperor was just as one-sided then as it is now. We could visit the Land of the Rising Sun without restrictions; however, it could not be facilitated until two months after the study was scheduled to be over. What a coincidence!

The trips across the timelines of the world completed, Holy Week of April 4 brought us to the St. Clair Inn where 99 former strangers had become 99 craftsmen of an idea whose time had come! We had four and one-half days to take the world and consense on how it should be run. That first night in St. Clair, with the floes of ice unceremoniously seeking to end the movement of freighters on the river, we talked and hugged, drank and ate, prevaricated without harm – and bonded – friend to friend, not caring from where it was we came, intertwined by the force field of Machiavelli, never to pass this way again, but making sure that this trip was worth the future. For somehow, many of us knew, we were betting our careers on it.

This integration process, where we would meld our reports into one, was very suspect to all of us who would actually do it. We didn't know until it was consummated that Keith B. had no more practical certainty of success than we did. No one had ever done anything like this – actually take the animals and let them create the zoo! It was almost half a decade before I realized that somehow Keith B. had simply rolled the dice of fate to bring to life the axiom:

It takes courage to push yourself to places that you have never been before, to test your limits, to break through barriers.

We created what we intrinsically knew all along – commitment comes from involvement!

That first morning – after the homage paid to Pan, with the stories embellished to the point of absurdity, the ice in our glasses more lethal than the ice on the St. Clair River by nature of the alcohol that melted them – brought the clear, sobering realization that the trip being ended, the fellowship bonded, we must now pay the piper with whom we had danced. The payment was the tune of substance and application. For our theoretical machinations must now be agreed to in a manner that had never been done before. We must agree not only on the new course of action, we must convince two adversaries that collaboration, not compromise, was the path of the future.

For four and one-half days, many resembling the agony in the Garden centuries before, we too struggled with what was before us – could this be done another way? But, alas, we all knew – this, too, must come to pass. At least two members of each subcommittee would meet on each item in each ring, thereby making sure that their team was represented. They would come to a consensus on the best recommendation embodying the combined and diversely represented feelings and findings of each team. They would then bring their piece of the future back to the entire body for consensus. Here is where it truly dawned on me that we had learned that, regardless of which herd we came from, we realized the value of each other; for the reports of seven were becoming the voice of one. The real gold in our alliance resided in the valuing of our differences!

The emotions ran high in three large group consensus sessions as this new order of things began to unfold. A few in each herd had "traditions" that they were very reluctant to let go. These values from the past were very long on endurance for they had come from the "Land of the Adversaries." They were born of the battles of scientific management and were resplendent with scar tissue and medals of valor, respectively. These traditions, so painstakingly earned, lingered long in verse laden with the past, for these good and honest souls who saw the "world of change" in our travels did not fully understand yet that there could be no sacred cows, if we were to truly leapfrog our competition. They melded their golden calves with their idolatry to seniority, classifications, executive dining rooms, preferred parking, and unilateral decision making. As the days became nights and then days again, consensus ruled. "The Process" worked its powerful magic and brilliant ideas hid their beautiful heads until conflict reached its peak, and all had a chance to say their piece. "The Process" with its inherent demand for consensus wouldn't let us give up until we discovered an idea that everyone could buy into. In this second to last bonding experience we had during the study, the intensity of those four and one-half days brought the realization that who was rep or non-rep was inconsequential. What had become more important was the blending of seven books into one. Time after time, rep and non-rep would find themselves speaking up to present or support the other's perspective, but more important, to ensure that the other's point of view was heard. "The Process" gave us two more bits of learning that would last a very long time, both of which took us over the top of many hills down the road. The first was the "Vision." By adhering to the process, the vision remained bright and clear in everyone's mind and always was our superordinate goal. The second was that we truly understood the power in our differences and the tremendous knowledge transference when one listens to a different perspective with the intent to understand it – not disprove it.

Keith B. and the steering committee dutifully captured the essence of the collaborations and put it in appropriate verbiage for "the book" to be presented to Don and Al. With a classical musician's ear they listened, for their literature rivaled the Bard of Avon when reviewed by Don and Al. I wish I could have overheard them after the steering committee presented our results in slick flimsy format. Just to imagine them in their favorite reading places expounding adjectives of amazement as the realization crossed their cerebrums – this is so radical, it just might work!

We all departed the St. Clair Inn that holy Thursday night to the four corners of America, vowing to keep in touch with our bonded companions. We were feeling a strange anxiety at the ending of such an Alice in Wonderland trek, awakening to the realization that it was over, and that I – we – may never see these wonderful people again, but much more disconcerting was a feeling of lack of control over the outcome – what will "they" do with it, this legendary piece of work?

The wait was very short lived, for we were all contacted to return to Detroit on May 2, 1984, with our spouses or significant others to be feted in truly historic GM style by Don and Al. This gathering was to bring formal closure to the study and to praise these architects who had expanded the envelope of what is possible when it comes to working relationships. As Frankie Valli once crooned, "Oh, what a night!" The atmosphere was electric with speculation, for none of us had heard what "they" had thought of our child – born of 2 million miles of

18

travel and 50,000 hours of labor. We greeted the wives, husbands, girl-friends, and boyfriends of our fellow trekkies with appropriate respect and solemnly swore to all the lies they had been told of the happenings "on the road." Cocktails and dinner complete, we all directed our undivided attention toward the stage as the sound of silence grew deafening, waiting to hear how the fruit of our historic quest was received. The lights dimmed, and the soundtrack from *2001: A Space Odyssey* began playing as 21 slide projectors flashed shots of the "Magic of St. Clair," group photos of each subcommittee, and classic pictures of individual 99ers in Chaplinesque endeavors. As I glanced around in the darkness, I could pick up unmistakable prisms of moving light on the rapt faces. Tears of sadness, joy, and wonderment welled up as we relived in our minds those days and nights traveling the world, and the fantastic four and a half days at the Inn on the River. At the tumultuous climax of the video show – now accompanied by "The Voice" crooning "My Way" – as the saying goes, "the joint exploded!" When the applause subsided and the hugs and kisses ceased, Don and Al took the stage.

What would their words be? Now that they had time to digest the potential of this imaginative undertaking, did they come to the same conclusion we did? That this was too unique to become "just another joint study" to be relegated to that black hole of bureaucracy, never to be viewed again. Perspiration appeared on the faces of the males in the herds, while the females – who don't perspire – merely glistened, as Don approached the dais. What a great man of vision, this humble mill-wright from Framingham. He could see the future like no one I had ever met and haven't still; but an orator, he was not. Nevertheless, in his wonderful Boston brogue, he hinted at what we all had so desperately hoped. These clean sheets of paper he had given us were now covered with something very intriguing. He followed with more words of subtle innuendo that still left us wondering – well? Then he turned it over to Al. Now Al, who did not have Don's incredible vision but had come to trust and believe in it, did possess the greatest voice, vocabulary, and delivery of any public speaker in the country.

When he began with his quiet quotes from Socrates, every eye and ear was acutely tuned to receive the message we had all hoped for. This was too spectacular not to deserve follow-up. Pandemonium erupted and his oratory took a forced but brief pause. With order restored, he delivered the final line, "We're not sure what it's going to entail, but

19

some of you will be coming back. We don't know when, but the Rings of Saturn will be landed on again."

The formal festivities ended with each 99er, one at a time, triumphantly gliding to the stage to receive a jacket and plaque in this final scene of the study. Informal festivities continued through the night with much wondering about who would come back, when and what would happen. Again, as we had at the Inn on the River, we gladly and sadly headed home across America – only this time we knew, a new future had truly been formed.

The Second Phase

It was a dark and stormy night with the
Captain being called by the bridge. Captain,
Captain, there is a light in our sea lane, and
it won't move. Tell them – "Starboard, at
once," the Captain replied. The message
flashed out, but the reply came back,
"Starboard yourself!" The Captain, upon
hearing of this brazen retort thundered,
"Tell them who we are – the mighty
Missouri, greatest battleship to ever sail the
seas. Starboard at once!" The message
flashed out and the reply came back, "This
is the lighthouse!"

Stephen R. Covey

3

Several days later, it seemed like a month, I received a call from one
of the International reps on the steering committee. Would I be interested in coming back to Detroit for a meeting to discuss what to do
with the study? It took me one hundredth of a second to give my
answer, "Tell me where and when, and I'll be there early!"

The two members of each subcommittee who had been on the main
committee were each called by the steering committee to attend this
meeting. Those that couldn't or wouldn't were replaced by another
member of their committee, be it a labor or management declinee,
respectively. So Bob M. and I were reunited, as were many other pairs

of informal leadership; but a few, new to the main committee but not new to us, joined in to design how we were to proceed with what Al so eloquently called "follow-up."

The steering committee, after limited direction from Don and Al, was again charged with championing how it would work. Owen, while also ultimately sanctioning Don, had remained selectively removed from association with what was going on; and although Roger had publicly announced the original study, we felt he didn't understand what was really going on and was only paying lip service, unless something was ultimately presented to show him how he could benefit from it. With much satisfaction and admiration for the subcommittee members, the steering committee left the planning to us. They had learned from the quest that if they wanted to recreate the magic, they knew they had to involve those that created it in the first place.

So we went about our task. How many did we need? How were we going to pick them? How long would they be needed? Where would we work? What was to be the end product? The steering committee had done some prep work, anticipating the aforementioned, and presented its recommendations. Their approach was to have the original main committee members assigned to this phase, and if their home plants or units objected, to have Don and Al use their considerable influence to just make it happen. This approach was countered by the main committee members, who pointed out that people who were forced to do something were not usually as creative or committed as those who chose willingly to serve. They were reminded also that heavy-handed tactics could jeopardize careers of many management people who would ultimately have to return from whence they came. We suggested that all main committee member's be asked if they would like to serve further, and if they did that was fine. But if they didn't, we needed a process to replace them with other members of their subcommittees who wanted to come back.

So there we were, Keith B., the six-member steering committee, and fourteen from the subcommittees set to make consensus decision making work again around our philosophy and mission, but this time there were lines on the paper. It wasn't a clean sheet anymore. This time our sanctioners, Don and Al, had decreed that we didn't need 99 to put meat on the bones of "the book." We shouldn't need more than a third.

Well, anyone who has ever used consensus should know what followed, "Who are they to tell us how many we need?" Form should follow function. Structure should follow strategy. And so the gauntlets were tossed and the verbal battle ensued with the steering committee wearing the armor of Don and Al and the main committee wearing the colors of the soulmate families they were there to represent. After several hours of representing the stakes and equities of their respective constituents, the process again proved that if you value your differences, not view each other as different, you will achieve decisions that no one group would have ever arrived at alone. To top it off, because you collaborated rather than compromised, the acceptance level was far superior. So here was the process.

Twenty of us would decide, subcommittee by subcommittee, who should be brought back, based upon what had to be accomplished. The task was to research and write; but the first order of business was, of the fourteen of us there that day, how many were willing to stay? The entire event was facilitated by Keith B., whose words always reminded me of what Goethe said: "What you can do, or dream you can, begin it. Boldness has genius, power and magic in it." That was the approach to the original study, and why not now? "Who among you will stay?" So the call went out. What many were thinking, but did not say, went like this, "Who would roll the dice again and bet they'd make another winning pass? What if it didn't make it? Can I be away from my job, for who knows how long, without endangering my career?" These questions weren't asked, but I saw them passing through the minds of my non-rep (nonunion) friends.

Those who were on "the fast track," very eloquently and politely, provided a litany of reasons they were irreplaceable at their home facilities or were in consideration for new "opportunities" in the Land of the Adversaries. And, with their newly acquired knowledge, gained from the study, they could be "missionaries" of the 99 to better change the system from within. Those who weren't on the fast track were even more eloquent and polite in providing a remarkable inventory assuaging as to their value in pursuing the furtherance of the quest. My partner, Bob M., a general superintendent, was the first to beg off. In retrospect, it was a good move for him as he is now the plant manager of St. Catherine's, where the new Camaro and Firebird are being built, but at the time "family and desertion of his plant manager" were his reasons for breaking up our duet. It was very good to work with him again that couple of days, for we had developed a close friendship and admiration for each other's styles and viewpoints. But I wasn't surprised when he chose to stay in the old world, for he was one of those at the Inn on the River who paid homage to some of the traditions. A bright and fine man he was, and still is, as are all those who stayed and those who became missionaries, but these times taught me a lesson I have never forgotten, all that is worth cherishing in this world begins in the heart, not the head. Myself and my other UAW subcommittee members were all willing to stay, now that we had a fair and equitable process, agreed to, on bringing back some of our team members. We saw an opportunity that wasn't available to us back at our home facilities – to make a change, a change that could finally give those who had become a part of the machine control of the machine!

It's not that our careers were not important to us, but they were not the driving force. Our philosophical bent was more influential. The belief that our role was not to serve ourselves but to be of service to those for whom we went on the quest in the first place – the men, women, brothers, sisters, friends, and neighbors, who from the time they first walked into the bowels of the auto machine would never be the same again. They would enter and exit the machine every day; but slowly, gradually, they changed from caring human beings to either cynical critics of everything, or nonverbal automatons seemingly devoid of life. We had a glimmer of hope now. The opportunity of breaking this brutal pattern was within our grasp.

So the decision was made team by team. Those in the room who agreed to stay were considered onboard. Then the arduous process began to replace those who chose not to join us. The input of everyone in the room was heard. One by one the departing members were replaced until the original number of fourteen was achieved again. This task out of the way, we undertook with great vigor the naming of one more, plus two or three alternates, if the first choice declined, from each subcommittee to round out the initial team. This was more difficult for the represented folks than the non-reps. They were used to discriminating based on objective criteria, but that was not how our herd was used to doing things. We had always relied on loyalty, friendship, how you had earned your stripes, and blind trust as our selection criteria, not on whether you had the requisite skills needed to be successful. Subsequently, it was very difficult trying to sort out rationally whether someone had what was needed, or were we thinking of them because they were good soldiers?

With much perseverance and determination, this task, too, came to closure; and then it was onto, "How long should Phase II last? Where should we work? When did everyone need to show up? Who was going to contact them? If they accepted, who would get them released from their home facilities?" After spirited dialogue, we consensed on a list of givens that would enable us to kick things off. Don and Al would decide on the duration of this phase, based on periodically scheduled meetings. The steering committee would secure working quarters, contact the selectees, and their leadership. And those who could make it should be here next Monday. Pleasantries exchanged, with prophetic words of parting to those who chose not to return and encouraging commentary to those who had accepted, it was back home again to prepare our families and ourselves for our renewed trek into the future.

As I drove toward Flint, the sun going down with its most spectacularly beautiful, optically pleasurable display, the realization came over me again. I will never be able to work at Chevy Metal Fab again. The world I had seen with all of its untapped potential was permanently etched in my imagination. There were no trains home to the Land of the Adversaries for me. A cold chill crept up my back as the thought coursed around the circular walls of my intellect – What if this doesn't work out? What will I do? I'm not prepared to throw 19 years of service out the window! What if? What of? How come? – My wife and three sons – what of them? Was I putting my disdain for the system ahead of their welfare? What if? What of? How come? As the question marks began flying before my eyes, like flakes of snow in a blizzard, a calm returned; for I knew the answers were never going to be easy. These were the hard questions of change. It's never a walk in the park when you create a new order of things.

The drive back to Detroit Monday morning was fraught with anxiety. The weekend was spent with my wife, talking over the endless list of uncertainties, culminating in general agreement that we would watch life unfold and deal with it on life's terms. I felt a tremendous anticipation about building onto the study and having these breakwith ideas grow into the razor sharp steel of change that would slice through the petrified armor of tradition with a boldness so great that the only response the "powers that be" could have would be, "Why not?"

Those first couple of weeks back were very enlightening to all of us, but especially to me. While we were getting everyone freed up to return and all the associated logistics attended to, we were housed in a garage across the street from the GM Technical Center in Warren, Michigan. The steering committee had not yet secured a permanent home to house this phase of the study. My first flash of enlightenment occurred while we were here in our "temporary" quarters. Why not house the engineers, who were working on the technology, and the study team, who were working on the integration of people systems and technology, together? That way we could build on the relationships we initially developed with many of them during the first phase of the study, and we could really learn from each other the reasons why our plants didn't work like they were designed to work. The answers came back too quickly. There really isn't enough room; the time to develop a prototype to show Roger B. was too short for distractions; more engineering resources could not be freed up to help them; the study team needed time to hone its initial findings without diversions, and so on.

Someone was afraid of something! Who were "they"? Why the reservations? Were the tentacles of change that gingerly inched from Saturn that threatening? The answers to these and many other questions that developed over the summer would come to be answered in the fall. Some of the reasons, among others unnamed, were that the Tech Center had too many leaks for such a sensitive project; there was still too much distrust between labor and management; and some feared career damage if this turned out to be another boondoggle.

The steering committee did their job. All the selectees being freed, they channeled their energy into finding us a home. The search was done very quietly, as the study results were not public knowledge. There was a keen desire to keep what was being developed away from the press so as not to tip off observers that the General was up to something. Everything that happened in GM triggered a feeding frenzy among the fourth estate in Detroit. Our home turned out to be a nondescript building on the Stephenson Highway corridor in Troy, Michigan. It was nestled among the many job shops so familiar in the area, with a high-bay in the back and office space in the front. In we moved, armed with our study and high spirits, tuned toward creation, holding onto the reins of this race horse of change that was champing at the bit to hurl full force into the fray!

So what should be the first order of business? What should we call ourselves, seeing as how we weren't the 99 anymore and the Study Center had been disbanded? How should we organize ourselves to flesh out this skeletal innovation? Who should work on what? Should our mission and philosophy be adjusted? Given our collective solid schooling on the importance of philosophy and mission, that was where we began. For our new mission, we would have the steering committee, 15 full-time members, and as many as needed part-time. Satisfied that these would remain unchanged, we turned our focus to a name. Although our travels would be considerably reduced from what they were during the study, we concluded that subject matter expertise would still need to be sought out; so when we went a-seeking, we had to have an identity that would suitably open the doors of those we were looking to borrow from.

Consensus reached, we would be known as the UAW/GM Saturn Resource Center. Our charge would be, we concluded, to explore all the resources of our intended organization – physical, financial, and human – so we must not impose a self-induced constraint on ourselves like just being called the Human Resource Center. We also agreed that our involvement with the project engineers, both product and manufacturing, must be more closely knit, so how we organized ourselves would be critical if we were to truly take a systemic approach to this phase of the development. However, the best-laid plans of mice and men do sometimes go awry. Due to a lack of establishing up-front expectations between the Resource Center members and the project engineers, what a blowout we had in early October, just days before we were to present our research to Don and Al. I will discuss this in more detail later, but to say it was a significant learning experience on everyone's part is a serious understatement.

Our "core group," as we became known during this phase, consisted of 15 people and a consultant who would work full-time. As we progressed, many other 99ers came back part-time to work on the ring committees as we added meat on these bones of concept. Our key objectives were to continue to integrate people and technology and test the concepts established in Phase I. During this fleshing out process, we assessed the impact of the concepts on the people and the organizations (UAW, GM, and Saturn). Our vehicle to do this was our S.T.E.P.S. Organizational Planning Model (on page 29) which we established in Phase I. The model contains five rings; but the philosophy and mission Bull's-Eye ring being already agreed to, we would focus our efforts on the other four radiating rings. To do this we established ring committees to address each element in the respective rings and collectively to address the interrelatedness of all the rings. We also determined that the entire 99 needed to somehow be involved in the Phase II development. To achieve this, we organized the following:

- All 99 would be kept up to date by a Project Saturn newsletter, which we would publish monthly.
- All 99 were to be invited to come to information/consensus meetings to be held in July and September to review the work of the core group and ring committees, to provide input and reach consensus on all appropriate items, and to get updated on the overall status of Project Saturn.

Secure in our feelings that these efforts would carry on the synergy of the original study, we budgeted our best "guesstimates" and secured a million dollar plus fund to operate this phase from GM and the UAW National Training Fund.

We in the core group divided ourselves up into teams to oversee the ring committees, as well as to manage the interrelatedness issues of the five rings; to coordinate the writing and editing of the final report; to prepare, edit, and distribute the 99 *Newsletter*; to plan and coordinate the July and September consensus meeting with the 99; and to plan and conduct periodic reviews with Don and Al as work progressed.

Planning and organizing being done for the moment, the core group teams began structuring the development of the four rings. The teams were chosen, based on background expertise relative to the respective ring elements and also, I believe, more important, sincere individual passion for the development of those elements if we were really going to achieve breakwith thinking.

Those who chose Ring One were deeply driven to rectify the inappropriate blend of people and technology that existed back in the Land

•SOCIAL • TECHNICAL • ECONOMIC • POLITICAL SYSTEM (S.T.E.P.S.)
ORGANIZATION PLANNING MODEL

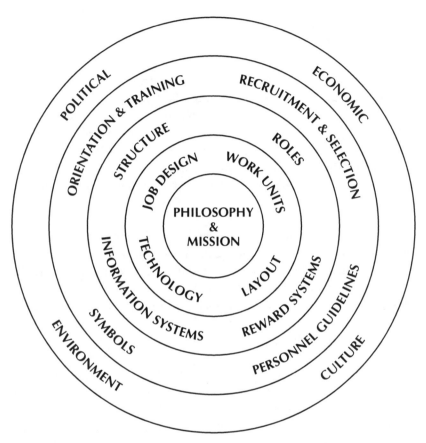

of the Adversaries. They knew we had to reinvent the plant layout, how the physical facility was developed, and more important, how the site was selected. The development of the basic building block of our organization – the work unit, or W.U. – had to be planned. What would a typical work unit look like? How would it operate? What would a W.U. technician be responsible for? What would be the role of the W.U. advisor? Who should resolve personnel issues? How did the work unit fit into the business unit? And what would the business unit look like? What about job design? Should there be buffers and banks? How would the tradesmen be organized, and how would they interact with the operating technician? What about preventive maintenance and relief practices? How many shifts should be worked, and what were the tremendous implications on training for all of the preceding? How would the Project Center engineers get input and feedback on the critical rings development? And, if we go forward to a Phase III, what challenges can we anticipate?

Those who opted to pursue this first ring were devoted to finding a way to stop the dehumanization cycle that had plagued our brothers and sisters since Mr. Ford introduced the assembly line to America. Through their travels around the globe, they had seen other corporations break the pattern of industrial "zombieism" perpetuated by the mismatched blending of people, machines, and structure. They truly believed that they could build a new foundation for the house of industry that would treat all its members as functional caring adults who could and would perform.

Ring Two attracted its own zealots, those whose burning fire of enthusiasm is fueled by how an organization is structured. What should be the appropriate roles within that structure? How in the world could the information systems be integrated in a way to support these new roles within the structure? And, last, a different method of rewards must be developed that would not only support these new approaches but demand commitment to them for the rewards to materialize.

Ring Three was where I chose to focus most of my energy for this phase of development. Those who joined with me to expand the envelope of human technology believed as strongly as I that the people system development would ultimately be the deciding factor in our success formula. The importance of how we went about attracting the "right" people was a point vividly driven into us during the study by every world-class organization we had the good fortune to borrow from. The recruitment and selection process, we learned, should not focus on screening out undesirables, but rather be designed to screen those in who want a new order of things. In this new environment, they would thrive and have a very high likelihood of being successful both personally and professionally. Once the choices were made on these million dollar team members, we knew that how they were oriented into this socio-technical juggernaut of change was critical to the effective blending of all the rings together. Training would be the easy part if we designed the aforementioned properly. The only challenging aspect we foresaw in educating the work force was to design training that is competency based and to convince the GM and UAW leaders of the importance of training as a lifelong endeavor.

The next element we tackled had deep emotional baggage tethered to it from decades of use in the Land of the Adversaries. Symbols of division must be changed for effective innovation to have a chance. The years of outward expression of differences among people must be transformed into what will bring people together. The golden calves of the adversaries – executive dining rooms, privileged parking, suits and ties, time clocks for some and titles and offices for others, separate restrooms and break areas, and so forth – all must undergo a metamorphosis, not unlike the transformation of the larvae into the butterfly. All aspects of segregation must be driven from the good ship Enterprise, if we were to go where no man has ever gone before. Last, a few broad and flexible personnel guidelines must replace the endless volumes of policy, practice, and procedures that had relentlessly self-reproduced over time. Armed with the philosophical belief of the inherent good of people, the 42 shop rules, designed for the abuser, yet implicating all as dysfunctional, must be banished forever. A code of conduct must be ordained that demonstrated belief in the dignity of all people, or we would merely replicate the past under a different name.

Ring Four, the final ring of Saturn, was the one we added to Professor Walton's Bull's-Eye Model during the study. The elements within this ring, we had discovered, would ultimately determine our success or failure in moving from a project to a duly sanctioned entity. We also believed that, were Saturn to become a viable organization, the attention paid to this ring in planning and execution would have a dramatic effect on the long-term life expectancy of the organization. The staffing of this ring was primarily the steering committee, based on the committee members' respective career paths through GM and the International Union and their ties to the individual government relations staffs of their organizations. We informal leaders of the other three ring committees, however, met with the steering committee on Ring Four development weekly. We knew that politics, economics, environment, and culture must have input from the 99 if it were to be properly blended into the overall system; but more important, we would bring new ideas and perspectives to areas that were traditionally the domain of leaders, and everyone knows what a "wonderful" job has been done in this vein by just looking at the track record.

Those of us who had spent most of our careers in the plants knew. We had to insulate ourselves, somehow, some way, from GM and the International Union. We knew we had to develop new relationships with government at the local, state, and federal levels. It was obvious that our relationship with the fourth estate must undergo a total transformation. It didn't take a rocket scientist to see that the open checkbook of Roger Smith, since his ascension to the helm of the 14th floor, was a harbinger of doom, for the short-term financial payback mentality that the financial staff of GM had forced on the organization was choking its creativity into oblivion.

We all knew that, should Saturn become a reality, we must seriously alter our thinking in regard to the environment. The decades of industrial abuse of America had taken its toll, and we all realized that a new approach to the construction and operation of a world-class manufacturing facility was needed if we were to truly break with tradition. The last element of this ring was extremely critical, for it was the cultural aspect of the other three. How the rings were managed would ultimately spell victory or defeat. GM, the International Union, the Europeans, the Japanese, the government (local, state, and national) would all be averse to our cultural revolution. We knew in our hearts that if we did not prepare ourselves well to anticipate every possible attack from The Establishment and think through how we wanted the future to be – so clearly in our minds that it was virtual reality – we would be overtly or covertly subverted before we had a chance to prove the validity of our mission.

All the committees being formed and staffed, we were all set for the long, hot summer grind of another 50,000 hours of debating, reaching a consensus, writing and editing, interviewing, and building on the ideas of the interviewees. We traveled back to the origin of the concepts, over and over again, until it was time to meet with Don and Al in mid-October.

Before we get to that historic meeting, I must return to the point I made earlier about the lack of communication and involvement between the project engineers and the Resource Center. There were many reasons for the ultimate showdown at 31623 Stephenson the night before we were to present our Phase II Report to Don and Al – none of which were insurmountable – but they were eye-opening for all involved and helped us, in the long term, better understand that real commitment comes from real involvement. So let's explore the intricacies of intrigue that led up to the first Battle of Saturn.

The origin of discord, we discovered, lay in two supposedly innocent decisions. The first was one made by the GM Organizational Development (O.D.) staff, where two O.D. consultants with different styles, backgrounds, beliefs, and a mutual dislike for each other were assigned to Saturn. One, with a deeply entrenched academic background, was a self-proclaimed theoretical expert of socio-technical systems. He was assigned to the project engineers. The other had roots in the factory, starting in the bargaining unit, pursuing academics by necessity, but gradually gaining stature while developing and applying an intolerable ego. He was assigned to the Resource Center. This, in and of itself, would not have been unmanageable if the two of them could have put aside their egos and agreed to work together for the common cause; but, unfortunately, a trait of their breed, especially in GM, was the fight for who would get the most credit for what. That mindset led to divergence and a lack of meaningful communication. Exacerbating the situation was that we in the Resource Center didn't even know about the engineers' consultant until the week of the big blowout; therefore, we were also unaware that the engineers might be getting direction different from ours. Not knowing this led to our inaccurate assumption that the committee members in Ring One were successfully bridging the knowledge gap created during the study. I guess that's what you get when you assume.

The second seemingly innocent decision, again, unknown to the Resource Center, resided in the GM staffing approach to projects like Saturn. As we came to find out, to get engineers to commit to long-term projects, the standard practice was to promise them leadership positions, should the project become a viable entity. No wonder they had so much energy about what we were proposing. Our "new order structure" had hardly any of the positions they had been promised if they stayed with the project.

So these two separate, yet intertwined, decisions taught all of us some very important things. One, you can never "assume" that the right things are happening simply because everything is in place for them to happen. Two, if you don't have all the information necessary to make the correct decision, that is, two consultants instead of one, GM project staffing practices, you will not make the right decision; and more important, the decision will not be accepted. The third learning we had was probably the most important; namely, that change is very difficult when the change involves you personally. We learned that most people who say, "Let the chips fall where they may," figure they won't be hit by a chip; and if they are, they do not accept it well. Last, the part of our philosophy that states, "All people want to be involved in decisions that affect them," had been grievously violated. Unintentional or not was irrelevant. Of greatest importance was whether people felt violated, and that had to be dealt with.

So, here we were, the night before we were to meet with Don and Al, burning the midnight oil in preparation for what we knew would truly amaze them, when in walked one of the project engineering leaders, Joe Joseph. Joe was the head of manufacturing engineering for the production of the car, and he was livid about our impending meeting. We had to postpone the meeting with Don and Al. Disagreements between the two groups had to be ironed out before we made any more recommendations. Furthermore, if we proceeded to meet with Don and Al tomorrow, they (the project engineers) would disavow any knowledge of what we in the Resource Center had been doing and would do everything they could to put the project on hold. It didn't take a genius to figure out that emotion had overwhelmed logic, and this was not going to be bridged over a cup of coffee.

The call went out for pizza and drinks, as well as to many home fronts, for we knew we were in for a long night. The only means available to combat emotion is data. So the battle lines were drawn around facts about the various elements of our report, the work being done by the engineers, and how well we had or had not communicated with each other from June through October; but then we got to the structure. At last, the real source of the emotion came to the discussion table, "Who gave us the right to decide how engineering should be organized?" "Where did we get the authority to decide how the plant should be structured?" "Who died and made us King of Saturn?" This was going to take some time.

The pizza arrived; the drinks started flowing; and the discussion gradually evolved into, "How many engineers were promised jobs?" "What level were these jobs, and who had the right to promise in the first place?" "Weren't the engineers aware that the only reason we were here was that Don and Al liked what they heard in the Phase I report?" After many pizzas, drinks, and verbiage impassioned enough to make a sailor weep, we reached an accord. We would meet with Don and Al and present our "draft" of the Phase II report with the caveat that the engineers had not bought into the structure as designed, and more "high-level" dialogue was needed to resolve our differences! Catastrophe avoided, we all retired for a couple of hours of sleep before the big meeting. I don't know about anyone else, but I didn't sleep at all that night.

The meeting took place in Al Warren's office in the General Motors Building in Detroit. Al was in attendance with three handpicked members of his staff, and Don was there with both of his administrative assistants. We were represented by the steering committee and two representatives from each of the ring committees. We had prepared transparencies galore, an executive summary, and individually bound copies of our report for Don and Al. For some reason, the room felt tense. I tried to lay it off on the night before; but as I looked around the room, there was a strange anxiety on the faces of those who had confidently entered the room a short time before. The steering committee started the executive summary, and things went well for about five minutes. I hadn't noticed it at first, but while the agenda was being covered, both Don and Al were speed reading through their copies, and serious frowns were appearing on their faces. About halfway through the introduction of the first ring, Don very abruptly asked, "How many copies of this book are there in print?" When told only the two he and Al were holding, he relaxed somewhat. Then Al unceremoniously queried, "Who has seen what you're presenting today?" The response being, "Only those in this room and the two project engineering leaders." This brought the meeting to a halt. Ah, a blinding flash of the obvious! One of the engineering leaders had gotten to Al, and Al had talked to Don. The ensuing dialogue didn't directly say so, but it was obvious by what was said. "We expected you to be bold; but you have been bolder than we ever imagined," Al eloquently stated. Don, however, was not so eloquent. "You are out in front of your interference. I agree, you have really stretched; but no one can see this book until the path is prepared. If this leaks out, this project will come to an end. Put all your papers under lock and key, and before you talk to anyone, clear it through Al and me first." At that, Don and Al got up and left, and our much awaited meeting was over without actually making the planned presentation.

It was a long drive back to Troy that day, but it was also a reflective time. What had we learned today about Ring Four? Politics and culture were alive and well in both the GM building and the UAW Solidarity House. Our new order of things had enemies who had done well under the old order. A great awakening came over those of us who understood, and now we must teach those who hadn't. The weeks remaining before the Christmas shutdown were spent refining what we presented to Don and Al, and meshing the collective thoughts of the engineers and ourselves with daily communications with Don and Al. The time passed relatively uneventfully, and before we knew it, December 23 arrived; and we were once again faced with returning to the four corners of America, not knowing if we would ever see this dream of ours become a reality. The word had simply come down, "Good job! Go home and enjoy the holidays, and let us take it from here. If anything develops, you'll be contacted."

The heartfelt good-byes were mouthed with the promise that whoever heard anything first would contact the others. Then it was home for the holidays again, with all the anxiety of an expectant father pacing the waiting room for news of the birth.

The Corporation

JANUARY 1985 - SPRING 1985

How monotonous the sound of
the forest would be if the music
came only from the top ten birds.

Author Unknown

4

ome for the holidays was an ambivalent time after 11 months of
seeing the potential that the future could hold. It was relaxing to
face a couple of weeks of leisure with my sons, with no cities to visit,
no hotel rooms to flop in, and no companies to study. Just 14 days of
nothing to do and all day to do it. In a blink of an eye, Christ's birth-
day had passed. The new year was ushered in with the pageantry of
Pan. All the Bowl games were concluded and the Gridiron National
Champion crowned. Suddenly, it was time for me to look at the past
through the eyes of the present.

Having heard nothing from Saturn, I had, I thought, mentally prepared
myself for my entry back into the zombie maker in the birthplace of the
adversaries. But as I slowly approached the ominous orifices that led to
the bowels of the beast, the stark realization hit home. If Saturn didn't
become a viable entity, this would be life for the next 10 years. I said to
myself, "I'll never make it!" If Saturn didn't call, I would have to move
on. So I vowed to myself, I would give it two weeks; and if I hadn't heard
anything by then, I would call Joe Malotke, the lead UAW International
rep on the steering committee, and see if he could offer any news.

37

That first week in the beast was a nostalgic sojourn to the pain of the past. The déjà vu I experienced after almost a year of travel around the globe watching the world progress was very sobering. The meaning of the phrase, "The mind once stretched by a new idea never regains its original dimensions" was clear to me now. I had been blessed with an experience that showed me a potential that would never allow me to step backward and acquiesce to the old order of things. I could not consciously sit idly by and watch this dignity-stripping, dehumanizing play unfold again and again with the players expertly tuned into their roles, slowly but surely taking themselves to the brink of extinction, without standing up and saying, "Stop this madness! Can't you see what you are doing to yourselves?" But, alas, poor Yorick, to no avail did my pleadings for change have any retention in the minds of the adversaries. On the contrary, my overtures were met with suspicion and hostility by both herds. My union brothers and sisters accused me of being brainwashed by management and generally heretical to our history, while the management herd unanimously branded me as seditionist, agitating, and bent on causing dissent among those who were "rightfully put in their place."

So during that first week back, my job and my physical well-being were both threatened many times. "Who did I think I was! That "fairytale" world I'd been in for the last year was not reality, boy! This is the *real* world!" Row well and live, Ben Hur! Needless to say, this full frontal assault did not go unanswered. My best defense had always been a good offense. So full frontal assault met full frontal assault and lose-lose was fully enjoined.

With the first week over, I sat at home reflecting all weekend on, "Why couldn't they see the rut they were in? Why wouldn't they listen? Why were they so afraid of change?" Lord, how I wished I could plug my brain into a TV monitor and show all the vivid, candid scenes of the future I had experienced so they could understand. Lacking such technology, I knew the only way was patience, pain, and crisis. To readily embrace change, one must be not only able but, more important, willing. The two herds were making the same mistake they had made for decades – each waiting for the other to change, but neither willing to make the first move. I retired for the night hoping that my dream maker would do what it often did – deliver a subtle epiphany across the chasm between the conscious and subconscious that would show me the way to reach them.

I awoke the morning of January 7 with an unusual sense of calm, especially after that turbulent week inside the beast. My benevolent dream maker had done its job, I thought, as the revelation swept over me that I must cease my offensive and model what I wanted them to see. I must demonstrate the change I wished them to emulate. Suddenly, the TV drew me sharply back from my sojourn into the mysteries of the gray matter. My reticular activating system had picked up the words, "Roger B. Smith, Chairman of GM, has called a press conference..." My pulse began to quicken. "Could this be *it?*" I could barely contain myself until the time of the conference. I must have called half the 99 by airtime. Finally, it was time. Roger B., Chairman of the Board of GM, strode to the microphone and enunciated these historic words, "The GM Board of Directors is proud to announce the formation of Saturn Corporation, a wholly owned subsidiary of GM, and the first new nameplate added to the GM fine line of automobiles since Chevrolet was added in 1918."

I was in orbit. My phone rang nonstop between my calls to my family and friends. I did not remember feeling this way, ever, in my life. The closest feeling I could relate it to was when my sons were born. That awe-inspiring sound of a baby breathing – a new creation on this earth with the potential to be whatever it chose to be. Then a sobering thought brought me down from my orbit. The quest was over – the grail was in our hands now. What we dreamed, we could now do. What we imagined, we could achieve. Later that day, an esoteric, recurring thought emerged again from my subconscious. Well, they did it. But do they (GM and UAW) have the wherewithal to do this right? Who are the champions going to be? How strong will their commitment be? I somehow knew the critical importance of these questions, so I vowed to myself that when I returned to Saturn – not if, but when – I would unceasingly drive the "process" until it was institutionalized.

But, back to the press conference. The first leaders were named to the Strategic Action Council (SAC). Joseph Sanchez was named president. John J. Wetzel was named as vice president of product engineering. Guy Briggs was named vice president of manufacturing. Tom Manoff was named vice president of finance. John Middlebrook was named vice president of marketing, sales, and service. Edwin Dilworth was named general counsel, and Reid Rundell, who was the Project Saturn leader from June 1982 until this natal day, was named executive vice president of strategic planning. I mentally noted at the time, and later successfully verbalized, that three very important functions were missing: human resources, public relations/corporate communications, and organizational development. So here was half the brain trust of the future, seven men and an AMEX card. Although Roger had committed $5 billion to Saturn, there was NO budget, NO place to call home, and the union leadership was unnamed. Here came that esoteric query again. How well was this thought out? Was this first decision the harbinger of their commitment to do this right?

Well, on with the joy of the birth. I knew now that I could reenter the portals of the beast called Chevy Metal Fab, for my days there were numbered. It was just a matter of when they sent out the call to return. I knew it would come, but I also knew I would call Joe Malotke before the day was out. He was the lead international rep at Saturn when we left for the holidays, and I would volunteer my services. This was actually just a courtesy call because Joe and I had become very close during the last year, and he had already intimated that I would be the first one of the 99 he would call.

As the SAC started functioning, I went back to the zombie maker to prepare for my departure. Every evening I would go over and over in my mind how I wished my family could share this excitement with me, but we had separated four months previous to this, and I could never seem to correlate my exuberance for Saturn with the demise of my marriage, although I suspected a relationship between the two.

Five days later (it seemed like five weeks), on January 13, 1985, the call from Joe came. "I've cleared it with your plant. Be here tomorrow at 8:00 A.M. I want you to do an interview with the *Detroit News*, and then we'll start planning how to get the 99ers back." How many, who, and so on, I was thinking as I headed south down I-75 at 6:00 A.M. January 14, never to look back – the first 99 Bargaining Unit UAW member to join "Saturn Corporation" – six days after its birth.

After the interview was over, Joe; Chuck Stridde, a 99er and personnel director for GM; Neil DeKoker, a Project Saturn steering committee member; Marty Storm, 99er and production manager of Detroit Gear and Axle: and I, Jack O'Toole, set about the task of organizing the logical return of the 99ers. After completing that task, we made plans to meet with the SAC on Friday January 18 at the temporary headquarters in the GM Tech Center to give the new officers a general overview of the evolution of the project that landed them on the planet called Saturn. What an eye-opening experience we had at that meeting! I knew that there would be a sizable knowledge imbalance, but I was totally unprepared for what happened. Having become accustomed to meeting with people who would say, "Why not?" it seemed ominous that we were met with so many whys. "Why would we want to do that?" "Why was that so important?" And, alarmingly, "Why are you telling us this?" Leading this barrage of whys was the president of Saturn, Joseph Sanchez. I'll never forget my thought that day: How in the hell was this guy picked to create a new order of things? It sure seemed like he wanted to do what we'd always done and just call it something else, which as Einstein says is "the significant problem." It also became painfully obvious that the other five SAC members were not going to question the president even if they had some inkling as to why they should. That just left Reid Rundell, and his countenance expressed what a job was ahead of us.

I never got the opportunity to understand Joseph Sanchez any better, for he had a heart attack soon after that meeting; and then another while still in the hospital, which was fatal. A new president was named. Before his appointment, we met with the other SAC members to expand on the issues pointed out at that first meeting; that is,

99ers: "Why wasn't there a H.R./O.D. [human resources/ organizational development] function named?"

SAC: "You've got to be careful with those types, or you'll lose control"

99ers: "Why are you averse to bringing back UAW technicians right now?"

SAC: "What purpose would they serve? We're not building cars yet!" (ugh!)

The list was long, but we had faith that, properly presented, they would come to understand, and then they would be asking, "Why not"?

Naming William Hoglund as Saturn's new president could not have made us 99ers any happier than if it had been Reid Rundell. We knew Reid was right for the job, but this was our first real taste of GM corporate priorities. The track record of Bill H. was very promising. He had a justifiable history of close involvement with the union, being very open to new ideas, and as general manager of Pontiac, was lauded by both the corporation and the International Union as the one most responsible for putting the "excitement" back into Pontiac. So his arrival was greeted as Pontiac's loss and a definite gain for Saturn. I, and others, also noted the subtle change in the rest of the SAC. Their rigid "why" mentality was suddenly tempered with, "Why don't you tell us more about this partnership, consensus, and so forth?" We added more 99ers that first week back, then the next and the next. In all, 35 chose to come back to the future; but the same phenomenon occurred that took place at the start of Phase II in March 1984, and it would happen again in October 1986 when the Bargaining Unit members could officially join Saturn – the rationalization about why they could not commit to what they had helped create.

When everyone who had volunteered came onboard, we all convened and laid out what we thought the number of UAW technicians and non-reps needed to be in this critical formation stage. What kind of expertise was required that was lacking in the 35 99ers? We knew three things for sure:

1. It was clear that UAW technicians would not be offered permanent employment at Saturn until a memo of understanding was negotiated.
2. The SAC officers would begin staffing their respective functional organizations with non-reps.
3. The lack of H.R./O.D and P.R./Corp Comm. [public relations/ corporate communications] functions on the SAC would leave valuable resources, both rep and non-rep, out of this genetic boiling pot.

So the order of the day became this: Form follows function and structure follows strategy. We must let no stone go unturned. So out came the Bull's-Eye Model again. Every one of the returning 99ers was placed in one of the model elements and then we looked at the gaps and asked, "Who do we personally know from the Land of the Adversaries that would, from both a technical and social aspect, not only welcome the challenge of this historic undertaking, but, more important, have the skills to challenge without alienating?" We needed the bright minds and hardened skins of experience; people who had always believed that there was a better way to manage an organization to success; those who believed in the inherent good of *all* people in an organization; and who could hit the deck running, for we did not have six months to bring them up to speed on the project.

Saturn engineers had not disbanded at the end of Phase II as the 99ers had. The SAC members were staffing their respective groups without partnership input; and here, a year later, the SAC and technical staffs were in one place and the 99ers were way across town. This "must" change! We knew it would be a while before we had common working sites, so it became critical that we get the right people in with "them" before decisions were made that would have to be changed. My thoughts at the time, although tempered with thanksgiving at having the opportunity to bring the vision to reality, were hardening between a slow burn and spewing lava. After spending a year with my 98 comrades and as many, or more, brilliant engineers, we forged bonds that would take decades, or never, to achieve in the Land of the Adversaries; but here we were separated still. And, now, a new crew of players cast ominous shadows of uncertainty across the rings of our rising planet. Here we were, damn it! We'd spent 100,000 plus hours of research, writing, editing, interviewing, rewriting, more editing; and spent over $3 million doing it. We had been successful enough and articulate enough to launch this "wholly owned subsidiary," and now we were doing that age-old American labor/management dance. "I don't think I like the message you're delivering, so I will attack the credibility of the messenger" was what we were hearing. I knew that this dynamic was not endemic to the auto industry, and that every change agent in any organization in the world had to experience this ritual of metamorphosis, but I was really feeling angry about the way our ideas were being received.

January passed to February and rocketed into March. After the first quarter of a year of our existence, we had finally convinced the SAC that we needed a human resource function at their level of the organization. Although GM still used the archaic term "personnel," we had shown that world-class organizations knew that the human resource was the most valuable of any resource they had. We also drove home the point, through the use of data, that the single most important success tool at any organization's disposal was the recruitment and selection process. We would be in the hiring mode for the next eight years, at least, and it was critical that we do this for the right reasons. The goal was to screen people *in* who wanted to work in this kind of environment, and who would thereby have a chance at success; not to screen *out* undesirables.

We weren't successful, yet, in getting organizational development professionals onboard to help deal with the change process. So four other 99ers and I agreed that we would do anything necessary to bridge the gap until we could hire the right team members. For all of us had worked and taught in the Quality of Work Life process back in the Land of the Adversaries. So there we were, five at the time, semi-professionals facing the formidable task of aligning new organizational behaviors with old-world paradigms at the highest level of the organization, with a newly selected vice president of human resources, Jim Lewandowski, whom we knew would not come in and immediately alienate the rest of the SAC officers by supporting our plea for external O.D. help. A phrase quickly came to mind: "When you walk through a storm, hold your head up high, and don't be afraid of the dark..."

"Heed this – change agents out there!" Our premise was soon proven true, the week after Jim came onboard. He was only "officially" loaned to Saturn, for the power realm was still not convinced that H.R. was really necessary. We convinced Jim to "convene" the SAC, so we could make another assault on their aversion to having O.D. specialists simply "loaned" to us for a "defined" period of time. We felt this approach might be less threatening and would still achieve the desired results. Not! We were warmly received, attentively listened to, and then the skeletons came out again. The VP of manufacturing said, "We've got to be very careful here – with those people [O.D.]. You can easily lose control." An interesting response, I thought, when we were trying to create an empowering organization. The VP of engineering said, "We're hiring the best engineers in the world, and we certainly don't need to be distracted by all that touchy-feely stuff." Was this the precursor of throwing designs over the wall to manufacturing, again? The president's comment was, "Our team believes in you, and we feel that you can get the job done without outside interference!" Was there

a good understanding here of the scope of this task? Our on-loan VP of H.R. remarked, "I have been thinking about this since you first approached me with your rationale, and I feel like the other SAC officers. We're too chaotic right now for those people to come in here. We need time to get our feet on the ground, and then we'll reevaluate the situation." Was the criticality of the socio-technical balance *that* misunderstood here? And, last, our International Union representative on the SAC, Joe Malotke, who only the evening before, had pledged support for our proposition chimed in, "Well, after listening to how the rest of the SAC feels, I guess we could give it a little more time." And Caesar said, "*Et tu, Brute?*"

I remember my emotions welling up almost to overflowing and thinking, I should just calmly get up and kick my chair over, make a lightening sweep of my arm and knock everything on the table in front of me across the room; and, in as threatening a tone as possible, demand to know if they are all on drugs or merely summa cum laude graduates of the school of incompetence. My non-rep friend and associate 99er Laurie Danko must have seen Beelzebub in my eyes, for she quickly stood up, put her hand on my shoulder, and calmly said, "Thank you all for your input. We'll certainly go back and discuss this with the rest of our team, and then sit down with Jim." At that, we got up and left – quickly.

On the drive back to the Resource Center, across town, I made an oath to myself – if the mountain won't come to Mohammed...I knew I would call Keith Brooke the moment I got back to my desk. I would be meeting him before the day was out, and anyone who wished could join me.

I coined a phrase that afternoon. I saw the obvious; however, it was in retrospect. I would never make that same mistake again. I knew that you get people to do what you want, not by bullying them or tricking them, but by understanding them. Prior to a year and a half ago, I didn't regularly travel in the circles of these people of influence, so I must get help in learning what makes them tick. How do they make decisions? In their own heads? Do they value opinion or fact, both or neither? The greatest desire of humankind is to be understood. So being from the real world, I knew I must understand them before they would seek to understand me; and Keith Brooke was my mentor.

THE SITE
AND THE MEMO

**Do not follow the beaten path. Go where
there is no path and leave a trail.**

Author Unknown

5

I can look back now at all the frustration I was feeling. How ironic that after a year of seeing what the future could hold, a long year of convincing Don and Al there was a better way to organize and lead an organization, we did it well enough for Don to convince Roger B. to launch Saturn. With the gold within our reach, we were now trying to convince the newly appointed officers of this once-in-a-lifetime opportunity that they didn't have to reinvent the wheel that had just been reinvented. This new invention didn't look like what they thought a wheel should look like, and they were not about to change its shape until they understood why it was shaped the way it was. Once they understood, the process was there for them to make improvement suggestions.

Their approach, however, was all too typical of GM's arrogance: "We know how much you care about Saturn – your ownership and all – but reality must still be faced. We have been 'chosen' to bring this organization to life and a product to market because we all have track records of success. The bottom line is that decisions are going to have to be made, and when that happens, we'll make them." I could contain myself no longer. Mt. St. Helen's blew. I jumped up, knocking my chair over backward and thundered, "I knew there was going to be a sizable learning curve here, but I didn't know we were going to face such a blatant case of cranial-rectal inversion. You keep your pompous attitudes and make your brilliantly wise decisions, but I can guarantee you, they will *all* be revisited, gentlemen! For this is *not* business as usual under a different name! It's going where none of us have ever been before!" I then picked up my briefcase – after having closed it with the force of a Sonny Liston right cross – and walked out of the room amidst murmurs of, "Who in the hell does he think he is!" "He can't talk to us like that!" "What does he know about running a billion dollar corporation?" Once I had my back to them, I smiled as I walked out. Touché! Keith Brooke had counseled that win-win was not in their hearts and minds yet. Maybe a dose of what they understood – namely, state your opinion loudly and clearly with no question of surrender – would open the passageways in their cerebrums that were very clearly occluded with the plaque of the past.

The Memorandum of Understanding discussions at Al Warren's and Don Ephlin's level were going on starting in January. Ephlin always argued principles, but now they were getting down to the nuts and bolts level. Don and Al agreed in principle on the general nature of what should be "understood," but now it needed to be put in print with what we all knew must be cloaked in vagueness to effectively deal with change; ambiguous enough not to be overtly constricting and with flexibility built into its very core so that if the wrong decisions were made, with the best intentions, they could be quickly addressed and rectified without waiting for an expiration date. The SAC wanted to be on the memo team themselves, but Don Ephlin's tremendous vision showed through again as he pointed out so appropriately, "The people who need to put the memo together are those who understand what really needs to be at its very core – a mission, a philosophy – and who better to do this than members of the 99 with support from the GM and UAW staffs respectively." So the memo team was named. For the UAW, Joe Malotke, lead international representative and member of the 99 Steering Committee. Jim Wheatley, a 99er and international representative servicing Cadillac, and Jerry Mills, an international rep servicing Flint plants. Although not a 99er, he was someone for whom Don Ephlin had the utmost regard and who proved to be the wisest of the three. The corporation named Dick Huber, an industrial relations staffer and member of the 99 Steering Committee; Neil DeKoker, a high-potential engineer from the Tech Center and member of the 99 Steering Committee; and our very own 99er, Chuck Stridde, whose keen understanding of the vision would really help the non-rep side. The memo team was rounded out with a process consultant, none other than Keith Brooke from the GM organizational development staff who helped the Steering Committee sail the uncharted waters of the 99er quest.

Anyone who knows anything about the auto industry in Detroit knows that whatever GM is doing is newsworthy, so the first order of the day was to find a place for the memo team to work that would be unknown to the fourth estate. Not an easy task to do, for the *News* and *Free Press* have some of the best investigative reporters in the nation, and as historic as this agreement was felt to be, it was the hottest topic in Motown. The first clandestine meeting place was at St. Mary's Convent, a celebrated, old nunnery in Detroit. This worked fine for a week, but was found out by the hounds of the *Detroit News*, and so the backup site was activated, Bay Valley Country Club, about 80 miles north of Detroit, where the seven members of the memo team were sequestered until they came up with the plan for the planet Saturn. Those of us who were back from the 99 were consulted, almost daily; and whenever we, or anyone from the GM/UAW staffs, were needed, an ingenious plan was implemented to duck any tails that might be after us. We would never drive straight to Bay Valley. We would switch cars at least twice; drive only imports; and never, ever, would anyone show up in a suit or logo jacket, for that would clearly show his or her identity.

The new site and strategy proved very effective because it was implemented the way it was planned. The memo team was able to function devoid of the pressure of exposure, free to exercise what Albert Einstein profoundly extolled 40 years earlier, "Imagination is more important than knowledge. Speculation, more important than fact." Buoyed by the process of consensus that spawned this historic "negotiating" team, the creativity that is so strong in Americans was able to flourish, because those who were chosen for this task had learned very well that if you value the differences rather than point them out, the possibilities are unlimited.

The importance of secrecy was critical for two reasons: First, a site for the plant would not be announced until the memo was done. Second, Joe Malotke was also on the site selection team, which was simultaneously pursuing where this historic memo would be implemented. A later discussion of the thinking behind the site selection is important to understanding the systemic thinking that was integral to the Saturn formula for creating change.

Keith employed a technique with the memo team that he had used with the Resource Center members and the engineers prior to the night of the blowout on Stephenson Highway. Instead of sitting on opposite sides of a table issuing demands and receiving counterdemands, he helped them focus on the needs of each side. He coached them to seek to understand why the needs of the other were so important to them, and for each group to work for a way each respective need could be met. There could not be winners and losers, only winners.

The memo team made a strategic decision very early on. The members of the team knew the product of their labors would be unmercifully compared to the GM/UAW National Agreement. Also, their goal was not to ignore the 50 years of collective bargaining embodied in that agreement but rather to make sure that the respective commitments of the parties, or lack of commitments, were not merely matched in the memo, but understood so well that the Saturn Agreement could not be challenged in any way as being inferior. So the entire 1984 GM/UAW National Agreement was dissected and placed in the elements of the S.T.E.P.S. Model with a strong emphasis on mission and philosophy, with assumptions about people that led to a transformation from one page in 1937 to over 600 pages, with addenda, which is its current form. What revelations came out of this task of letting the wind of understanding sweep over the wings of change!

The stark reality of the depth of animosity between the adversaries shone as it never had in the past before the hawk eyes of these agents of change. The distrust and disdain for each other, having never been addressed over the last five decades, had taken form in voluminous verbiage with all the tones of parent (GM) talking to child (UAW) and the human characteristic of, "Tell me how far I can go, so I can figure out how to go farther without being caught." As the 14- to 16-hour days passed into a week, an intriguing point became very clear. One paragraph very close to the front of the Agreement of the Adversaries seemed to have generated the hundreds of pages that followed, and a tiny paragraph at that. It was the Management Rights Clause, which follows:

GM/UAW National Agreement, Paragraph 8

The right to hire; promote; discharge or discipline for cause; and to maintain discipline and efficiency of employees, is the sole responsibility of the Corporation except that Union members shall not be discriminated against as such. In addition, the products to be manufactured, the location of the plants, the schedules of production, the methods, processes, and means of manufacturing are solely and exclusively the responsibility of the Corporation.

It didn't take a calculus professor to figure out that 80% of this large agreement consisted of exceptions to that tiny Paragraph 8.

The memo team again displayed the wonder of synergy that can be unbounded when the purpose of disagreeing is to ultimately agree to a third alternative* an answer neither side would have come to alone. The brilliance of picking out the lack of mutual or individual commitments in the traditional agreement, and then making respective commitments the cornerstones of the memo (commitments from the Commitment Evolution Research Document [C.E.R.D.]) was the "breakwith" thinking that allowed Saturn to crest every monstrous wave of resistance it faced in those crucial forming years.

After six weeks of intense creativity, an agreement was presented to Don and Al for their review. Confident they were that it would be heralded as historic, innovative, and "too vague," the seven designers were much taken aback when the word came back – "too specific!" "We'll never get this past our respective executive boards." Another dose of reality was meted out. *Change agents of the future take note of the following:*

1. When engrossed in a world of collaboration and mesmerized by the charms of synergy, don't ever forget that the world as a whole is not where you are. The daily reenactment of the first battle of the adversaries, repeated for decades and honed to Oscar nomination form, will go on. For no matter if, esoterically, each adversary was desirous of a different approach, all their respective

51

herds hold them unwaveringly accountable to defend their win-lose, and even lose-lose golden calves of the past.

2. When creating "a new order of things" in which no one losing is the ruling norm, remember that we all came from a zero sum-based world. Someone has to lose for me to win, and every day we wake up in this world and come back to this world. So, we must wear two opposing hats while we incrementally eke out change with our work family and our nuclear family, gradually influencing both to the point of action that will sustain this abundance thinking, and then fan out and start changing their respective spheres of influence. All the while, we must be mindful not to ever let one hat start to feel too comfortable or be reluctant to don the other when necessary.

The Memorandum of Agreement, so Don and Al and their respective "inner circles" set to making the little gray book acceptably grayer. Through their well-honed political instincts and machinations, the memo that was sent back had all the dominions of power assuaged to the level of, at least, begrudging acceptance. This was the last week of July 1985. All that the memo needed now was the site to be named where it would be implemented. As mentioned earlier, the search for land was going on simultaneously with the construction of the little gray book. The system thinkers that created Saturn had planned to announce the site and the memo at the very same time. A gap between the two would lead to too much speculation around which drove the other, a speculation that had no merit except in the hearts and heads of the herds on the plains of the adversaries, the razor-sharp pens of the fourth estate, and the intricately pompous and confused industry analysts and economists, and last, the academicians of higher education, who for decades have been turning out superstar MBAs and MEs, the would-be saviors of American industry. By the way, they still are, and yet year by year our manufacturing base has been getting smaller and smaller. You will see as we go further inside Saturn that this speculation would serve no purpose other than the killing of trees for the production of paper.

The search for land wore the cloak of secrecy, for the first new nameplate added to the GM stable since Chevrolet was acquired in 1918 was a plump jewel to be garnered, especially in light of Roger B.'s much ballyhooed $5 billion investment promise. The Economic and Community

Development staffs of 50 states were salivating to the Pavlovian stimulus of potential revenues, taxes, direct jobs, service and supplier jobs, construction of the plant and houses, and the rest. The question of a landing zone for Saturn was kept small by design to minimize detection, but more important, to look at all the available sites with the same eyes. The entire SAC, the president Bill Hoglund, all the VPs, and International Union rep Joe Malotke were joined only by a small group from Argonaut, GM Architecture and Real Estate Division, GM Legal Services, and superstar financial wizards from the Corporate Finance staff. We 99ers had weekly input and feedback sessions with both Joe Malotke and Jim Lewandowski to ensure that, for the first time in the history of GM site selection, people's needs were kept in the forefront of thought in the making of such a decision.

For 11 months in 1984 the 99ers never visited an organization without meticulously detailing where their facilities were physically located in reference to the community, roads, rails, housing, the topography of the area, and how they were logistically located in relation to process flow, inventory transference, and most important, people flow. Where did people – all people – park in relation to their point of use job? Where were the break areas and cafeterias positioned, the lavatories, up in the rafters or down in the bowels? All these issues were of strategic importance if we really intended to create a new order of things. For we knew if the SAC made the site selection the way it was always done, Saturn's orbit of origin would eventually spin out of control. All the change agents preceding us had dutifully issued the warning.

What was done under the veil of secrecy, to avoid a bidding war, all came to naught when Governor Jim Thompson of Illinois came to Detroit to present the chairman of GM, Roger B. Smith, the pen he used to sign the Illinois Mandatory Seatbelt Law. "What evil lurks in the hearts of men" could be aptly applied to this "innocent" and "apolitical" visit. It just so happened that after presenting Roger B. with the historic signing pen, Governor Thompson then added, "Oh, by the way, Roger. I'd like to let you know that Illinois would be proud to be the new home for your Saturn car, and we would more than make it worth your while." We Saturnians were aghast with indignation at this blatantly secular approach to the Shrine of the New Order. What a wonderful opportunity this so well-orchestrated little statement created for GM's financial staff – a multistate bidding war. *Change agents take note:* We 99ers were so caught up in the internal focus of development, we naively lapsed into that pink-clouded wonderland, where everyone is pure and true, and we did not objectively evaluate two elements of the outermost ring of the S.T.E.P.S. Model, economic and political. Our parent organization had, however, and how well did the site selection team veil the secret searches: all the while publicly chastising Governor Thompson.

Thirty-eight states generated "very" lucrative incentives for Saturn to land in their domain. Minnesota topped the scale at a total package exceeding $1 billion. Within 24 hours, we were back on track doing our own focused lobbying so that the final decision about the Saturn site would be made by us and not by some remote "bean counters" who didn't understand or care about the significance this decision would have and who would base it only on incentives. I said to myself when Minnesota's proposal came in, "How in hell will we ever get anyone to relocate to the Ice Planet Hoth?" This proved to be the stimulus we needed to check our commitment of togetherness, determination, and perseverance to reach for our common goal.

How could we be most effective? Who were the optimal players to focus on? How often would we target them? Who would focus on whom? What and who were the resources available to utilize? Last, but not least, where were the ever-so-critical timeline and milestone charts that must be meticulously planned and executed to perfection? We strategized that for optimum effectiveness the number of people involved should be small, so that the chance of negative press being generated, even remotely alluding to a business as usual GM plant selection, was totally eliminated. The optimal players had to be Roger B. Smith and Don Elphlin, for the stakes in this game were success or failure. There could not be even a minute chance that the players we targeted could be second-guessed by anyone. We, after much discussion, settled on weekly targeting. Our daily access to these champions would be limited by our geographical separation and their 16-hour day work schedules. However, those who were advocates of status quo site selection were in close proximity and would utilize that advantage. We then settled on who would focus on Roger and Don, respectively. Chuck Stridde would head up the target Roger team and Jerry Mills the target Don team.

From a resource perspective to help in this lobbying war, we were quite formidable in both the rep and non-rep arenas. Our president, Bill Hoglund, came up through the GM financial staff, so he and Roger had a natural bond as well as a solid personal relationship. Ironically, Don Ephlin was also an excellent resource available to us in relation to Roger, as they had developed a very good rapport, and Roger genuinely valued and listened to Don. In respect to Don, we were also blessed with three International Union reps that he valued highly, Joe Malotke, Jerry Mills, and Jim Wheatley; and we also had a non-rep ally with superb credibility with Don, Keith Brooke from the ORD staff. Last, we had the "partnership". While the partnership was not a physical entity, it was a real life force that, properly utilized, would be the most formidable resource at our disposal. Armed with the Phase II Report as the battle standard, we could effectively rattle the saber of change and hold the sanctioners' feet to the fire to implement what they had agreed to in forming this company.

The timeline was set with an end date of July 31. That meant weekly reviews from May onward. The milestones highlighted each week were twofold: A weekly debriefing after lobbying with Roger and Don, and updates on the progress in the memo team's negotiations. As I mentioned earlier, the site was to be announced only when the Memo of Agreement was signed off on by the appropriate executive boards of each organization. Focused we were, as we pulled our research papers from the Phase I and Phase II Reports of 1984. Anything and everything that even remotely touched on system thinking for choosing a plant site was handfed to the SAC as well as put into the hands of Roger and Don lobbyists. There are only two effective ways to change people's thinking, a significant emotional event or spaced repetition. The latter was our only viable option. So, methodically, with determined perseverance, the message was relayed. Make the choice with people and their needs in mind; again, make the choice with people in mind. What is the climate of each locale? What is the moral fiber? What are the school system's academic standards? Are there adequate universities near by? What is the price range and quality of housing, both single-family dwellings and apartments? Are there adequate shopping malls and recreational facilities? How are the roads? What kind and how many churches are in the area? What about the quality and quantity of hospitals and doctors? Oh, by the way, don't forget that this will be a true

55

"just-in-time" manufacturing facility, and we won't make the same mistake as Hamtramck and Lake Orion and put in 50 railroad spurs, only to dig them out and fill them in to make truck docks later. Right? Week after week, we repeated these questions. Think about this, think about this, think about this.

Well, as the saying goes, luck is when preparation meets opportunity. We were very lucky. The memo, duly sanctioned, was announced to the world on July 29, 1985. The very next day, with the press speculating between Michigan, Kentucky, and Tennessee, as *the* site, the home of Saturn was announced: Spring Hill, Tennessee. A small, 1,300-person farming and horse-rearing community 40 miles south of Nashville. Saturn would occupy 2,500 acres of rolling middle Tennessee land, and 37 other states were agonized and indignant, "Spring Hill, Tennessee! Are they nuts! There's no industry in Tennessee! What a bunch of flakes!" For the next six years, flake was our collective name, but we knew the wisdom of the decision. Saturn now had a chance at success. The ghosts of battles past, between the adversaries, would not lurk around every corner, waiting to strike at the jugular when conflict arose. The first J. D. Powers surveys in 1991 changed our name from flake to formidable. Green, green is green they say on the far side of that field....On with the development!

THE DEVELOPMENT

JULY 1985 – DECEMBER 1989

First we form our buildings.
After that they continuously form us.

Winston Churchill

6

The trek to Tennessee began with much pomp and circumstance. As stated earlier, the memo was announced on July 30, 1985, and the next day Spring Hill was announced with a full-blown press conference in Nashville. Governor Lamar Alexander hosted the gala event with Bill Hoglund, the Saturn president, and Don Ephlin, vice president of the UAW, sharing the dais with him. I was asked to be in attendance by Jim Lewandowski, our VP of human resources, for we had developed a good relationship over the months of memo preparation and the search for land. The press conference was a sight to see. Every major newspaper, all three networks – ABC, NBC, CBS – plus CNN were there. As usual, the political platitudes and promises flowed like water off a rock, but for once, I felt that there was some sincerity offered that was truly meant. That first day and evening, excitement was everywhere, as everyone was enthralled with their individual vision of what this meant to them personally – and how could they get in on the ground floor. The next day, however, was a different story. The reason we were in Tennessee was to negotiate. All the niceties being said before the rolling cameras and the staccato pens of the written word aside, the state negotiating team, of which I was a part, was here to get the t's crossed and the i's dotted with those who requested we locate in their fine state. What a delightful experience this turned out to be for two reasons: One, negotiating with our new Tennessee friends was so enjoyable because they play the "I'm just an ole' dumb country boy routine", but anyone with any experience dealing with Tennesseans knows that is 180 degrees from the truth. They are very tough negotiators who continually make you repeat yourself with the hope that you will talk yourself into what they want. The second reason was getting to know the players on our team in the way you really get to know coworkers. We were under the pressures of timelines, goals, and implementation of strategies while almost living together for six months. This way, you get to know someone in a manner you never would if you worked in the same office for 10 years. There were four people on our team that I really got to know, and for me they were the most enjoyable. They were Bill Hoglund, our president; Gary High, who was hired to manage training for us; and Joe Koch, who set our Tennessee friends on their heels with his absolutely precise, methodical, meticulous calculations on the cost of training our work force. The last member of our particular group was Laurie Danko, whom I already knew well, for if you will recall, she was the process consultant for my subcommittee at the Study Center.

Getting to know Bill Hoglund, our second president, was a real treat for me, personally, because he was so down to earth. The rest of the SAC officers were OK, but they were so caught up in how important they were, with the all too typical GM arrogance, that Bill was an exciting contrast to the typical Detroit executive. Bill was not only approachable but downright friendly. From the first time he walked into the room, I knew he was just what Saturn needed, for the whole climate in the room changed – from cold or cool to warm. He had that glint in his eye, which all good leaders have, that signals, "I take my job very seriously, but I don't take myself too seriously. We can get things done and still have a good time doing it." Bill had put the excitement back into Pontiac while he was the general manager there; and, as I alluded to earlier, he came very highly recommended from both the International Union and the Pontiac locals. I believe the trait I liked most about Bill was his willingness to listen to the union members of the 99 and truly value what was being said, as well as the perspective it was coming from. Although he was labeled as a progressive leader, his background was still from the Land of the Adversaries, and he was much more comfortable listening to his non-reps and then presenting options for the union to pick from. He adapted to this mode so well that it would make one think that, if he had been able to in the Old World, he just might have operated this way. Over the next seven months, Bill and I developed a good relationship, one that lasts to this very day. Every time Bill comes to mind, I think about one day when we were in a pretty heavy negotiating session. It was getting on into the afternoon on Friday, the day we went back to Detroit every week. I saw Bill write something on a piece of paper, and the look on his face was strained. I was sitting off to his right at the next table back, and the note got to me after being passed through three people. I opened it anxiously, wondering what brilliant tactic he was asking our opinion about. After reading it, I could barely restrain myself from laughing out loud. Hastily written in pencil was: vodka, scotch, bourbon, or beer? Place your x next to your choice. It looks like we're going to be here until the last minute, so I'll stop on the way to the plane. When I looked up from the note he was staring at me, and there was that glint, just dancing across his eyes saying, "I'm sure looking forward to that plane ride home."

Gary High was the second person on our negotiating team who I really enjoyed getting to know. Gary was another career GM manager who didn't act like the typical GM manager I had come to know over the years. Gary had spent most of his career in traditional personnel functions, primarily dealing with non-represented salary administration, but he had also been on a fast track to the unclassified ranks, so he had the opportunity to spend time in labor relations, hourly personnel administration, training, health and safety, and the GM Europe personnel staff. When Saturn hired him in the spring of 1985, he was the personnel director of Detroit Diesel/Allison Division in Indianapolis, Indiana. It was kind of ironic because we also interviewed his boss from DDAD for the same job, and we picked Gary because he was much less pretentious and very honest. When we asked him what he knew about training a work force he replied, "Not very much, but I know people, and if you check my references, as I'm sure you will, you will find out I have had a very good rapport with every local Shop Committee that I've worked with. You can teach the training business, but it's very hard to teach someone how to get along with people." I really liked that response because I had said that myself over 20 years ago when I applied for my first job as an appliance salesman during my first summer in college. Another reason that response was so welcome was that we on the interview team had already decided that we didn't want someone to head up our training team as a non-rep who was steeped in GM education and training history. So Gary fit the bill very well. We had a minor problem with Jim Lewandowski, the VP of H.R., because he didn't want to break with tradition and hire out of the chain of command, but we convinced him that this was what Saturn needed. He handled the whining of the Personnel Administration and Development (PAD) staff in the GM building, and on we went.

Over the years, Gary had built up many friendships that proved very helpful in the next few critical years of development. He got us equipment dirt cheap or for nothing, and he managed to get access to people in the corporation who could be very hard to get to sometimes. The greatest part of getting to know Gary, however, was his absolute honesty. The man was incapable of telling a lie. He would always tell you the truth, knowing full well it was not what you wanted to hear, but you got the truth nonetheless. His most endearing trait, in the way he handled people, was that he would always do it with consideration for one's feelings – making sure that the truth didn't alienate you or crush you, so that when you finished talking to him, you walked away saying, " He's OK!" Gary spent hundreds of hours with me, helping me understand the GM corporate political system as only an insider could. That personal tutelage has proven invaluable over the last 10 years and is something I will always remember, for it was given without any strings or demands for quid pro quo. Gary and I meshed very well because we both believe in the value of people, and that people are the only resource any organization has that can leverage synergy to make the other two resources, physical and financial, quadruple in value.

During the seven long months of state negotiations, Gary and I spent an untold number of hours, planning, plotting, scheming, and sometimes orchestrating covert undertakings to get what we needed for Saturn to be a success. Very few people in Saturn really comprehended the importance of securing enough financial support from the state to train our new work force in the manner we knew it needed to be done. We knew that to be ready to take on the Japanese, we would need to triple the amount of training corporate America was currently doing, and that was a pitiful half of a percent of a person's total working time. The first six months of Saturn's existence had shown me that, and when

Gary came onboard in April, he saw the same cryptic writing on the wall. The corporation wouldn't fund what needed to be done, and not just during start-up, but, more important, during steady state, when we were building cars. Their track record with this was very well documented and very easy to predict. So working with Gary on this issue really cemented our relationship, and we were able to do what needed to be done. The dollar figure wasn't as important as the kind of relationship we established with the Economic and Community Development people with whom we were negotiating. If they found us to be inflexible, "me" focused, typically arrogant, large corporation bureaucrats – as they assumed we were at the genesis of these discussions – we would have gotten the initial money but no more. We convinced them that we were in this for the long run, a hundred-year car company was our goal, and we sincerely wanted Tennessee to benefit and grow from our locating in their state. With that demonstrated and understood, we began a very good working relationship with the state that lasts to this very day, 10 years later, and this relationship is the result of Gary High's dedication to doing the right things.

The third member of the state team who was a pleasure to get to know was Joe Koch. Joe came to us from GM education and training. He was on loan back at the Study Center before Saturn became a corporation. He originally came from AC in Wisconsin, but had been single-handedly building technical training programs in the plants for the past 15 years. He had no staff, budget, resources, or support, but nonetheless, he had helped build a formidable technical presence in back rooms, closets, storage areas, and occasionally, if he were lucky, even an old office. Joe was an engineer by training and worked hand in hand with NASA on the moon program while at AC Milwaukee. His name and the names of several other people are on a plaque to this day, sitting in the Sea of Tranquillity. When the space program slowed down, Joe's love of the mysteries of the universe took a forced hiatus and his work on guidance systems for navigation came to an end. We both shared an eager desire to explore the unknown, and we talked for hours and hours about what a lifetime opportunity he experienced getting Neil Armstrong and his fellow astronauts to the moon and back. These talks would always evolve into what we had an opportunity of a lifetime to do at Saturn, and Joe would always end our conversations with, "See how lucky I am. Most people pass through life and only dream of having the chance to change the course of history, and here I am doing it twice in 20 years. The Good Lord has truly smiled on me." Joe would be smiled on again in the next five years, for he developed congestive heart failure, and became, at that time, one of the few, fortunate, successful recipients of a heart transplant; and to this day, he is deservedly enjoying a happy retirement.

It wasn't by chance that we sought out Joe's services. The Study Center research had clearly pointed out our need to build technical expertise from within, and we were not going to leave anything to chance in preparing our team members for success. Get the best, if you want to be the best. The next seven months working with Joe clearly proved to me that we not only made the right choice, but that the Good Lord truly was smiling on Saturn. The thing I liked most about Joe was his absolute obsession with detail. I had always found detail painful, and I dealt with it reluctantly; but Joe thrived on it. He would, day after day, set the state team on its ear with his absolutely precise, calculating, and systematic attention to letting nothing slip through the cracks. When our negotiations with the state came to a win-win conclusion, Joe Koch, as usual, did not stand in the limelight, but we all knew that we would never have done what needed to be done without him. Joe has always epitomized for me what Dr. Martin Luther King, Jr. once said, "If a man is called to be a street sweeper, let him sweep streets as Michaelangelo painted, as Shakespeare wrote or as Beethoven composed, so that the hosts of heaven and earth will pause and say – 'Here lived a great street sweeper who did his job well.'" Joe was a great trainer, thinker, and doer; and those who were fortunate enough to work with him would all say that he did his job to perfection.

The last member of our negotiating team, and by far not the least, was Laurie Danko. Being one of the 99, Laurie had Saturn ingrained in her soul. She also possessed something we had all come to value during the Study Center, the female perspective. Women see the world differently from men and if manufacturing would have listened to them 20 years ago, we certainly wouldn't be in the negative position we are in today. Women intuit, or sense and feel, that which men try to solve with logic, data, and fact. We generally come to the same answer, albeit considerably later, and often after the window of opportunity has closed. Laurie came to Saturn from Pontiac, where she worked on the Organizational Research and Development staff helping to implement the Q.W.L. program in the plants. Laurie did not come from an auto industry family, so she didn't have built-in adversarial tendencies. Her father was a college professor, and she started her working career in a lawyer's office in Boston. Laurie was not callously hardened by the auto wars and, thereby, brought a pleasantly naive approach to her work, which helped tremendously during our state negotiations – for many of the people we were dealing with were battle-hardened career government veterans, and they bent over backwards to explain anything she questioned. Notwithstanding, being in a state where a well-turned heel rarely goes unnoticed, her pulchritude was an additional asset.

The next seven months were exciting and exasperating, as we worked many, many 12-hour days; and then, no matter how tired, we had to accept the Tennessee hospitality until the wee hours, for we learned very quickly just how proud Tennesseans were of their state and themselves. They took every opportunity to show us Detroiters that they were formidable in their goal of making Nashville the automobile capital of the South. The majority of our team's discussions took place in a small office housing the Tennessee Industrial Training staff, which was a part of the Economic and Community Development Office. It really is ironic that, while most of the high-level (ugh) discussions were taking place in or around the governor's office, much in the public eye, with topics like bonds, taxes, or pay in lieu proposals, the strategies that were planned, agreed to, and ultimately implemented from our tiny little office would prove to be the most critical.

If you recall, as stated earlier, continuous, lifelong education of a work force was not comprehended in the upper echelons of GM. It was something nice to talk about, but planning it and then making it happen was not of any concern to our SAC officers. It was something that those H.R. folks could handle; and when it didn't work, they could take all the blame. For any manufacturing manager worth his salt knew that what really mattered was getting out cars with as few people as possible. Continuous improvement meant reducing the number of people it took to assemble an automobile. What a blinding flash of the obvious it was going to be – when we had the time and their undivided attention – to show them that our team members were going to be *fixed* assets, just like the plants and machinery and equipment. The result of our seven cramped months in that office, in the shadow of the State House, was arrived at very satisfactorily due to the whole team's effort; but, primarily, it was Joe Koch's meticulous, detail-focused mind that won the day. I don't mean won in the context of win-lose but, rather, getting across to those we were negotiating with that this was not going to be a "get all you can approach" so that you don't have to plan and then execute to that plan. It was not going to be, as the state initially thought, simply doubling what they allocated to Nissan to train their workers.

We had to have them understand that we were faced with changing 50 years of tradition, and simply giving people technical skills was not going to get us that quantum leap in attitudinal change required to really leapfrog our competition. All the research we had done, when the site selection had been narrowed to a short list, paid off handsomely. We knew generally what the state had committed to Nissan, Bridgestone, and over 90 other foreign corporations. So we were well prepared when they suggested that we could wrap this up quickly if we just agreed to doubling what they had allocated to Nissan. That first week that was spent orienting them to what we were trying to do fell on deaf ears, as we thought it would; so when we respectfully declined their offer, much to their dismay, we started over with the mission and philosophy of our original study, systemic approach, history and potential, and most important, our vision of the future. The old adage of having only two ways to change one's thinking, a significant emotional event or spaced repetition, proved true. So day by day, over and over again, the picture began crystallizing in their mind's eye. I have said this before, and I'm sure I'll say it again, commitment comes from involvement. Involve me and I'll understand.

The weeks passed into months very quickly. By October we had graduated from working with staffers on the Industrial Training Service team to working exclusively with the director of the group, Robert Parsons. Bob was a great person to work with, for he was just one level below the director of Economic and Community Development, thereby avoiding the political cleansings of new administrations. He could focus on doing the right things, getting people what was promised them, and making sure that, if the situation changed, he kept an excellent relationship with his director. He would secure whatever was necessary. Bob also liked to cut to the chase, just like I do, and talk about what it was going to take to get this wrapped up. This is where Laurie and I were of the most help. For we understood socio-technical systems and what advantages were hidden in the blend of people and technology.

We knew that Bob didn't really comprehend at first, but slowly and surely he was open enough to embrace new ideas, and he had a very large "ah-ha." He then became our supporter. The more Joe kept talking – just when Bob thought he was finally finished, "And now here's the next step" – the pattern started to take shape in his mind. This is not what Nissan, Bridgestone, Calsonics, and many others had done.

They trained in hard skills like SPC, JIT, material handling, welding, design for experiments, and on and on. They merely put people alongside machinery. How the two interacted was important but only in reference to productivity. The picture now emerging was one of "They don't expect people to be merely an adjunct to the equipment; but, rather, masters of the machines." The key was the blend of people and technology so that the optimal balance was achieved, thereby allowing synergy to drive toward feats never accomplished before. Laurie and I never missed an opportunity to reiterate how far we had to go just to catch up to where the competition was now, let alone to overtake them and become the market leaders. We did have one significant handicap to overcome. Our vice president of manufacturing, in all his exuberance with announcing Tennessee as our home, made a verbal faux pas. He said we would like to make half the jobs in our factory available to Tennesseans, a decision Don Ephlin quickly pointed out to everyone at the press conference that was not his call to make. Yes, it would be great to hire Tennesseans, but, at the present time or in the foreseeable future, that option was not open to Saturn, and it would be determined by GM and the International Union. Unfortunately, all they remembered was what our VP of manufacturing had said, and Don's statement was ignored. We debated this over and over again for the next 10 years, especially when one of the established firms moved its operations elsewhere, which happened with all too much frequency.

All the rest of the negotiating teams were making about the same progress as we were, for they, too, had to convince the respective state teams that this was not business as usual in any area of negotiations. I speak of negotiating, but in actuality, it was not traditional negotiations. Everyone, on every team, had the same role and that was to help our new friends understand what we were trying to do with a whole new culture and very fixed attitudes. Slowly, incrementally, and with the patience of Job at times, the lights would finally go on and then an entire staff's attitudes would change. They started to see that they were part of history in the making and almost to a person the swell of pride could be seen taking over their countenances. When agreement was reached on any issue, they would look at us and ask "Will this meet your needs?" When told yes, they would almost unanimously state with unadulterated pride, "See, we told you that you made the right decision in coming here." These were the times that I always look back on, and thank the Lord that I had the good fortune to be part of it all.

Although we were told, when we first came down, that the state was planning a Homecoming '86 festival for the next year, showcasing all the resident talent of Tennessee, we didn't comprehend the tremendous emphasis they were placing on these festivities. So just as we had painstakingly and patiently explained the "why" to what we were doing, they in turn helped us to understand what significance this had in reference to all their energy. During this negotiating process, we really came to understand just how proud they all were to be Tennesseans. They shared the legacies of Daniel Boone and Davey Crockett; the long heritage of volunteers for any worthwhile cause, hence the state name Volunteer State; the battles of the Civil War that took place in Tennessee, many of which were the bloodiest of that infamous struggle; the notoriety of having James K. Polk and Andrew Jackson, both presidents of the United States, as native Tennesseeans; as well as a distinguished a list of senators, congressmen, secretaries of state as any state in the nation. One could start to see that the pride they exuded was very deeply seated in their hearts and minds. As hard as they fought for the Confederacy, they were ever noble in defeat. Once that struggle was settled, they set about to rebuilding our shattered Union in the true democratic process, by getting involved in making America truly the home of the brave and the land of the free.

Not too many people know that Tennessee is actually three states in one. West Tennessee is known for some of the best jazz music in America. East Tennessee is home of the fabled Hatfield and McCoy feud; but, more important, it's the home of the University of Tennessee's main campus and some of the most beautiful land in all of America. Middle Tennessee is home to the Grand Ole Opry and the state capital of Nashville. The state flag bears witness to this, as emblazoned across it are three stars in a circle, one each of West, East, and Middle Tennessee. Each of these respective areas is rich with tradition in its own right and ruggedly independent in thought and action about every issue of its statehood. Legend has it that not that long ago members of the "other two states" were not heartily welcomed in each respective locale. It was almost ironic for here we were, GM and the UAW, having done battle for over 50 years joining forces in a state that was still doing battle with itself. We paid attention well, for we never missed an opportunity to study and understand how they resolved differences among their triadic adversaries, and it helped us immensely, when we would get into conflict situations, to use them as a model for collaborating on common goals. For no matter how much they disliked each other, distrusted each other, or sought purely personal gains, when it came down to what was best for Tennessee as a whole, they always reached agreement.

The year 1985 went by so fast it was hard to believe that it was December again, and we were all readying ourselves for the Christmas shutdown. Only this year we would not return to our homes wondering if we would ever see each other again or if Saturn would go any further down the path of destiny. This Christmas we had already received our present, on January 8, 11 months earlier. We could go home and really enjoy the holidays this time, for Saturn was now a wholly owned subsidiary, a legitimate enterprise that we all knew was destined for greatness. The last week before we left for our respective homes, all the UAW-represented team members were still on loan and living in Detroit on per diem. We rehashed the year in review, almost waiting for someone to come in and shake us and say, "Wake up! You have been in a coma for almost a year, and the project is really over this time. Get on with your lives. Saturn has been aborted." Every evening we would go over the events of the preceding year. January 8 was our anniversary date. We had a tremendous gala on February 1 at the Westin Hotel in Detroit, where there were only three speakers: Roger B. Smith, chairman of General Motors; Don Ephlin, UAW vice president; and Ross Perot, the newest member of the GM Board of Directors. This was the first time Roger dropped the bomb about when Saturn was expected to launch its first vehicle. Up until February 1, we were a "no year" vehicle, destined to come to market when we were ready. Of course, none of us really believed that, but those who had a date in mind had kept it a very closely guarded secret.

On this cold and bleak winter night in Michigan, only four days shy of a year after the Study Center started its famous quest, Roger B. let it be known that he fully intended to drive the first car off the assembly line in Spring Hill, Tennessee, before he retired. It didn't take a calculus major to figure out that Roger had to retire in 1990, that was the GM rule. A small but very perceptible chill ran up the necks of all those associated with Saturn. The challenge has been made. Now it was put up or shut up. There were the 99ers, surrounded by the top 500 executives in GM, 14 of us were table hosts to members of the GM Executive Committee. I hosted Don Atwood who was head of the Automotive Components Group at that time (who later became assistant secretary of defense during Ronald Reagan's second term), and I spent the entire evening explaining to him and his wife what went on at the Study Center, how we came up with the almost mysterious structure and organizational breaks with tradition. Don Ephlin was the second speaker, and he, too, dated our car. He let everyone know that he fully intended to be in the passenger seat of the first car before he retired. Don also spoke of how historic this evening was in building "a new order of things" in labor-management relations.

The last speaker was Ross Perot, who talked about how much Saturn's genesis was very similar to how he created Electronic Data Systems. He capped his remarks with yet another bombshell when he asked Roger and Don what did they think they were doing in his car. For he fully intended to purchase the first salable vehicle and auction it off to a lucky Saturn team member. Ross had not yet totally alienated himself from the Board of Directors, and his enthusiasm and candor were highlights of the evening. None of us would ever forget that evening, for if you didn't feel that something great was destined to happen when you walked into the Renaissance Center, you surely felt it when you left. We relived the building of the memo and our guarded fear that it wouldn't be creative enough or would become too watered down to let us really achieve our potential. The site selection process, shrouded with all its mystery and intrigue, and the almost comedic bidding war that took place to guarantee its landing in 1 of 38 states. We marveled at how well the negotiations with the state of Tennessee had been and the walks we had taken across the fields of the horse farms we had purchased, vividly trying to picture in our mind's eye what the site would look like when finished and meticulously picturing what would be going on inside those newly formed factories of the future. We marveled in recollection at how much we learned about ourselves and our newly formed partnership with the state of Tennessee during our intense seven month's of negotiations. The bonding of old friendships and the formation of new ones, realizing that no matter how much you think you know about someone, when charged with a task that has lofty goals and no predetermined outcome, you will see a side of each other that you had not been cognizant of.

The longing of family and friends awaiting our return home was foreshadowed by what was ahead of us on our return in January 1986. Our timeline had been set back, and although preliminary discussions had been going on in many areas of development, I believe that, at this holiday season, the scope of what was before us, for the first time, really registered in our minds. A \$3.5 billion corporation was to be built from the ground up, and those charged to do this were all from the corporation of the past and present. But the more we talked and reflected on what had been done so far, we knew that success was in our control, for we had institutionalized two key mindset over the last 23 months:

1. No force is greater than an idea whose time has come.
2. The empires of the future are the empires of the mind.

I think the most sobering thing that we discussed was that, over the last year of 1985, it became very obvious that the rest of GM was of two distinct mindsets in their attitude toward Saturn. First, the other car groups, CPC, BOC, Truck and Bus, the Automotive Components Group, GM Overseas, and the GM Technical Center were very jealous of our notoriety and our funding; and, second, no one in GM and the UAW, other than Roger and Don, took us seriously. Our competition were polite on the outside, but inside they were openly laughing at the folly of those arrogant Americans. How could you take someone seriously when they were going to "design and build" a car that had no parts in existence anywhere in the world – except a few nuts, bolts, and fasteners – then build it with UAW workers, in a brand new plant, in a "right-to-work state," which, by the way, the union had jointly selected.

Now talk about arrogance, we had said we were going to utilize processes that had never been set into production before, like lost foam casting for engine blocks, heads, and cranks. We were going to build automatic and manual transmissions on the very same equipment lines. This had never been done since the creation of the automobile. We were going to use plastic panels for the skin of the car, built in 7,000-ton injection molding machines, of which there weren't any in existence. A new paint system would be utilized with a clear coat and top coat that was water borne. Now, get this, we were going to do this with the union as a full partner in all the decisions that were to be made, utilizing a whole new people system that was without supervisors, and last but not least, we were going to revolutionize how a vehicle was marketed. Yes, our parent organizations and our competition sat back and waited, waited to gloat and have the opportunity to say, "We told you so. Who in their right minds would ever have tried to do so much at one time." Our mindset, however, was only buoyed by this evident disdain. We viewed our adversaries as our friends; for if you do that, they will steel your nerves and critically sharpen your wit.

January 1986 would bring all our collective creativity together for an all-out assault on the bastions of status quo. The sourcing of machinery and equipment while preliminarily started had to be pursued with great vigor, as well as sourcing of all the parts we would not make in Spring Hill. The most dynamic recruitment, selection, and relocation program in the history of industrialized America had to be designed, developed, and delivered – bringing onboard more union-represented people, four years before scheduled launch, than had ever been done in the history of the auto industry. Engineering of the car had to be done in lockstep with marketing, sales, and service development. Although the GM executives liked our car, until we held clinics in the heart of import country like California and New York, we really didn't know how much engineering remained or for that matter, reengineering. The site having been picked, the colossal task of preparing land for the production of 500,000 units a year loomed massive on the horizon. The design of the physical facilities would for the first time be done with people in mind, not just the most purely logical engineering approach.

A whole new people system awaited birth. With the fragile partnership between union and management having been agreed to in principle, it now awaited the operationalization of the detail relative to this bold move. Just the thought of creating a human resource organization that would really care about people ran shivers up our spines. We talked about all the elements of our organization, but this was, beyond a doubt, the topic that meant the most to those of us who were represented by the union. Imagine, we could design out the labor relations department; we could eliminate the segregation of salaried and hourly personnel; and we could relegate the role of committeeman to the Land of the Adversaries and put decision making where it belonged, in the hands of those who must implement the decisions. We could unite human resources and organization development into one focused group, seeking only the development of our most valuable asset, our people, rather than have two groups competing for the most notoriety in achieving the organization's goals.

The process of breaking in the SAC would continue in the new year with renewed hope, especially after we had spent the last week before going home reflecting on all of our opportunities when we returned. We reflected on the importance of our champions, Roger and Don, and how we would never have come this far, this rapidly, with so much more lurking right over the horizon in the new year, if they had not been there every time we needed them. We also reflected, with much less enthusiasm, but ever with a wary eye on the future, about that time when they would both be gone, for champions do not stay forever and life must go on. That is as certain as summer follows spring. Yet, we were still buoyed by the prospect of what awaited us in the new year. Don Ephlin had clarified what we were really out to do the last time he had spoken with us. He made the most profound statement about Saturn that I had ever heard and still the most profound to this very day. He looked at us with those marvelous eyes of vision and said, "We are not here to build the world's cheapest car or the world's highest quality car. We are here to prove that we can build an automobile with UAW workers and GM managers that is competitive in quality, cost, and customer satisfaction and do it without lowering our standard of living. We are playing on an uneven field of wages and benefits; tax structures that encourage foreign investment; and retirement programs that don't need funding because no one could or would retire from the transplants for 30 years."

Yes, Don put it in a very clear perspective. One that made us even more determined to show the world that Americans, union members and not, could and would rise to the challenge. Although all the hard bargaining with the state had been successfully resolved, we looked to the new year for the formalization of our endeavors with all the bells and whistles that our friends from Tennessee so loved to use. The last thing we talked about was not a reflection but rather an anticipation, for we all knew that, since the memo had been approved by both GM and the UAW, 1986 would be the year when we, the UAW, represented team members would be formally offered jobs, after being on loan for over two years. We laughed and joked about who would stay and who wouldn't, mockingly challenging each other's commitment, and every person swore that, when offered, he or she would sign on the dotted line. But we all knew that some would go back to the Land of the Adversaries, very reluctantly, but go back they would, for their spouses had made it all too clear that they had no intention of moving to Tennessee. Still others, who could survive on loan with the safety net of being able to return to their home plants always at their beck and call, trumpeted loudly how they would jump at the chance to become permanent Saturn workers; but we collectively knew who they were and knew that when the time came in the new year, they would leave.

Those of us who had already made that mental commitment knew that we would miss them, would not begrudge them, and would always think of them fondly, for we had become family since February 1984; and no matter how much we would want them to stay, we knew they had to leave. So, when the time came, we would make all the lovely promises about keeping in touch with each other, hug and squeeze, cry and laugh, then wave good-bye, fully understanding that when rejoined with the attendant difficulties of the old world, they would call less and less frequently, just as we would, being totally immersed into forming the future. We all knew also, that many of the 99ers who couldn't stay on loan would relish the chance to join, if offered permanent status, and how much fun it would be to renew those dormant friendships. Yes, 1986 was going to be a great year. The trips home to the four corners of America would drag on endlessly we mused, esoterically wishing that the holidays had already passed.

The reverie with family and friends now fondly tucked away in the microprocessor of the mind, we were back – rested, recharged, relaxed, and raring to roar headlong into the future – armed with the belief that "No force is greater than an idea whose time has come." The month of January passed relatively uneventfully, with everyone toiling diligently in his or her own little ecosystem, vacillating between ecstasy and shock at the wonderful opportunity we had and having scope and complexity of totally integrating people, technology, and business systems become overwhelming. Before anyone really noticed, our coldest month of the year in Detroit, February, was on us for the second year with Saturn; and it lived up to its expectations with daily temperatures below zero. Something was in the air, besides the frigid wind, but you couldn't put your finger on it. It was there, nonetheless. It seemed like February would always be our month of change.

If you recall, it was the month that the group of 99 was summoned together in 1984; the gala ball at the Westin Hotel in 1985 thrown by Roger; and now something was going to happen, but what? We didn't have to wait very long, for Bill Hoglund, our president, and Joe Malotke, our lead international rep, called an all-Saturn meeting for February 6 at the styling dome of the GM Technical Center in Warren, Michigan. The purpose, as announced, was to take a picture of everyone who was working for Saturn – permanent, on loan, temporaries and STAR students, interns from universities all over the country whose bright young uncorrupted minds we were utilizing to create our new order of things. Everyone would receive a copy of the picture as a memento of Saturn's appreciation for the 16- to 18-hour days they were working until we could hire more resources in a much more expeditious manner. So, gather we did, everyone in sartorial splendor for posterity would harshly judge those in tacky outer accoutrements. Many of the represented team members were not used to working in suits and ties; but at this point in our development, we were spending the majority of our time at the Technical Center, the GM Building or O.E.M.s (original equipment manufacturers) with some of us also visiting universities and other organizations' human resource departments.

Another key reason for business attire ruling the day was that we had not yet clearly established our culture, where what you do, not who you are, would determine your worth. So the attire from the Land of the Adversaries was accepted, for the time being. It was a good stroke of business for us union-represented folks, because people would tell us things, dressed as we were, that they never would have divulged if we were in the "normal work clothes" of labor. Many times a valuable lesson was learned about people we were dealing with, whom you could trust and whom you couldn't, ludicrous as it was, just from the way you were dressed. All the conversations completed with those we didn't get to see on a daily basis, 500 of us lined up on the styling dome stage, and the picture was taken. Then we were asked to sign a large blank card that the picture would be married with so everyone would get a copy with all the signatures on it. All of us also received a commemorative clear glass coffee cup from the Westin Hotel in honor of the occasion.

This being done, Bill Hoglund and Joe Malotke ascended the stage with another person I'd seen before, but I couldn't place a name with the face. Bill took the microphone, and in his absolutely devilish voice said, "Another milestone for Saturn, huh? How about this, a year ago, there was only the SAC officers and now we are 500 strong and growing. I have a short announcement to make and then Joe, Skip, and I will be available to answer questions." The sound of silence suddenly became deafening. "I wanted you to hear this from me because it is going to be announced to the public later this evening. I have been promoted to the Executive Board of General Motors as an executive vice president in charge of the Buick, Oldsmobile, Cadillac Group (BOC), and my replacement is here between Joe and me – Skip LeFauve. Let's all give him a spirited Saturn welcome." The ensuing applause, though heartfelt, was considerably reserved given the circumstances. Bill Hoglund had made many friends while coleading us, and he would be sincerely missed, but the looks on the faces in the crowd told the whole story. Written across their brows, you could almost read the thoughts behind their eyes, "What does this mean about corporate commitment to us? Who is this guy? Did the union know this was coming? Did Bill ask to go? Why a change – so fast? What does this 'really' mean? I know I said change was OK, but this is too quick." (Several of us 99ers had been told about Skip several weeks earlier but were sworn to secrecy until it was official, because you could never tell in GM when something was for sure until it actually happened. It was a long couple of weeks, but no one spoke, and it was fun looking completely surprised – as if we really were.)

Joe Malotke brought everyone back to the present when he stepped to the mike and said, "Bill and I have discussed this for several weeks, and Don and I genuinely support Skip. When you get to know him, you will also." That brought another reserved round of applause, and then Skip, in what would become very familiar to all of us, confidently stepped to the front and with those ice-blue eyes and a wonderfully disarming smile said, "I can't replace Bill Hoglund. No one can. I can only be me. Ever since this corporation was formed I've hoped I would have the opportunity to just be a part of it, but never in my wildest moments did I think that I would be named president and have the opportunity to lead such a fine group of people in such an exciting undertaking. Let me also set the record straight, right up front, I did not come in here to make wholesale changes or disrupt your fine work with a bunch of meddling. I believe you will find that I am a team player, for I have believed for a long time that cooperation is the way we will beat our competitors – not confrontation. I'll be here in the styling dome for an hour or so and will meet as many of you today as I can, but if we don't talk this afternoon, we will talk, because I want to meet each and every one of you." Applause again resulted from this brief speech, only this time it was more enthusiastic. Skip's low-key voice and demeanor were successfully disarming – as he had come to know so well – and with that, our newest milestone was ushered in, the typical Saturn way, with all of us gathered together, up front, no deception or veiled truths, and on with our quest for the future.

Needless to say, our new president's arrival was the talk of every cubicle for the next few days, but given our monumental undertaking, it was relatively short lived. Soon all were deeply engrossed in what they were doing prior to Skip's announcement, and the creativity of hundreds of minds was again totally focused on our new order of things. The benchmarking we had done showed us some very good practices in all aspects of an organization, but no one had put them all together. Also, if we simply replicated what the successes of others were, we could only be as successful as they were; and we could not settle for that. We had to leapfrog everyone in the small car market at the same time they were going full speed ahead at getting better, and this was going to be quite a feat to pull off. We were very aware that one of our strengths lay in our ability to accept change and grow from it. In the next five years, it would remain the only constant. Every idea that surfaced would face a juggernaut of challenges, "Was this good enough? Why do we want to do this? How does it integrate people, technology, and business systems? Does it support the original mission and philosophy? Will it help us clearly leap ahead?" Of course, no one knew the answers to these challenges, but nonetheless, every idea would be subjected to their rigorous onslaught. All we could do was be willing and open to each other's ideas and build off them, make the original idea better than the person who thought of it could ever do alone, and then commit to making it work. Our critical success factor would always be taking the time to get the buy-in up front; we could make anything work that we believed in.

FORMING THE FUTURE

A little over a month after Skip became president another major change came to pass. (I was privy to this one also.) Don Ephlin, Joe Malotke, Jerry Mills, and Jim Wheatley from the International Union had been working for several months to put together a start-up team of local union leaders who were progressive thinkers and would embrace building a strong local union leadership as well as provide the needed continuity in decision making while we expanded very rapidly. New engineers were being added weekly to develop our product from scratch. Finance was staffing up, busily building the financial systems of the future, and facility engineers were being lured from all over GM to design our world-class manufacturing operations and on and on in every functional group in Saturn. Decisions were going to be made, challenged, made again, challenged, and made again; and there were only 35 of the 99 to carry the partnership across our rapidly expanding enterprise. To further complicate things, the lion's share of the 35 had little or no union leadership experience; and while their hearts were dripping with Saturn blood, they did not always understand the ramifications of some of the decisions they would come to a consensus on. Some of which could put our champion, Don Ephlin, in a very compromising position, especially if they were made public before he could run interference for them. As I look back on this announcement of our appointed local union leaders, for several years afterward and to this very day, it still makes my temperature rise. There was no calling the entire Saturn team together for a unified announcement. The people represented by the union were called together and introduced to their local reps, and then the reps were introduced to the SAC, but that was it. It may have been true that the partnership was embryonic at this point; but the person who was appointed president of a local, which was not even going to be chartered for a year, would have a tremendous impact on all of us. It did and still does border on criminal, how unceremoniously he was ushered in. More on this later, but the union's local leadership team was announced, comprising many local presidents, shop chairmen, and shop committee members. Leading this team was Michael E. Bennett, a local union president from my home town of Flint, Michigan. (He is the person who leaked the Al Warren report to the press on using the Q.W.L. process to circumvent collective bargaining. This happened while I was at the Study Center, and it almost shut the Study Center down.) Bill Sells, a shop chairman from Hamtramck, GM's new megaplant, was also named, along with one of his shop committeemen, Cliff Cantrell.

76

Three were named from plants in Alabama: Jim Mills (no relation to international rep Jerry Mills), Jackie Teague, and rounding out the group was Grady Cook. This assemblage had over 120 years of union leadership, collectively, to bring to bear on our partnership development, but they must face the learning curve that all new team members must navigate. How quickly and completely this navigation would take would depend entirely on their willingness to learn and their reluctance to ready, fire, aim. Many of the represented team members, who had already been on loan, felt discouraged that they were not considered for these appointments. But, with the passage of time and the leadership demonstrated by some of these individuals, especially when the magnitude and the scope of integration that must be managed in tandem with organizing and implementing a brand new chartered local became all too obvious, envy for their responsibilities and hectic schedules evaporated with the obscurity of condensation and was replaced by, "I'm glad I don't have that job!"

Another milestone in our journey passed by. Our movement on the road to the future picked up speed, as each day that passed, in the blink of an eye, brought us closer to the day when all the design, development, and implementation must work. We would not have the luxury of making a good second first impression. So on we went, like a formula one race car driver with maximum acceleration on the straightaways, then downshift and deceleration for the next curve that must be traversed, before again feeling the tremendous rush of full force acceleration. Almost overnight, it seemed, we were assembled again, only this time in Spring Hill, Tennessee. The gala event was the groundbreaking of the manufacturing site that would be home to almost all of us, someday, and it was only April 1986.

To those of us who had walked those fields of dreams only nine months earlier, the twinge of ambivalence again surfaced its ugly head. We gathered at the temporary construction headquarters, where the awesome earthmoving devices stood poised with their engines roaring like prehistoric beasts of prey waiting to swoop down on an unsuspecting herd, screaming, "Let me at this land that I may use my blades of steel to change the face of this beautiful rolling hillside into the home of the future." We all thought, "It is so peacefully picturesque here. What a shame." But our vision of the potential of the future won out, and forward surged those land eaters, forever changing the landscape from tranquillity to progress. In the next few months, millions of cubic yards of earth were removed and saved, for utilization later, to get down to the layer of rock that would be dynamited and crushed to form the pad for our plants and the base for all our surface roads. In the end, $5 million was spent on dynamite alone to prepare the base for the four plants, the truck roads for just-in-time delivery, parking lots completely circling the complex, the main entrance and egress route from Highway 31, and the five-mile spur off I-65 that we negotiated and called the Saturn Parkway.

Then it was back to Troy, Michigan, for all but those overseeing construction, as the clock kept ticking toward 1990. Square footage for each plant had to be calculated, equipment processed, and so on. Every aspect of our infant organization had to be analyzed anew to fit against our benchmarking, knowing full well that by 1990 almost every aspect of our corporation would look different from what we envisioned that day. This is one of the marvelous aspects of the change process. The future state never ends up looking like what you planned because if it did, you would not be in the future, but merely replicating the past. The flight back to Detroit from groundbreaking was very sobering for many of us, but the challenge facing us now that the plant was under construction also awakened the spirit of the pioneer – inherent in all Americans – but highly tuned in all those we had searched out. The thrill of heading the wagons West, not at all sure what one would find over the next hill, around the next bend in the road, or the next day that would dawn. That exhilarating tension between "bring it on" and trepidation about what it would really be like.

Again, the thought of Oscar Wilde flashed across my mind. We were artists, the pioneers of Saturn, and as he so well stated, "Artists don't see things as they really are, for if they do, they cease to be artists." We must see things as we want them to be and have the commitment, dedication, and perseverance to make our mural of the future come to fruition. Back in Detroit we all came to the same conclusion; that is, we needed to break out the S.T.E.P.S. Model and, functional group by functional group, look with a finely tuned eye on our dependencies, independencies, and interdependencies. What had we learned from our travels during the study? Every element in the model was interrelated to every other element in the model. You could not change one without having an impact on all the others. The SAC, left to itself, now earth had been turned, would put pedal to the metal at building little fiefdoms and putting line after line on our clean sheet of paper. Week by week more and more engineers were brought onboard full time: first, product engineers, then process engineers, followed by manufacturing engineers, and industrial engineers. The financial staff, now but a handful, grew like grass in spring, watered by the rain of money to be controlled. Sales, service, and marketing staffs, charged with creating a revolutionary buying experience, multiplied like rabbits before Easter.

Human resources bulged at the seams with developers of recruitment and selection, orientation and training, benefits and compensation, wellness and fitness, child care and structure programs. Every month more people moved to Spring Hill, almost under the cover of night, to do what? Heck, the first plant wouldn't be ready for at least two years, but move they did. I'm not sure exactly when it dawned on us, but two distinct cultures were being created that at a point in time would battle for control of Saturn. The outermost ring of the S.T.E.P.S. Model told us that. As did the brightest academicians of America, when control finally surfaced, its inevitable head, for now, was somewhere in limbo between the two growing entities. People in each functional group would be promised things by people who wouldn't be able to deliver when the devil came to call.

Yet, promise they would. For to get the talent that they needed (or at least felt they needed), the bidding war would be undertaken with the divisions that currently had the talent and those who wanted their talent. In the next four years, the managers would choose the car while the union would choose the people, but the *process* would ultimately bring us back together when the time was right. *Take note, you formulators of the future.* The process is what change is all about; not technology, not people, not the business systems but, rather, the integration of the three systems into a megasystem, one that would cause many things to happen merely by the fact of its existence. If this megasystem were not guarded closely, by the only resource that could control it, it would veer off on a path of its own and no telling what it would look like or where it would stop. Which resource, you ask? Physical, financial, or human? They are the only three resources that any organization has. Yes, *people* manage the process or it manages them.

Given that we were creating two cultures, one bordered only by geography and another bordered by our values, the latter being much more motivational than the former, necessitated our energy around a total system check of where we were headed and what were the indicators for potential conflicts that could be avoided. We would certainly encounter enough that could not be avoided. Our undivided focus must be on systemic thinking or balance between the three systems. As aforementioned, exacerbating the situation was this steady influx of new non-reps, and the fact that we 99ers were rapidly being outnumbered by new team members who did not necessarily receive the "real vision." Our challenge in human resources became one of how to get the right balance of 99ers spread across this rapidly expanding megasystem. Our second, and equally as important, challenge was to secure the appropriate support for a new team member orientation, so that all those who were already onboard could get focused in the right direction and all those who would follow could get focused properly in the first place. Last, we had to continue to bridge the gap that still existed between the Project Saturn engineers, who had come onboard full time, and the Resource Center team members, who had not been grounded since the October 1984 blowup over our structure recommendations in the Phase II Report.

So here we were, 35 99ers, 800 non-reps, and 6 new local union leaders, all equally devoted to building Saturn Corporation into a world-class organization but from clearly different points of view and physically separated locations. No one ever thought this was going to be easy, but when you stopped to survey the battlefield, the opportunity facing you could seem to be overwhelming. There was no room except for brave hearts. Too much was at stake. I could see the handwriting on the wall if we were to fail. "We told you, you can't let the union get involved with running the business. They're not professionals." As the saying goes, adversity reveals genius while prosperity conceals it. There was no doubt in my mind that, whatever it took, we would be successful. The battles in the Land of the Adversaries had taught us much. We knew what was wrong – why our plants didn't run the way they could – and come hell or high water, the sheer force of will would produce a winner for us if we remained aligned and focused.

Within a month, we had a fantastic orientation program put together in H.R. and were at Skip's and Joe Malotke's desk with bells and whistles, sales techniques abounding, prepared for a tough sell. But, much to our surprise, they simply said, "Show us what you've got. We really need an awareness of what to expect not only for new people, but everyone already onboard." We were very pleased with the ensuing presentation, took their suggestions for improvement with due sincerity, and left with a mandate to put our plan into action as cost effectively as possible, but to do it immediately. The primary architects – Laurie Danko, Patty Martinec, Dennis Bowman, Ken Duncan, Dora Mack, Gary High, Larry Hales, Dave Smith, and myself – were ecstatic. The people system would get a push toward the balance scale, so we had to coordinate our effort with folks in the technology and business systems sectors; and, incrementally, the megasystem would come together.

The technology system development was championed by international rep Jerry Mills, Mike Bennett, and from the 99, Bill Brake, who was a crusty man with 25 years of adversarial battles firmly etched in his memory but a real example of the talent we had in the rank and file. Bill could uncannily cut through any amount of traditional engineering verbosity and unerringly pinpoint the problem – not the symptom, as was a recurring event in the GM system – and with determined perseverance surface potential solutions. Next was Al Brown. Al was a trades technician from my hometown of Flint, Michigan. I think everyone in the world knows at least someone like him. While he was a very good technician, nothing that came to his mind stayed there long. It was always an instant flush, and that flush became the trademark for him, no matter where he went or who he met. This book could never be complete without at least one description of what I mean.

In the spring of 1986, while driving to work one morning, I happened to catch a traffic signal, and while stopped just casually glanced to my right where a red Corvette convertible was also waiting. The driver of this car was a young blonde woman in her middle to late twenties. When our eyes met she smiled and blew me a kiss. I returned the same, and the signal light changing, we both continued to wherever we each were headed. That was that. As I drove on, I reflected for a few moments on how that spontaneous gesture from a total stranger made me feel so good, and I vowed that every opportunity I had to do the same for someone else, I would, and did, almost every day. I was talking about this incident a few days later over morning coffee, when Al, out of the blue, said, "Jack, you just figured out another way to pick up girls, you rogue bachelor, but I'm married and I don't think my wife would like it if I was blowing kisses at strange women." I reiterated to him and everyone else who was listening that this was not the case. It just made me feel good and was a great way to start the day, having another person just share a brief moment of warmth with me. I further explained that I was not attempting to even meet her. Whether they were young or old, beautiful or not, it didn't matter. It was merely a good way to get your endorphins flowing in the morning and invariably started a day off that was very productive and satisfying. Al still didn't buy into this but vowed to try it himself to see. About a month passed during which I would ask him almost every day if he had tried it yet, to which he would always reply, "No", but would swear to do it the next day.

The last week of May, on a Friday, Al came in and was very upset. I inquired as to his agitation, and he did, as he always did, an immediate dump. "I told you it wouldn't work for me Jack, you louse," he shot out. This was vintage Al. He went on, "I did exactly what you said. I stopped at the light about three blocks north of here, looked over and a gorgeous redhead was sitting in the lane next to me. So I rolled down my window, looked over at her, smiled, and blew her a great big kiss." I questioned what was wrong with that, and he replied, "She didn't smile and blow me a kiss back at all. She rolled her window down and spit on my car." There were about 10 of us having coffee during this delightful dissertation, and we all fell out of our chairs. After composure returned, we offered Al our condolences for he was genuinely hurt. He was really a decent, caring human being who unfortunately had a style that brought out the worst in people.

The third 99er in the guard of the technology system development was Mikey Gifford. Mikey hailed from Kokomo, Indiana, and was a mechanical trades technician. While being a gifted machine repairman, Mikey had the heart and mind of a poet. He always looked at things through the emotional side of his mind, even though he was as logical and analytical as anyone I ever met. He was a perfect choice for heading up the daily interface with the engineering community, as he was every bit as left brained as they were; but, as I said, he could mix emotion and dreams with their Cad tubes to help them understand that what looked good on paper most often didn't work when it got to the plant floor. Here is a summary of the Study Center that Mike wrote in late 1984, which will give you an idea of what I'm talking about:

TOGETHER

Saturn....Where can I begin? Well, let me reach into the throes of my memory – You know, it seems like only yesterday that it was the first of February; and now, it's almost February again. Yeah, we've seen the seasons go around....Together.

Anyway, initially we met – most of us total strangers to one another. After short introductions, we got acquainted, listened to an orientation, were given a mission, and sent out into the world to investigate our charge....Together.

Travel? Yeah, to the likes of Grand Rapids, Kansas City, Milwaukee, Atlanta, Chicago, Tuscaloosa, Rochester (N.Y.), to name a few, and back to Detroit. Ah, Detroit, Motor Capital of the world. Acquired a little soft spot for the city, the excitement of the Tigers winning the pennant and going to the Series (Bless you, boys!) and the chance to see Solidarity House and the famed General Motors Building (No, didn't make it to the 14th floor!) The whole metro area and even the side trips to Windsor are an experience, but the longing for home is still there....Together.

Sacrifices? Sure, but that depends on whose definition is used. A few particular to me were not seeing my baby son shedding his diddy (diaper) and ba-ba (bottle), now standing like a little man and drinking from a cup. Not being there for the middle daughter's excitement of getting on the school bus for the first grade, and missing some of the growing pains of the oldest girl maturing into a fine young lady entering her teen years. And the wife? Yes, the wife – holding down the fort, working her own job, maintaining the household, and pacifying those kids until Dad gets home! God Bless 'em all....Together.

To ease the pains and strains, we've been bowling, harness racing, swimming, dancing, singing, skating, jamming (air guitars), and sun bathing. We've played golf, volleyball, basketball (highball), the lottery, and even a little trivia. We quit smoking, started smoking, quit drinking, then drank more. We've gorged and feasted, then dieted and fasted. Thank goodness for Tums and fresh fruit! We've been stranded in airports, hotels, and traffic jams. We've had no luggage, no hot water, no cars, and then crashed a couple too – though not our fault!...Together.

83

Educational? Definitely! That's something they can't take away from us. We've been into the likes of Webster, Brittanica, and Roget's to name a few. We've been reading, proofreading, writing, fighting, searching, researching, typing, griping, word processing, computer programming, budgeting, fidgeting, and even widgeting. We've been editing, crediting, cussing, and discussing, sharing, caring, stretching, reaching, learning, and teaching. We've also been perusing, bemusing, composing, and decomposing (reminds me of a song I once wrote), calculating, costing, charting, graphing, investigating, digesting, questing and testing, scanning and seeking, planning and tweeking. We've worked first, second (afternoons), and third shifts, weekends, holidays, (remember we've been through Easter, Memorial Day, July 4, and Labor Day thus far) and we've even worked while on vacation. Not many trials and tribulations have escaped us – Hell, we've even been on strike....Together.

And so it goes in the "real world," and knowing in our hearts that our destiny lies in the powers that be. We only hope we leave them with the lasting impression that the strengths and courage of our unity is...

"Together"
To Jack
From Mike (11/14/84)

The business system development was being spearheaded by Chuck Stridde. Chuck was a personnel director from Kokomo, Indiana, who had spent nearly his whole career in human resources, except for a very short period in manufacturing. Chuck was not a traditional GM bureaucrat, although he knew very well how the system worked. He had a real penchant for procrastination, not in the form of putting things off to be adversarial but more, "Let's make sure we covered all the bases so we don't have to revisit this." This mini procrastination was also a part of Chuck's whole style, though. He was probably one of the most laid-back people I have ever met. During these critical forming years, Chuck was very instrumental in getting people on all sides of an issue, especially many of the emotional ones, calmed down and listening to each other simply by staying calm himself and not allowing them to get him upset or rattled. He was also our resident expert on the Saturn structure, having worked on it extensively at the Study Center.

84

Being keenly aware of how much impact all the functional parts of the organization had on manufacturing was an issue we talked about daily.

So Chuck's role was to interface with key leaders from product engineering, marketing, finance, material management, and strategic planning, while being a key leader in human resources. Integration of this system with people and technology would be one of our key success factors, and we also knew it would be the hardest to integrate. The functional groups had a long history of autonomy and unilateral decision making and to crack this tradition was going to take a tremendously focused effort. An example of what I'm talking about is finance. General Motors is run by the finance staff. For the last 30 years, the chairman of GM has always come from finance, and many of the decisions that adversely affected manufacturing were made by a short-term payback on investment mentality. Cost, solely, would drive decisions, not quality or customer enthusiasm or buildability, and the result would always be the same, a product that was less than world-class and tremendous expense in redesign. One would think that after 30 years GM would learn, but that was going to be one of the benefits of Saturn to the rest of GM, if management would listen and learn, when we were successful.

The champion of people systems was Joe Malotke, our lead International Union rep, who was joined by me, Ken Duncan, Dennis Bowman, and Dora Mack. Joe sat on the SAC, so we had an ace in the hole in pulling this three-system integration together, with a "people first" focus. That may sound contrary to system integration with people first, but in all our travels we consistently heard from one successful company after another, "Don't let the other systems drive the organization and then work on the people issues. Err on the people side, and it will be easier to compensate later." In addition to getting an awareness up and running, our most important task was the recruitment and selection process. We were finalizing how we would get all the represented people, who had been on loan from their home plants since 1984, onboard full time, as well as all the others who would follow. From one-on-one conversations with each person on loan, we knew that not all of them would stay, so we had to get new team members identified and into the organization who would stay when D day came. It looked like that was going to be around the fourth quarter of 1986. In addition, the compensation and benefit system had to be refined enough to let people make an informed decision and, last, but of significant importance, was training. This is where we would have the greatest opportunity to leapfrog our competition. In the late 1980s corporate America was training its team members less than 1% of their work time. In the auto industry, our competition was besting that by over 1%. That was why we chose 5% as our training goal. We simply could not match our competition and hope to catch them. Our training system would encompass all three elements of our organization and this was going to be our greatest challenge, to thaw, change, and refreeze.

Around June we decided that a more focused UAW presence needed to be put forth in Tennessee. First, Tennessee was not a UAW stronghold, for many reasons, and it would be an opportunity to show middle Tennesseans what we were really like, which we were sure was much different from what they thought unions were about. Second, the plant was being built without our input, except by phone or a one- or two-day trip to the site. This may not sound important, but many things can change on a blueprint in a blink of an eye. Once concrete and steel are in place, it is very difficult and costly to resolve differences with, "Oh, I'm sorry. I didn't know that's what you wanted." So Jim Wheatley, the third International Union rep and 99er, volunteered for this assignment. Jim was born in Tennessee and had migrated to Detroit during the auto boom years, so this provided a welcome opportunity for him to move back home. Jim had started in the plants of Detroit and worked his way up through the local union structure into the International Union. He had developed a reputation as a tough negotiator and the years of battle in the adversarial wars had left a tough and gruff veneer, which he showed to the world, but once you got past his facade, you would find a heart as big as Tennessee, a wit that was very down to earth and funny, and a mind that was sharp as a razor. Jim would be perfect to lead this two-pronged assault into the heartland.

It was also decided that the newly appointed local union leaders should join him, as many of them were thought to have key roles in manufacturing in the future. So Mike Bennett, who was earmarked to be president of the local and all the other appointees were to go south, but one thing had to be fixed first. When they were appointed a few months earlier, the business teams in manufacturing were still being organized; and at the time the decision to move south was made, there were not enough local reps appointed for the number of business teams that had evolved. (This would be an ever-changing number over the next couple of years.) So, before the move south, several more appointees were named. Mike would head the local team and would be joined by Henry Campbell in stamping, Grady Cook in the body shop, Jackie Teague in paint, Bill Sells and Jim Mills in general assembly, Cliff Cantrell in vehicle interiors, and new appointees Ken Duncan (a 99er) in casting and Dora Mack (a 99er) in transmission and engine. (These last two additions from the 99 had eased much of the tension that was created when the original appointees were named.)

Off they went to become a team, shape the design of the manufacturing facility, and build the UAW image in middle Tennessee. Remember earlier when I said that one of our strongest points in Saturn was our ability to be flexible. Here is a prime example of what I was talking about. They all moved lock, stock, and barrel to Tennessee. I mean they bought houses and moved in. However, their stay was very short lived. After about three months of watching concrete being poured and steel raised, it became painfully clear that one person could satisfactorily watch the blueprints. The real design and development work was still being done in Michigan. It was not a total waste of time, however; as a good deal of team building was done and some key relationships developed that would serve well in the coming years. By September they were commuting to Michigan every Sunday and going home every Friday to Tennessee, and this would continue until about 1988, when the trend would be reversed as equipment started arriving in Tennessee.

October arrived and after two years on loan, for many of us, the time had come for the decision to be made. Were we going to join Saturn full time and leave GM or were we going to go back to the plant we came from? There would be no more loaning of people to Saturn. Even though we weren't funded yet, as of October 24, 1986, if one chose to join Saturn, it would have to be permanently, if one were represented by the UAW. Non-reps did not have to quit GM, because they would not have all the rules of the National Agreement to fight their way through, such as leaving one bargaining unit and then returning, local area hire pools, guaranteed income stream, and the like. This was a sore point for many represented team members for quite a while, until we were up and running, and it came time to downsize the non-rep work force.

All of us who had been on loan for 31 months thought all along that this would be an easy decision when the time came, but oh how wrong we were. I can speak only for myself, although others confided later they had the same roller coaster of emotions, but this was much more emotional than I had planned. As much as I disliked the Land of the Adversaries, when it came to signing away 20 years of seniority with no way back, I flinched. But only for a moment, maybe 30 seconds. The real issue to me became my sons. Although I had been divorced since the fall of 1984, I still saw my two boys every other weekend. I knew the move to Tennessee was still a couple of years away, but it was very sobering to think of living 700 miles away from them. After much rationalization, which was not always objective, I made the decision that I always knew I would make and signed on full time to Saturn.

In the end, only 17 of the 99 signed on, and no one felt bad about anyone who didn't, other than knowing we would miss them. It was an individual decision for me, but most were married and their families had not had the opportunity to eat, sleep, and breathe Saturn like we had. When presented with having to sell their homes and leave behind all their relatives, their favorite baby-sitter, all their friends, and, oh, by the way, quit GM, many families said no. Of the other 50 reps who were borrowed during the last 18 months, only 12 decided to stay. All for the same kind of reasons as the 99ers. Here we were, two months away from a brand new year of 1987, and we had 27 union-represented people to spread out among 800 plus non-reps who were growing by 20 to 30 a week. Finding good replacements for those departing became a real focused effort.

At the same time that those on loan left, the sourcing of machinery and equipment became a very hot item. Opportunities always seem to run in threes. Facilities were in need of design, hiring was a top priority, and now machinery and equipment (M&E). The allocation of resources was a critical issue for us now, for decisions made about any of the three without integration in mind could prove disastrous down the road. Many of us would have to do double duty until more reps came onboard. The pipeline was full of people we had already processed for these roles who were unwilling to come until they could join permanently.

It would be the first of the year before they would be ready to accept the challenges facing them. The 3 international reps and the other 27 of

88

us sat down and put our plan together for communication, decision making, and coordination. Given the length of lead times to build some of the machinery, as well as sourcing lead times for the suppliers that we eventually chose to do their own M&E, we decided that the greatest number of people should be assigned to sourcing. It was very obvious that the engineering community, left to its own wiles, would source as it had always done, and we could not let this happen. We had 50 years of sourcing done this way with the same result, equipment that did not perform the way it was sold to perform, and engineers, and no one else, trained on troubleshooting problems once it was installed and supposed to run. This time, the people who had to maintain it as well as use it every day would be partners in making these sourcing decisions.

A second and equally important reason for having trades and operating technicians involved in these sourcing decisions was to ensure that the union-represented suppliers in America were given equal opportunity to bid for these contracts. It had not taken us very long to figure out that the lead non-rep in sourcing, Alan Perriton, was less than enamored with the GM Allied Divisions. He, like many others from GM, felt that all of GM's problems were directly associated with wage and benefit packages of the *hourly* worker, completely forgetting, or purposefully omitting, the sorry state of competitive engineering from both a design and development aspect. The Allied Divisions would get a fair chance. The importance of this lies in that we could not be successful in the short or long term if we did not help the rest of GM realize the importance of being competitive, not only within, but to compete for business outside of GM. "The General" had been making overtures with regularity since the early 1980s about selling off the components group and outsourcing what it formerly produced.

The union had fought this effort effectively in the 1987 National Agreement but knew it would resurface in 1990. Outsourcing to this level would put GM on even par with Ford and Chrysler, which had been outsourcing their components for years. Our charge, with Don's wisdom and support, would be to show that we could be competitive in America, Saturn and GM, with UAW workers, helping the Allieds to see how uncompetitive they were in global components' design, development and production, and then working with the division to make it a formidable force. This was one of the union's goals. Actually thousands of jobs were at stake, as well as the standard of living for the families tied to them. Exacerbating this wonderful opportunity even more was that engineering and materials management non-reps did not feel that trades and operating technicians had the skills to be involved in these decisions.

Without our Memo of Understanding, we would face the same plight as the locals in the components group. Ours, however, guaranteed that we would make these decisions together. That our sourcing would be done with a long-term focus on UAW/GM success, not just Saturn success. This was going to be a critical struggle and was another key reason we had to get the right people assigned to this effort. We had to have people who would say "Stop! This isn't right!" and bring in reinforcements. The importance of this undertaking had me, Mike B., Jerry Mills, and Don involved intimately with each and every one of the sourcing decisions. To categorize the conflict that resulted from this effort, one would have to use a Richter scale, not only at the epicenter but at the collateral reaches as well. We in Saturn and GM learned a great deal through this sourcing process, but unfortunately, those in Detroit did not retain it as well. What we accomplished in this process affected us all for the next decade and beyond.

To this day GM and the International Union still claim amnesia to the fact that our sourcing process saved or created 3,500 bargaining unit jobs, dozens of joint ventures, as means to get the Allieds competitively thinking and focused, and last, we have the highest North American content car produced, at 95%. Of the offshore content, 4.5% comes from Europe and only 0.5% from the Pacific Rim – quite an accomplishment in itself, not to mention all the local unions that got involved in helping make their plants more competitive and secure. It was also critical how we went about managing this conflict, which was both on the surface and, more important, below the surface.

We learned many lessons over the next two years that helped us in the longer term deal with three very key ingredients in cultural change: How do you handle bad news? What do you do when you are at an impasse? And, how do you communicate about these first two to your entire organization? *Change agents, lend me your ears!* Here is where I believe we made a break with tradition. It is not because I am a UAW member that I say this, but rather we had only to gain from this partnership. The engineers were losing traditional power, but we were the major catalysts because we did not lose sight of the fact that we were not "gurus." It was not our job to provide *the* answers but to be a powerful change agent by providing others we worked with the opportunities to discover their own solutions. If we imposed our beliefs on the engineers, we would inhibit both of our growth processes. We knew that we had to allow those we were dealing with the dignity of self-discovery. When we disagreed or had alternative suggestions, we could *not* let the situation become adversarial. We had to hold fast to our belief in the inherent beauty and strength in all human beings and not assume that we knew what was best for everyone. Instead, we would model decisiveness, strength, security, and inner peace that would be absorbed by all those around us. *Again, change agents,* these are principles I am talking about. Reach agreement on principles and all the details will be easy.

With a snap of the fingers, it was Christmas shutdown again. Wow, where had 1986 gone, we wondered. Here it was, time to go home for the holidays again, only this year we didn't want to go. "Couldn't we stay and work through the holidays?" Well, the answer to that was pretty obvious, but nevertheless the desire was there. The countdown to 1990 was ringing in all of our heads, like "Jingle Bells"; and although it was three years away, the ticking of the clock grew louder and louder every time we thought of what had to be done in comparison to what had already been accomplished. When we eventually departed to our homes across America, we knew we needed the break, but we would anticipate 1987 throughout the entire holiday season.

It was January 1987, and we were back, all energized and enthusiastic about getting on with the creation of Saturn. In what had become a yearly ritual, all of the UAW technicians gathered the first day back, and we went over the mission and philosophy. These were our two pillars of strength that we always used to guide us through the development of this "partnership" that neither rep nor non-rep really understood, for the simple reason that we were developing it as we went along. When we struggled, almost daily, there was no one we could call and ask for help, for nowhere could we find anyone doing what we were attempting to do. Within our mission and philosophy were the answers, if we would only use them as the guide they were designed to be. Our mission told us that we would be successful if we "integrated people, technology, and business systems"; and the philosophy told us, "We believe that all people want to be involved in decisions that affect them" – so these had to be the two tenets that we build the Saturn house on, and this annual first-of-the-year gathering must focus us all on that one goal. Decisions were going to be made this year of our Lord 1987, and they would be made together, for that is what would ultimately determine whether we were just another car company or a really new way of doing business.

By early spring over 6 million cubic yards of dirt and rock had been moved to make the pad that the plants would be built on. Some really innovative undertakings had resulted from collaboration between the rep and non-rep team members in Spring Hill, Tennessee, and our general contractor Morrison-Knudson. We had made a commitment to Governor Alexander that we would not do what Nissan had done in Smyrna, Tennessee; that is, build a huge white monolith in the middle of the beautiful middle Tennessee rolling countryside. We designed our plant to be hidden from view by the passing public. We mounded the dirt that was removed into two huge hills that totally obscured the plant from Highway 31, which runs parallel to the site. Being likewise concerned about the surface roads that would be destroyed by thousands of cement trucks rumbling across the county roads delivering cement, we built our own cement batch plant on the back of our property near an old rock quarry. In addition to all the rock that was dynamited to create the pad, we had ready access to more rock if it was needed. All the surface roads at our site and all the building foundations were made exclusively from our own land.

This initially upset many of the tricounty cement contractors, but when they calmed down and listened to the logic of not destroying their road system, it ended up being OK. The first building foundation completed was the Powertrain Plant, which had the first equipment scheduled to arrive in early 1988. The Body Systems Plant would be next, followed by General Assembly and Vehicle Interior Systems, Northfield, and then Service Parts Operations. Although Northfield had not been designed yet, we had earmarked a piece of land for it and were comfortable that the size and scope of services would be successfully resolved before groundbreaking needed to be undertaken. Northfield had many opponents within Saturn, being championed primarily by our vice president of manufacturing, Guy Briggs. With Guy, everything was a control issue, not because he didn't believe in people development, but rather his concern was with *who* was in charge of people development. Northfield would be a bloody battle in the end, but there was never a doubt in my mind that it would come to fruition. For all things are designed twice. First, and most important, in the mind and then on paper. Northfield, with its training facilities, child care, wellness center, communication center, banking, pharmacy, flower shop, beauty salon, post office, and maybe, just maybe, an on-site union hall, would truly be the *"cultural center"* of Saturn. Hmm, more on this later.

January fled to June in a New York minute, and as had happened in 1986, an Awareness Orientation was taking place on a weekly basis for all the new team members coming onboard and, interestingly enough, many of those who had been onboard since 1985. Word had gotten around, as we had hoped it would, that this orientation to Saturn was really good, that it displaced many of the myths that were products of some peoples' imaginations and could really help make sense of this massive undertaking. It became so popular that by mid-June we were running concurrent sessions every week just to accommodate all those who had come in before it was required to be taken. This was very positive for our embryonic organization, because everyone was being hired in Troy, Michigan, and month by month the exodus south was increasing. We would probably not move the Awareness Orientation to the plant site before 1989, and it would serve as an alignment tool to all those moving before that in the months and years ahead.

Around this same time frame, it became all too obvious that Skip and the other VPs on the SAC were meeting separately on developing the 10-year Saturn business plan. We asked Joe Malotke what was going on, but he merely said not to worry about it. Everything would work itself out. Well, we who would be charged with building the local union found that answer unacceptable and told Joe that we were going to put our own business plan together. He said, "Fine." So Mike Bennett, Ken Duncan, and I sequestered ourselves for a week and wrote the first draft of the UAW business plan, which would ultimately go through five revisions before we were successful in getting everything we needed in the Saturn business plan about 1991. Our plan was necessary because there were some serious flaws in the Saturn plan that no one seemed to want to address. The first was too many business units. The engineers had developed 12 different business units, geared around the various systems of the car and the processing of the build. A great deal of this was built around turf and who would be in charge of what. This could not continue if we were going to compete against the very mean and lean Japanese.

We deduced that the 12 units could be very effectively reduced to 3, at the same time realizing that this would not be accomplished without a battle with both the engineering community and our own people who had also been bitten by the "who's in charge" bug. Second, union integration into the traditional functional unit was not progressing the way we felt it should. Product engineering, finance, marketing sales and service, Electronic Data Systems (EDS), and corporate communications did not yet understand the value of having union technicians helping them make decisions. Too many decisions would be made by these groups that would ultimately affect those who would build the car, so integration into their midst was seen as not a nice thing to do but a very necessary thing to do. There were many emotion-filled meetings on this issue, but the union fully participated, win-win prevailed, and the development continued.

The last issue that was lacking in the Saturn business plan was, from our point of view, the most critical. How did we manage this entire change process? Skip had his ideas, Joe Malotke had his ideas, almost to a person, everyone in Saturn had his or her own ideas about how this would happen, but there was no organized plan to make change management happen. From my daily conversations with both Joe M. and Jim Lewandowski it appeared that this would be the responsibility of human resources, and that was totally unacceptable.

Every part of Saturn would be responsible for the change process or it would be a dismal failure. There would be no déjà vu here. When it didn't work, H.R. would wear the coat for it and be summarily flogged in public, and then it would be business as usual with each functional unit pointing the finger somewhere else in the organization for not stepping up and helping poor H.R. or, even more cleverly, after-the-fact questioning about why H.R. didn't ask for help. The stakes were too high. Every part of Saturn had to be responsible and accountable for managing the necessary change. Change was very easy to talk about, but oh so very hard to do, once it got personal. The key non-rep leaders of Saturn spoke very eloquently in public about how we shared power here, but that was at the SAC level where Don Ephlin sat. In the bowels of the organization, where the important day-to-day decisions were being made that would really shape this partnership, a full-fledged battle was being waged every day, and it had to be brought under control if we were to succeed. Power was not being "let go of."

We in the union were vastly outnumbered for all the aforementioned reasons, and we realistically did not have a strike option to utilize. So the tried and proven management tactic of secret meetings and stalling until the 11th hour and 59th minute before a decision needed to be made was very much in vogue. Unfortunately, the 99ers were the very few who really understood consensus decision making and the ability to block decisions. This was a trait learned through experience with so many Saturn decisions that could be reversed and were reversed in some instances. But, a lot of decisions could not be reversed, and a large proportion of them would haunt us down the road.

Leading the effort to create a full partnership with the union having equal say in making decisions was Mike Bennett, who had quickly gained the background information needed to be a fully functional Saturn leader. The phenomenal brain power of Mike Bennett was becoming totally obvious to those who interacted with him every day. As a result of his unquestioned competence and true dedication to the union and Saturn, the negativity that surrounded his awkward entrance into Saturn had dissipated. He proved to be a true champion of the cause. The following dissertation written by Bennett illustrates the extent of the man's understanding of the awesome responsibility that sits on the shoulders of the union leaders at Saturn as well as union leaders, in general, if they expect the union to be a viable entity going into the future:

THE CHANGING ROLE OF UNION LEADERSHIP

The increased demands of global competition, international capital flow, technological advancement and transfer, the changing role of government, renewed values in human resources, and the ever-increasing demands of public expectations from institutional values are bringing about profound changes in the American automotive industry. Certainly we can easily document these changes within the competing corporations, which include changes in product, process, business systems, organizational structure, and labor/management relations. It is the very result of this rapidly changing market, fierce competition, and technological advancement that has made the already complex and sloth-like information-gathering and decision-making structure of the American automobile companies more complex and less responsive to market needs. Consequently, with the passing of time and the lack of a significant permanent paradigm shift by the American auto companies and the UAW, they will more than likely remain more and more at a competitive disadvantage unless a change in thinking occurs. Faced with this consequence, the General Motors Corporation and UAW responded to this challenge and elected to collaboratively defend the American small car market in this automotive "Battle of the Bulge" with the creation of Saturn. The result of this totally American innovative partnership has raised many unanswered questions, one of which is: How will these changes and this challenge impact the role of the union and the responsibilities of union leadership?

Over the last 16 years of my own involvement as a UAW local union leader, I have often heard many of my colleagues proudly proclaim, "Management acts and we will react." A fundamental question now facing the union is whether or not a reactive strategy, or even a more recently proposed alternative reactive tactic, can serve the long range needs of the American auto worker and the auto industry.

In the AFL-CIO's study, "The Changing Situation of Workers and Their Unions," it was said that, "Unions have found themselves behind the pace of change, and are called upon to reconceptualize their role in order to deal with the emerging state of this continuous change in the international economic market." At the same time the future indicates the emerging structure of the "New Capitalism" or "New Management" is expected to have fewer levels of traditional decision-making layers and significantly fewer managers itself. In fact, this change is already under way, according to some experts. Sectors of the economy with the traditional sequence of product research, development, manufacturing, and marketing are being impacted by what Peter Drucker calls "Synchrony." Here, he says, various specialists from all the various business functions work as a team, from inception of the research to the product's establishment in the market. At Saturn we speak of it as a "cradle to grave" concept. In any event, it is maintained that "such a new decision-making system will require undoubtedly greater individual self-discipline, and increasing emphasis on individual responsibility for improved relationships and communications."

Today nearly all American citizens look to the business enterprise for their livelihood, growth opportunities, access to status and function, as well as personal fulfillment and achievement. The changing competitive nature of the auto industry has in reality made the completely manual labor worker obsolete and forced the company to rely more on the knowledge of the worker in order to remain solvent and viable. H. Ross Perot said it another way, "If you want to know what's going on in the business, ask the worker on the floor!" It is clear that from this point forward, management will not only be required to create in a timely fashion new products and processes through innovation, but must still be able to optimize products and processes existing in order to remain competitive. Accordingly, scientific management can no longer deliver both of these requirements while still increasing productivity. As a result, a "new" organization of work is about to come forth.

In the old management system the autocratic and authoritarian decision-making structure around the organization and the intensity of work induced conflict and promoted the adversarial relationship between organized labor and management. As a result, in many cases, the structural costs of worker surveillance, supervision, information gathering, and labor relations have now grown to exceed the cost of direct labor and made the enterprise more uncompetitive. This increasing burden cannot, in the long run, be sustained if the American business enterprise is to remain solvent.

It's long been known that individuals identify more completely with the goals of an institution when they are involved in the participation of its governance and when it is perceived as operating in their own best interests. Likewise, a shift to less control and surveillance of workers is likely to raise their individual contribution to work output. This releases the yet to be fully tapped creative minds of the enterprise's most important asset, its workers. Thus by lowering the control and surveillance burden and releasing the untapped energy of its workers, the business enterprise will receive a logarithmic economic competitive strength. This advantage will increase the proportional likelihood of improving the product and the product's quality and value. Such "new" organizational experiments, if successful, will change the structure of the economy as we know it. This is the arena, in my opinion, where workers, labor leaders, and labor unions must find their future. The reorganization of work will ultimately require the reorganization of the institution that represents the worker.

Because the business enterprise is primarily task-focused with profit as its first priority, a countervailing institution must be established, maintained, and accepted in order to fully optimize the work force in this new work structure – an institution whose first priority is the worker and centers on the safe effective organization of meaningful work. Such an institution within the enterprise must maintain its focus on the business's long-term viability, the needs of society, and the interests of the customer on issues of value, quality, and pricing; the reasonable expectations of the owners' return on the business institution's property; as well as the long-term job security needs of the enterprise's entire work force. Admittedly, this new balanced institutional relationship will mean the sharing of authority, economic power, and decision making within the enterprise. Although most of this ground is still uncharted, it will be only a matter of time before such an organization gains the experience and trust to move forward into this new dimension of the lasting partnership between labor and capital.

Ultimately, the survival of both the American business enterprise and the union resides within the ability of both to meet the needs of society in the 21st century. Union leadership, in order to effectively contribute and represent, must break the self-imposed historical bonds of organizational confinement and expand the arena of its perceived role. The union leadership will have to refocus itself on product quality and profitability planning in order to fully understand the impact it has as a union on the market and the customer. It will have to be champions of product value and work to ensure that organizational mediocrity no longer permeates the process between the inception of research to final sales delivery. Union leaders must be able to recognize and respond to the consequences of poor management or mismanagement itself in order to stimulate timely organizational response. The union, union members, and union leaders must realize that their own livelihoods and work-life careers are directly related to the long-term economic health of the enterprise. Union leaders must be able to assure the fair and equitable distribution of the generated collective wealth through the representation of the stakes and equities of all involved interests, including shareholders, workers, suppliers, dealers, consumers and the public. Only by doing so will the labor movement be able to ultimately represent the comprehensive interest of its own members.

This will mean, of course, that union members and union leaders must understand and learn more of the business. Tomorrow's labor leader and union member will need more formal education and experience in these matters. The business enterprise management system must accept the union as a full partner and recognize the need to move labor leaders and union members quickly up the learning curve in order to clarify the issues and solve problems quickly.

Finally, the membership, labor union leaders, managers, and the business enterprise owners must put aside the fear and distrust that has accumulated over the last century and embrace the new relationship, as in a marriage, where there is spiritual and legal unification in the exchange of vows between the bride and groom at a wedding. It is understood going in that both participants must be able to maintain their own self-worth, dignity, and identity in order for the partnership to survive a life-long commitment.

Saturn and the UAW today are exploring this new ground. The issue and quest of the desired partnership between labor and capital is not a new one. It has in fact been attempted many times before. It is our hope that Saturn and the UAW will carry America one step closer to the realization of this vision. There are dangers and there are risks involved in this experiment.

Of course, there are those whose purpose and needs require them to point to the errors of the past. These prophets of failure strive to maintain mankind in the past and undoubtedly would have counseled society against moving from the caves 10,000 years ago if given the opportunity. A great humanitarian, Jacob Bronowski, believed that man would continue to ascend, and ascend is what we are attempting to do at Saturn. The real long-lasting success of the American auto industry does not lie totally upon the design and quality of the car; it lies instead with the balanced relationship and definition of the partnership. We do not fear failure at Saturn or within the UAW, we fear complacency and stagnation.

Michael E. Bennett
UAW Saturn Manufacturing Advisor
March 1988

In August the first round of mailings were sent out to prospective Saturn retailers. This was the result of over a year's work including sales, service and marketing, the union, and 12 of the best GM retailers in America. This group had done what was suggested in the Phase II Report and systematically compared the best marketers in the world against how cars were sold traditionally and came up with the model, to be revised many times, that would forever change how this was done in the future. We sent out about 2,500 pieces in the first mailing, not knowing what kind of response we would receive back. It was believed that many GM current dealers would feel that they had a lock on a franchise if they so chose, which was not going to be the case; but it was the interest by those who had never owned, or wanted to own, a franchise associated with GM that was the unknown commodity. Our research had told us that these were some of the best retailers in all of America, and we genuinely hoped this mailing would spark an interest in a new way of doing business.

September 9, saw the first steel raised in the Powertrain Plant, and once that first piece was in place, it wasn't very long before one could recognize the building that was under construction. The Body and Vehicle Systems Plants were progressing on schedule with their respective foundation work, and the site was really starting to take shape. This ninth month of 1987 also brought a very serious concern to light. I don't know who surfaced it first or if it was a tripartite epiphany, but one day Ken Duncan, Mike Bennett, and I asked, "What is the matter with Joe (Malotke)?" He was a dear and wonderful friend who had our utmost respect, but something about him had changed. He had always had a memory that would challenge mine. (In Saturn my memory is legendary, especially among the non-reps.) Lately it seemed he would make a decision one day, and the next day he would do just the opposite. Invariably, when questioned about it he would casually blow it off and say we'd go with the first one, but, sadly, we knew it was much deeper than simply forgetting. We weren't exactly knowledgeable, or for that matter even remotely knowledgeable, about what caused this change, but each of us vowed individually to seek Joe out and express a genuine concern. In the meantime, in the event he felt he could not confide in us, Mike would seek counsel from one of the other international reps, his close friend Jerry Mills. Ken and I did not know Jerry well, but Mike had a long and positive history with him. Mike was also very close to Joe. We all agreed that the situation would be kept close to the vest but watched very carefully.

The last quarter of 1987 saw two more significant things take place. The car that the corporation had sold to the GM Board of Directors was to be "cliniced" in the hotbeds of the imports, the East and West Coasts. We needed to see what our target population thought of our new baby. It would have no identifying logo's linking it to Saturn and especially GM. We would show models that were hand built, without powertrains, that showed the exterior, a front seat with instrument panel, steering wheel, radio and air conditioner controls, and the rest (all of which were not functional), but we would still get a feel for how our product would be received by people carefully selected as being either a current import owner or intended import buyer. These clinics would be orchestrated by a firm that specialized in doing clinics, but for the first time, the union would be sitting behind the two-way mirrors listening to what these potential customers were saying. As I mentioned several chapters ago, the GM design staff back in Detroit was livid and tried desperately to stop us from doing the clinics. In the end, our champions, Roger and Don, showed their colors again and the clinics came to pass, but none of us were prepared for the results.

The most significant event of 1987 happened on December 7. Earlier, I described how we had not yet received corporate approval for our appropriation request (AR). All the work that was being done in Spring

FORMING THE FUTURE

Hill and Troy was being funded by the chairman's office – Roger! This was really very cleverly done because he had to have all the votes he needed to get our AR passed the first time it was presented to the board. If it had to be brought back, this could mean disaster for Saturn. Roger, being the shrewd GMer he was, took all the time necessary to get all his ducks in a row. Even being the most powerful chairman in GM history did not automatically guarantee approval of what he wanted. The politics on the board were no different than politics anywhere else, and he was very good at GM politics.

It wasn't just by chance that December 7 was picked as the date our AR was brought to the board. This was the very day 46 years before that the Japanese had attacked Pearl Harbor, and Roger was going to start his war with the Japanese imports on just such a significant day. The fourth estate tried to make hay with this, but everyone concerned simply stated, "What a coincidence. I really wasn't aware of the date." End of conversation. I can only tell you what I felt, and that was fierce determination. The imports had already cost 200,000 of my brothers and sisters their jobs and six times as many ancillary jobs. At that time it really didn't matter to me that it was our own fault. Labor and management had too long fought each other, which had resulted in our taking our eye off the customer. Our competition had become very arrogant, an example of which could be found in the book *The Japan That Can Say NO!* They thought they had us down for the count in the small car industry and were gearing up for the battle in the more lucrative large car market. I relished the upcoming battle for, deep in my very soul, I knew it was a mistake to take Americans lightly, especially when they were focused and united in a common cause. Our third corporate Christmas shutdown was up on us again. Where had the year gone, reverberated through the halls once more – 1988 was nigh and we were one year closer to launch. I could hardly wait to get back into the fray.

In the second week of January 1988 another key decision needed to be made. On the surface it might not seem important to the casual observer, but it was extremely important to those of us in the union. It involved what all the exteriors of the buildings on the entire site would look like and be made of. Remember the quote from Winston Churchill, "First we form our buildings then they continually form us." Well, our non-rep partners still had not grasped the importance of this. The facilities engineers, by training, were always looking for the most

102

economical way to do everything, which is very practical, but in this case, cost would not necessarily be the determining factor. We started this debate back in the fourth quarter of 1986 and still had not reached a win-win conclusion. The Powertrain Plant steel was scheduled to be completed on January 27. The first piece of equipment, a die casting cell for transmission cases, was scheduled to arrive around March 13, so the building needed to be enclosed prior to its arrival. The stalling tactics of waiting until the last minute when a decision had to be made did not work this time. The SAC, especially Guy Briggs, was supportive of the facilities engineers using the argument "Let's spend most of our money on the interior of the buildings. The outside isn't really that important."

We were absolutely livid. Here we were spending millions of dollars to make our site fit into the Tennessee countryside, and they wanted to actually put up corrugated steel that would look like a bunch of pole barns. The second reason we were unwilling to move from our position on the exteriors was that we were in the same situation, at impasse, on the interior of the buildings. Mr. Briggs's premise of really doing the interiors right had no credibility with us either. We held fast to the idea that the entire site must promote the atmosphere of attraction to those who would spend a considerable portion of their lives there, and, although Joe Malotke was with us, Skip and our VP of finance, Tom Manoff, were seemingly firmly behind Mr. Briggs.

I have spoken earlier, and will continue to do so, of Mike Bennett's brilliance, and here is another example of what I mean. Mike, while earning his undergraduate degree at the University of Michigan, had a professor named Colin Clipson, who was a recognized leader in workplace design. We discussed among ourselves how we were going to break this impasse and agreed that, to change the SAC's point of view, we must first change the facilities engineers' point of view. You know, let them discover the right answer themselves. So Michael, very diplomatically, invited Professor Clipson down to Troy the day of our next facilities meeting. As smoothly as silk, he introduced him to the facilities design team, and let Colin work his expertise.

At the end of the day, you could see a paradigm shift occurring in the demeanor of many of the engineers. His rationale had made a significant impression, so much so, that they asked for a day break before the next meeting, as we were meeting daily on this issue. We, of course, graciously agreed, knowing that they would meet by themselves and go over that day's events from a totally left-brain perspective. The next day we received a call requesting to have Professor Clipson back for our next meeting, which we had already arranged before he returned to Flint the previous day. We replied that we would try, but he was in very high demand and also had a rigorous teaching schedule.

The next day when we met, it was very obvious that they had talked to their leader, Mr. Briggs. Their questioning of Professor Clipson's ideas had a "prove to me this is really important" tone. True to his belief in modern workplace design, Clipson was brilliant. Every thrust was professionally parried. Then he began counterthrusting with crisp precise moves that could not be blocked, and the duel was over. The next presentation to the SAC would be done jointly, only this time the engineers would sell the sizzle. It would not be the union trying to sell it. We were becoming much more adroit at our role as a catalyst. As the country-and-western song goes, "You can lead a person to love, but you can't make them fall."

The power of self-discovery is so much better than beating someone into submission. I don't know if I can describe the feeling I experienced at the SAC meeting when the facilities engineers sold the scenario of having every building that would ever be built on site to look exactly the same. The exterior skin would be corrugated steel but would be painted a blue-gray, blending it almost totally into the sky. Around the top of each structure would be a distinctive red stripe the exact same color of the barns that were everywhere in middle Tennessee. The roof would be covered with fine gray stone to further enhance the blending with the sky, and the portrait was complete. The question of why all the buildings on site had to look the same surfaced many times from different SAC leaders, and none of us in the union had to answer even once.

The engineers handled them all, "Why, it was very obvious – one of the things we are trying to do in Saturn is promote symbols that bring people together, not create distinctions between them. The history of having the corporation headquarters look like a palace and the plants of obvious lesser design must not happen here. No matter where you go on site you need to feel part of manufacturing. After all, weren't we a car company?" I'm sure I was floating above my seat all the while, try-

104

ing not to beam with absolute pride at this professional, focused, and extremely effective presentation. The head facilities engineer, Dave Skiven, and I would work very closely in the next two years, and our relationship was shored on a firm foundation that very day.

At this point in our development the SAC was meeting every day. We would meet with Joe M. daily as well, either during or after work and, most days, both. Something was definitely wrong, and by the first of February, we knew that we had to talk to Don Ephlin – even though, at this point, we weren't exactly sure what we wanted him to do, but Mike set up the meeting and we went from there. The meeting took place in early February at Solidarity House on Jefferson Avenue in Detroit. This was a very emotional meeting for all of us, but it was especially difficult for me. Joe Malotke and I were closer than any of the other 99ers, and although I had talked and talked with him about his mysterious loss of memory, nevertheless, I felt like I was betraying our bond. We had actually spent thousands of hours together the last four years, and he had taught me so much about politics, power, and most important, life. He was a very unique and special man, and this meeting weighed on my heart heavily.

You see, the most important value in the union is loyalty. Loyalty to one another and to what the labor movement is all about: individuals collectively. I held out a glimmer of hope that a win-win could result from this meeting with Don, but I also knew Mike was at the end of his proverbial rope; and when he had enough, that was it. One of the things I liked about Don was that he didn't mess around with endless small talk. He always greeted you with that warm, disarming smile and a fine "How do you do!" with his Boston accent, but then it was right down to business. We laid out the data we had gathered to explain our concern and asked Don what he felt. What he said really shocked all of us.

Although we knew he was upset with Joe over the advertising agency sourcing process, we were totally unaware of how strained their relationship was. He told us that Joe did not like to communicate with him the way he liked to be communicated with. He revealed that they had many talks about this, with Joe always promising to do better, but the next thing he knew Joe would go off and make a decision. He'd find out about it after the fact, and they would go at it again. He would end up telling Joe that the seat on the Saturn Action Council belonged to the director of the GM Department, Don Ephlin, and Joe was only his surrogate, not the other way around. Even though you could feel the tension between them, you could also feel the respect that Don had for Joe's political savvy and his devotion to the Saturn vision. It was obvious by his nonverbal cues that this was very difficult for him. I sensed he knew something was going to be done that he did not necessarily want to do. When we were finished expressing all of our issues, he simply asked us what we wanted him to do. Kenny, John Michaud, and I almost fell out of our chairs when Mike said, "Remove him!" I glanced over at Mike in disbelief and saw that he couldn't believe he had actually said it either. Don just stared at us for what seemed like an eternity but was only moments. He said he'd take it under advisement, got up, and said he had another meeting to go to. Saying good-bye, he left the room.

It was a long ride back to Troy that afternoon, for none of us expected the outcome that had taken place. We thought, at the worst, that Don would sit Joe down and threaten him with drastic action if he didn't tell Don what was up with him. I didn't sleep well that night or for many, many nights to come. I daily sought counsel from my friend from Flint, Jerry Mills, one of the other two International Union reps and pleaded with him to talk to Joe. He said he had and would continue to do so, but Joe was denying that there was anything wrong. I also talked to Joe personally every day, but he did what he always did when I brought up the issue. He pooh-poohed it as inconsequential and said if Don wanted to remove him, so what? If Don did, he'd find out how tough it was to replace him. The next guy would be in the same position in the bat of an eye because he didn't understand just how complicated this new order of things was and how flexible one had to be. (In retrospect, whether he really knew what he was saying was so very true or it was simply rationalization of what he was doing, I'll never know, but his words ring in my head to this very day and I end up saying, "What a fox this guy was!")

The machinery and equipment began arriving on time in early March for Powertrain and was followed soon by M&E for the other two plants. All the work done by the engineers and reps (trades and operations technicians) was now paying off. Those teams that had built good relationships were proportionately successful in on-time delivery of their equipment. But, more important, by working with the original equipment manufacturers (OEMs) at their facilities through designing, building, testing and fixing, debugging, validation, tear down and shipping, receiving at our plant, unpacking and reassembly, debugging, and the rest, our teams had a real chance of success. Also, the start of the second quarter brought the data from the car clinics into a hard but realistic perspective.

Our target population thought our car was a cobbled-up Pontiac or something GM was trying to get over on them. This bothered us all but the engineers especially, for they had spent a lot of hard work and countless hours in what they felt was the new and exciting design of the interior and exterior of our "world-class automobile." In all reality, they had really stretched from how things were normally done, but this only pointed out again how stifled and inbred the GM design staff really was. The people we wanted to take out of Hondas and Toyotas made it really clear they didn't like the instrument panel design or location of the controls. They didn't like the seats, the windows, the slope of the hood; and they especially didn't like the trunk opening, which had a large lip you had to lift your luggage over. This could be a show stopper. How we addressed this was going to really test our metal. We were trying to select retailers to sell this product. We had plants being built to produce it on equipment that was being built and shipped by team members whom we were hiring as fast as we could get them in who must *quit* General Motors and move to Tennessee. And, at the same time, we were being told, "Your car sucks!"

As I described several chapters ago, we did the right thing – by utilizing the strengths and weaknesses of the partnership to get it done and likewise with the selection of our advertising partner Hal Riney & Associates. Needless to say, these were stressful times, over and above building an organization from the ground up. I frequently reflect on how we made it through them and marvel at the simplicity of it all. The only way then, and now, is that we always used the mission, philosophy, and values as our guidelines to make these very difficult decisions. We had two champions who trusted what we told them we needed; and we never, never, never pointed a finger at any group in Saturn with an accusatory "You messed up." We simply pulled together and said this is just another opportunity to be creative, never taking our eyes off the target. As the saying goes, "Obstacles are what you see when you take a skeptical eye off your goal." We simply knew that, if we really believed it, we would achieve it.

Recruitment and selection was in high gear, with the pipeline filled with potential team members both rep and non-rep. By the middle of April we were 2,000 team members strong in Michigan and 60 strong in Tennessee. While Michigan would hold the edge with team members for most of the year, the third quarter of 1988 would show the trend south picking up speed more and more as the buildings were completed and equipment began arriving almost daily. Everyone in the organization being involved in the recruitment and selection process had its advantages, but it also had its drawbacks. The pluses outweighed the minuses overall, especially when you considered the intense ownership that was developed by actually being able to hire the team members you would be working with. However, it was very time consuming; and it was a constant battle to get the non-reps to take the training that was necessary to do the job right, get them scheduled to do the interviews, the assessment, and team exercises, and then sit down and capture the entire process in writing so that, when we validated our selection criteria against job performance three or four years down the road, our actions would be legally defensible.

Our strategy for the Northfield Cultural Center was moving along slowly, as we imagined it would, but we had secured the required funding for the Training and Development Center piece of the project. Groundwork was taking place on an "agreed to" piece of land, and the details were worked out as we went along. The major conflict we had was the size, but I was confident that it could all be resolved.

The redesign of the car was well under-way, stretching everyone's creativity to the twilight zone, but all three systems being integrated were seriously complicated. Engineering was stressed to the max trying to figure out how all the changes could be made on time. Finance was frantically trying to cost out what all these changes would make in the business case to be presented to the GM Board and the ramifications to the return on investment formula. Human Resources was pleading with manufacturing to learn what these changes were going to do to the head count. Sales, service, and marketing were trying to determine what this would do to the retailer candidates that were being picked. We in the union were trying to reconcile the fact that we were already stretched thin with human resources with which to build this partnership, and now we had the whole issue of redesign to deal with. Last, the facilities group in Spring Hill was asking on a daily basis, "What does this mean to building configurations, floor-space allocation, and process realignment?"

April and May went by in a blur and the middle of June was upon us when Don dropped a bombshell. Joe was to be reassigned and a new guy, Dick Hoalcraft, was going to take over his seat on the SAC. Not a lot was known about Dick, as he had only been on the union's international staff since 1984. He came out of Syracuse, New York, where he had been both president and shop chairman of the local union, and was known as a fierce Ephlin supporter. Some of the team members we had hired from Elyria, Ohio, knew him when he was assigned to their plant as it became time to close their facility. They didn't speak really highly of him, but then what would you expect after they had gone through the emotional scarring of a plant's death and all the turmoil associated with relocating to another facility, in another state, with a relocation package that left much to be desired. They left behind their friends and relatives because they had no alternative but to go if they wanted to stay employed with GM. The only thing known for sure was that Don trusted him, but beyond that was only speculation about what this was going to mean to Saturn and this struggling, embryonic partnership. One consolation in this change was that Jerry Mills and Jim Wheatley were going to remain Don's appointees at Saturn and I knew that they would help in the transition. Hoalcraft's first couple of weeks were spent with Joe, Jerry, and Jim laboring up the education curve and then Joe was gone. He left just as he came in head held high and diplomatic as only Joe could be but you could see the sadness in his eyes at having to leave something he had given birth to and guided to where it was for four long, stressful, yet wonderfully learning years. I missed him the day he walked out and every day since, even though he has passed on to the Lord, for he truly was my friend.

Jerry Mills orchestrated the meetings with Mike, Kenny, all the other local appointees, and me with Hoalcraft. We had been very busy since the April meeting with Don, refining the UAW business plan we had written and putting together a structure for the local union that would stay in place at least until local union elections could be held when enough represented team members were onboard in the early 1990s. Joe, up until he left, and Jerry had worked with us on this structure but Jim Wheatley had not. Jim and Joe did not get along for many reasons, but mostly they both could not get past each other's ego. Jim had developed a deep bitterness that would last until he retired, I think, based mostly on Joe's demeanor of wanting everything to go through him; and also Joe didn't communicate with Jim any better than he did with Don Ephlin – probably worse. It also didn't help that Jim was in Tennessee overseeing the plant construction while almost all of the decisions about that construction were being made in Michigan. Last, and I believe most important, Jim had a difficult time dealing with the fact that this total development process of Saturn was not being done the way the International Union had always done new ventures in the past.

Saturn was going to be built internally, by the people who would have to live with it for decades to come. As more and more union-represented team members came onboard – wanting to be involved in decisions that affect them – this wore and wore on Jim. The International Union had always set up everything and just sort of turned it over to the local union throughout Jim's whole career, for there were never this many represented people onboard two years before the start of production. Mike Bennett was also a big concern to Jim, for Mike was not one to sit by and watch while what he was going to be ultimately responsible for was developed for him. He was also going to be involved in all the key decisions, and this created conflict with Jim as well. I'm not sure exactly when it happened, this summer of 1988, but Jim decided to take a different path, one that would have a far-reaching impact on UAW Local 1853 and Saturn as a whole. He decided to seek out the members of the local union leadership, those appointed with Mike, who could possibly share his view of how this great enterprise should be developed and set out to drive a power play for control of the local. More to come on this issue as it will become very evident later as to what an effect this had on our future.

The summer of 1988 heralded a significant announcement in our drive to take on the imports. On May 24, Hal Riney & Associates of San Francisco were presented to the world as Saturn's advertising agency. Out of a list of 50 agencies, which had been narrowed down to 3, Riney won the Jewel of the Nile. This caused much ado in Detroit because GM wanted us to use its advertising agency, but we held fast to our selection and the partnership weathered the storm of protest from both GM and the International Union. Consequently, the long, arduous, and wonderfully creative process of a new way of marketing a car began. The agency's lack of automotive advertising experience was key to why we selected it. They would not come in with preconceived ideas about how this should be done, and we could build the future together. Their presentations throughout the selection process showed us just how exciting an agency it was, but most important, they showed that they would not be a typical ad agency and just blindly do what the client said. The agency made it clear through the whole process that it would be a "partner," not an order taking lackey. The next two years were so exciting as we worked with Riney building toward the "launch." I will never forget them.

Change agents, here is another reiteration of arguing the principles. This was another key success factor that we identified. We could not be successful if we let the external forces dictate who would present our product to the world. We had to be in control of this, for remember what I said about the Pontiac Fiero? The people who ran the factory did everything that was asked of them, but it failed nevertheless. Determine what cannot be compromised and hold fast to those things. Principles are like lighthouses – you cannot break them. You can only break yourself on them. Spend the time up front to determine all the key success factors and then hold fast to them. You must be prepared to end the ball game before you compromise any of them.

The next issue to hit the airwaves was the heralding of the first round of retail partner selections. There were 26 announced on January 29, 1989, covering a wide range of market areas. The original plan was to announce the Southern California retailers first, followed in about 30 days by the New York retailers, but the franchise operating team (FOT) that was in charge of all retail functions decided to broaden the coverage area at the launch. As I mentioned earlier, there were over 2,500 applicants by this time, and although only a few had been selected, the energy received from the states of Tennessee and Michigan to be included in the first round of selections could not be ignored. The plan at this stage of our development called for a maximum of 250 retail partners, a message that had been already given to the fourth estate, so it was really easy to calculate that only 1 out of 10 would make the grade. So it was a good move on the FOT's part not to select all of the first round from just two states. *Change agents take note:* Although we knew we had to make quick and effective penetration on both coasts, the art of politics had to prevail in this situation.

This was an area in which having union partnership really helped the cause, because we understood the negative political climate that would be created by this kind of slight to the state in which we were going to manufacture our car and the state where our corporate headquarters still resided. Our non-rep partners learned much from this interaction, and it also was an excellent opportunity to further demonstrate one of our key success factors, involving all stakeholders in decisions that affect them. Traditionally, this decision would have been made by the corporation alone under the premise that the retailers didn't understand our strategic plan nor should they. Alienation would have occurred that would take years to correct if the original plan had been implemented, but by arguing the principles and teaching our partners the importance of good power utilization and politics, this was avoided.

Backing up to early July 1988, all of the meetings with Hoalcraft by Mills, Bennett, Duncan, Michaud, and me had accelerated the learning curve for him to the point where he was comfortable with what Saturn was trying to accomplish and had done a 180-degree turn from when he first arrived. The lack of communication between Joe and Don E. coupled with our meeting with him left Don with the impression that Saturn was a screwed-up mess. So he gave Hoalcraft marching orders to go in and clean the place up and get the partnership back on track. Our meetings with Dick had shown him the opposite. The structure that Joe, Jerry, Mike, Kenny, John, and I had developed to transition us to when elections could be held met with his approval, so he was charged with taking it to Don for approval. He knew full well that Jim Wheatley didn't support it and would be lobbying with Don himself to stop it from happening. Hoalcraft did not feel that Don would object to it when he told him that we were not screwed up, as he thought, but that we simply needed a little more structure. The real beauty of the structure we developed was in its simplicity. We combined the Bargaining Committee with the Executive Board positions, and from the outset eliminated the dangerous politics of having one group of people in a union hall managing the constitutionally required duties of running a local union which, by the way, was not a full time job, and the other group whose job it was to represent people and make partnership decisions for the membership as a whole.

Our structure provided for the president of the local also to be the traditional shop chairman but in the role laid out in our Memorandum of Agreement as the UAW Manufacturing Action Council (MAC) advisor. We had four union vice presidents, one for each plant: Powertrain, Vehicle, Body, and Northfield. The financial secretary and the treasurer were combined into one position, financial secretary, who was given responsibility for the partnership in both finance and sales, service and marketing. The recording secretary position remained intact but was given responsibility for the partnership in corporate communications and public relations. The other executive board positions remained as is in the constitution: sergeant at arms, guide, and three trustees. At this time, they did not have partnership responsibilities but would have them as we refined our structure and moved closer to the launch of our vehicle.

This was going to be a political risk for all of those who accepted appointments to these positions, for history had always shown that appointees who run in the first democratically held elections are never elected, regardless of how well they have done the job. A second risk also looming on the horizon was one created by Jim Wheatley's aversion to this structure. He had cultivated his own band of followers over the previous two years, and they constituted most of the appointees who came onboard with Mike. Jackie Teague, Henry Campbell, Cliff Cantrell, Grady Cook, as well as many of the team members hired from two plants that had been closed – Norwood and Hamilton, Ohio. The lobbying for these positions had begun over a year ago, with many of these people feeling that they should get the positions because of their past records of traditional bargaining, no matter how poorly they had performed since they came to Saturn, where they found self-management a very difficult role to play. In the end, after much "spirited" rhetoric that was laced with a great deal of bitterness, the Local Executive Board was selected. Mike Bennett was appointed as president/MAC advisor. Joe Rypkowski became the first vice president and had partnership responsibility for Vehicle Systems. Ken Duncan was assigned vice president at large and partnership responsibility for Powertrain. Henry Campbell was selected vice president at large and partnership responsibility for Body Systems. I was designated vice president at large with partnership responsibility for human resources, materials management and facilities and systems development. John Michaud received the nod as financial secretary with responsibility for representing the partnership in finance and sales, service and marketing. Dora Mack was appointed as recording secretary and partnered with corporate communications and public relations.

The rest of the Executive Board were picked initially without partnership responsibilities, though some of them were involved in this regard by virtue of the team that hired them when they joined Saturn. Furman Latimer was designated our sergeant-at-arms; Nancy Chisolm was the guide; and the three trustees were Tony Alferio, David Holman, and Lesa McClain. Though these were unilateral International Union appointments by virtue of the UAW constitution, they were done in partnership every step of the way with many lengthy meetings between Hoalcraft and Skip LeFauve. This took place in September 1988, after we had gone through many growing pains. The need for more structure was predicated on the fact that, although we had many reps in positions to make sure the sourcing, hiring, training, and facilities were being conducted in a partnership manner, many of these rep team members somehow had the narrow point of view that whatever they decided was final and no one was going to tell them any different. They refused to listen to the hard fact that decisions that seemed not to affect anyone else on the surface, quite often had serious interdependencies that must be coordinated before things were locked in that could not be changed. Many unscrupulous non-reps took advantage of this before we got all the "stuff" out of the way and the partnership positions filled. We then had the task of pulling all the leaders, both rep and non-rep, together to explain the difference between a UAW-represented team member and a UAW representative.

The last half of 1988 was spent implementing the new structure and trying to get a handle on all the ramifications of the car redesign that were turning up daily. Parts proliferation was going to add considerably to the workers needed, especially in Vehicle Systems, and Briggs and company were not willing to accept this without a fight. The pressure put on materials management to get all the new parts sourced and certified by June 1990 seemed one step next to impossible. How many more team members were going to be needed was the question on the lips of almost everyone in manufacturing. June, July, and August were two steps forward and three steps back on all of these key issues and everyone's emotions were riding the roller coaster of unmanaged change. In early September, Mike, Hoalcraft, and Skip met to search out ways to defuse the powder keg that was dangerously susceptible to any casual and unplanned spark. That meeting spawned the plan for a meeting with Skip, Hoalcraft, Briggs, Mike, Kenny and his partner Leon Wieland, Henry and his partner Jerry Gibbs, Joe and his partner Jim Peters, and me and three of my four partners: Alan Perriton, Dave Skiven, and Dan Juliette. My other partner, whom I lobbied hard to have in attendance, Jim Lewandowski, was not held in high regard by the leaders of manufacturing because he was a career H.R. guy, and it was deemed that what was to be discussed, and we hoped decided, did not have a direct impact on H.R. Therefore, his presence was not necessary. After sensing that if I kept up with my argument for his presence it could jeopardize the entire meeting, I backed off . This was just another glaring example of working around Briggs' ego and the obsequiously disgusting behavior of those reporting directly to him. I would be there to represent H.R.'s stakes and equities and would communicate thoroughly with Jim after each of the bloody five days of meetings. I was determined not to let happen to H.R. what had always happened in the past – having the "hard" side of the business make decisions and throw them over the wall with the inept directions, "Take care of this!"

The meeting took place at the Maxwell House in Nashville, the hotel I had spent nearly four years living in, and was initially planned for Monday through Friday with the weekend available if necessary. As with any group anywhere in the world that is gathered together to deal with very substantial issues, where conflicting viewpoints are known to exist going in, the morning of the first day was conducted with all the politeness and decorum of a church social. Neither point of view willing to be the first to shoot a warning shot across the bow of the other and just generally agreeing on the necessity of the meeting and going over the agenda. After our separate discussions during lunch we, the union, came back and launched into the issues we were faced with, in retrospect, too much candor, but launch we did.

One of our key issues, among the many we worked on that week, was the module advisor position, which is the most critical position at Saturn in terms of how the partnership will be implemented on the production floor; and we made it very clear that first afternoon that if this was not resolved in a win-win way, then the rest of the issues were moot points. One of the biggest stumbling blocks to resolving this key issue was the lack of trust between the union leadership and Briggs and those reporting directly to him. So the first order of the afternoon focused on

115

the people we couldn't trust and why. We pointed out that, if there was not going to be a change in how they do business, in our opinion, we would never launch the car before Roger retired. This became very emotional and lasted the rest of the day, with various non-reps storming out of the room, vowing not to return, and being corralled in the corridor by one of our two process consultants from our internal organizational development staff and ceremoniously ushered back into the fray. The non-reps never liked taking someone on in public, and still don't to this very day, preferring to go behind closed doors and rip their victim to shreds and then walk out like they are the best of friends. That didn't work for us and never will, for it always seemed to be duplicitous and would lead to suppressed feelings that would boil and bubble inside until they found a way to be released.

The overnight pause to cauterize and stitch up the wounds of the day brought a more focused group of team members back in the morning and every morning after that. We didn't need to utilize the weekend or even all of Friday to reach agreement on the majority of the agenda, but three key issues took time and were finally brought to resolution. One, the module advisor role was agreed to and a rate of compensation established. Second, the charter team member (CTM) role was defined and agreed to. And third, a UAW administrative rate was created and sanctioned. The module advisor's role was critical to be resolved, for if you remember, many of the engineers were lured to Saturn by promises of key jobs, promotions, and so on. Briggs and his crew had long viewed this advisor function as a way to close this loop. They also believed that it would be a non-rep job, solely, all along. They had a huge list of eighth-level names – in GM eighth level is a shift superintendent – to put into these positions. We came in knowing that our members, both those onboard now and more important those to come, would never stand for this. Non-rep module advisors would be viewed as bosses, and that would never work.

We ultimately agreed to there being two of them, one rep and one non-rep, with the non-rep prohibited from being more than seventh level, and they would have equal authority and responsibility for the socio-technical development. This was a tragic, bitter fight, but once we got past it, everything else fell into place. The CTM role was defined as a rep job and would be the first person hired onto each team with the selection being done by the module advisors. The CTM would then hire the next person, and the two of them would hire the third and so on. This position would stay in place until we transitioned to steady state and the work unit counselor could be democratically elected. To compensate for the tremendous compensation differential between rep and non-rep leaders, a rate for rep leaders was agreed to that we hoped would fill the void until the risk-and-reward system could be agreed on. We all left the weeklong marathon sessions feeling somewhat better than when we arrived on Monday morning, but the proof of what we agreed to would be tested two short days later. Monday morning, the selection of work unit module advisors (WUMAs) roared off the starting line so these advisors could begin the training programs we also agreed to; and they could subsequently pick the CTMs for their modules and get them into the training plans necessary to hire the next person. Then we could focus on launching a world-class car, together.

The rest of 1988 for Mike, Joe, Kenny, and Henry was focused on building working relationships with their respective partners and implementing our UAW business plan with the top priorities being leadership selection, processing, and head-count resolution relative to the car redesign. I had four partners to build working relationships with, even though I had worked with them for the last three years. I had to understand the GM executive mentality – there is a difference between working with them and being a partner with them, an equal in decision making. Two of my partners were easy to work with and the other two were more difficult. I, too, had to focus on leadership selection, having four partners, and although we had rep team members in all four of my partnership arenas, not all of them were the right mix for the tasks that lay ahead. Jim Lewandowski in H.R. would need most of my focus, due to the sheer quantity of team members to be brought onboard, put through orientation and training, relocated, and made to feel welcome in their new Tennessee homes. Alan Perriton who led materials management would be the most difficult partner, so he would receive the second most joy in my company. Dan Juliette, who handled all of manufacturing engineering and was Briggs's right-hand man, would rank third in priority, followed by Dave Skiven, who led facility development for us. Dave was truly a wonderful leader and would be the easiest to work with for he really understood what we were trying to do here and was not in this organization purely for his own self-actualization.

In what seemed like only a couple of weeks our fourth corporate Christmas was here. Eighteen months till the launch and so many, many things still had not come together. As for the past three holidays, the desire not to go home was strong, but common sense prevailed for we all knew that this year was a true bellwether of many years to come. A pause to recharge the batteries was mandatory for all those who hoped to be at full strength for the last leg of our developmental cycle. I, personally, was going to savor this holiday season because I knew this would be my last Christmas as a Michigan resident. The year 1989 would find me becoming a Tennessean.

January 1989 was upon us, and as each day clicked by we knew we were closer to the time when we would have to put our money where our mouths are. As each new year always was greeted with refreshed mind and hearts, this year was no exception. Buoyed by the anticipation, excitement, and challenge of taking on the world in the small car market had the atmosphere of Saturn more electric than I could ever recall. The first day back on my drive into work, slowed to a standstill in the horrific Detroit traffic, I recalled my thoughts during the holiday shutdown on what a tremendous opportunity faced us. We were poised to set the auto industry on its ear, and we believed that we would really do it. The training presentation I had made at the Sterling Inn flashed across my cortex, and I vividly recall the impact it had on the 99, for it was focused on our people. See if you can feel what I mean.

TRAINING PRESENTATION: SATURN CONSENSUS MEETING

We would like to address an issue very dear to us, the training of Saturn. Once, maybe in a lifetime, an opportunity comes along to dramatically alter the course of history. That time is now, 1984. Not the 1984 "big brother" of Orwell, but 1984, the year America and the automobile industry – which has been our love affair and life blood for over 75 years – are rocketed back to their rightful position: number 1 in the industrialized world. This great opportunity, ever so delicately balanced on timing and course of action, demands that we now say, the time has come for Saturn, and what Saturn entails – knowledge!

The course of action: We as one, must assert ourselves, and unitedly pursue the very essence of what makes Saturn so unique – people working together toward a common goal. With training unequaled anywhere in the world as the launching pad for our Saturn rocket. The only aspect that cannot resemble 1984 is our approach to training. Here is where we must truly leapfrog our competition. Through competency based training, designed and developed – based upon the true needs of our work force – we will become what our competitors believe we can't. Truly competitive!

Our opportunity of a lifetime is here and we truly fear that, if we do not reach, if we do not do this right, this time, we will never pass this way again.

Jack O'Toole – for Ring Three
9/17/84

This was the single most important ingredient in the success formula we were creating, our belief in ourselves. The tremendous individual talent we had was being transformed into synergistic teams that believed nothing was impossible. I had struggled over the holidays with my new role as vice president and the four partnerships that I willingly accepted, as to where to put the most emphasis. Each element was a critical success factor. Human resources would be my number 1 goal, but getting the right people into the other partnerships was imperative. I really felt calm this frigid Michigan morning sitting dead still on an expressway, looking around at all the angered faces of my fellow commuters, listening to the incessant honking of cars, and saying to myself, "I may miss some things about Detroit but this won't be one of them."

The three-system integration was still the foremost concern of the leaders of Saturn, but necessity being the mother of invention, significant parochialism developed around the car and how it was to be processed and people selection and how they would be developed. Shortly after Hoalcraft came onboard, the Saturn Quality Council that had been formed by the SAC in November 1986 was given more emphasis. Not that it had not been important, but until there was some semblance of a producible product to relate to, all the system development didn't need as much focused attention as it did the last half of 1988 and on to the start of production. It was totally revamped and five subcouncils were implemented: one each in Powertrain, Body, and Vehicle Systems; one for all the resource teams in H.R., finance, sales, service and marketing, and the other functions; and one for Michigan operations, which would incorporate both advanced engineering and all the resource teams' support that would remain in Michigan. The purpose of the subcouncils to institutionalize the quality systems as developed would be key to our success. Once we began, the learning that resulted would be shared with the main council, and this led to many, many system improvements. Not intentionally, but nevertheless, H.R. was to be the group responsible as always for people development. A year ago, I would have gone ballistic over this, but now I knew that, left with the keys to the vault, one must make good use of the resident assets. Also, if done properly, other groups would also be responsible for people development and not even realize it.

The first quarter of the year the hottest issues were keeping construction on or ahead of schedule, outsourcing the parts we were not going to produce ourselves in Spring Hill, determining a revised head count in manufacturing, and Northfield and South Park development. Also, on my personal agenda was the upcoming move to Tennessee, tentatively scheduled for April. In manufacturing, Mike and the other three VPs along with Briggs and his three minions were embroiled in completing the module advisor selection and beginning the CTM selection while methodically trying to resolve the redesign processing issues and deal as best they could with the emotionally charged head count increases that were surfacing every day. This last issue would not be satisfactorily resolved for years and would cause long-lasting scars that only time had a chance to heal. Mike, Briggs, and Jim Wheatley also performed yeoman's duty in keeping construction dead on track with tremendous support from Joe Rypkowski's partner, Jim Peters, who was brought in initially as our construction leader. I was acutely involved in three of these manufacturing issues with my partners – sourcing, facilities, and head count – but I also, with my other partner, worked closely with engineering on process changes from a support point of view. At least half of every day, was spent on Northfield and South Park development, with the main emphasis on Northfield. As you remember, we felt the key to success would ultimately lie with how well we prepared our team members for this assault on the status quo. So the Northfield Training and Development Center was a key factor in this success quotient. With all the plants under different stages of development, ranging from near completion to no wall yet, and more and more team members relocating every week to trailers that were already cramped, keeping Northfield's construction on track for a March usability date was critical. To exacerbate the situation, with all the emphasis on plant construction, it became almost a catch-22.

Perseverance and determination finally won out, with tremendous support from Mike, Jerry Mills, Hoalcraft, and Skip. Of lesser, but still important, concern was South Park, which was tentatively planned to house child care, wellness, hospital, fire station, and union hall facilities. This was a keen issue with the local union in particular, but the same energy was not shared by Briggs and company. However, I had the necessary support from my partners in H.R. and in facilities, so it never lapsed into a coma but did go through several transformations. Through the course of 1988 and ultimately 1989, the human resource training and development team, along with key individuals identified in the business teams, developed straw dogs (preliminary models) of curriculums for all Saturn team members.

Throughout this long two years of planning, developing, and revising, the words of Coach Vince Lombardi came out of my mouth so many times that people threatened to kill me if they ever heard them again, "Everyone wants to win, but everyone doesn't want to prepare to win. The greatest plans in the world are worthless if they are executed halfheartedly." Prepare to win was our battle cry that sometimes became a low agonized moan, when faced with the sheer numbers that kept evolving for training hours required. We had identified 390 hours of mandatory training for operating technicians; 550 hours for trades technicians; 700 hours for module advisors; an additional 200 hours for CTMs; 300 hours for engineers; and 500 hours for every leader past the module decision-making level. With an estimated 5,000 team members onboard by start of production, 18 months was about a third of the time we would require. With all these numbers being "guesstimates," it became critically important that the development of classes and instructors or facilitators stay totally on or ahead of the time line. The funds we negotiated from the state of Tennessee were a boon to us these two years and would be for the next four to follow.

The first quarter went by in a hurry and we were down to 15 months till start of production (SOP). Each day seemed shortened even though we had progressed from 12- to 16-hour work habits, yet no one complained, for the excitement could be felt rising incrementally each of these time-robbed days. I made my emotional relocation to Tennessee in the middle of April, but it was softened considerably by the fact that I would be commuting extensively to Detroit for the next six months and to a lesser degree for the next two years.

121

FORMING THE FUTURE

The first four months of 1989 brought some very unexpected and disturbing news, especially to those of us in the UAW. What had started out as a not-to-be-believed rumor was rapidly shaping up as a reality. Don Ephlin was not going to run for another term as director of the GM Department in the International Union but was going to retire instead. His heir apparent was Steve Yokich, the VP/director of the UAW/Ford Department. With Don's leaving a virtual reality, you could have blown me over with the wind from a gnat's wings. Shock is too mild to describe our local leadership's mental state at this revelation. Hoalcraft had hinted earlier in the first quarter of the year that Don was growing very frustrated with the lack of progress in moving relations inside GM to a more collaborative mode.

The situation had not gotten any better. If anything, GM had descended further into the paralysis of change; and Don, sensing in that remarkable visionary mind that it would take a cataclysmic significant emotional event or a decade of spaced repetition to bring about the needed shift, made his decision. What a situation we were faced with. We knew Roger was going to retire in August 1990, but we had planned on Don being there for another three years to champion our survival against the bitterly jealous other GM divisions, as well as the traditionalists within the International Union. Remember what I said about champions: they don't last forever. This is a fact of life, and we knew that we were going to lose the champion that sold the vision as well as the one he sold it to, but Roger was not really a concern because his heir Bob Stempel was an avid supporter and would do all that was necessary to ensure our survival within the corporation. Steve was far from being a supporter, and this could have far-reaching impact on our life cycle.

Champions are the superordinate protectors of any fledgling undertaking. Without them a project is naked and exposed to the onslaught of all its detractors. Many of these lie in wait, ready to pounce the moment an opportunity occurs and drive full force for the jugular. Roger and Don had been exceptional champions for over five years, and many would say that was long enough, but we hadn't yet produced one car for sale, and any glitches in our plan would open us up to immediate attack. We knew that there were flaws in the plan that was presented to the board, especially after the redesign, and now both of our guardian angels would be gone. The UAW has its triennial constitutional convention the year before negotiations on contracts with the Big Three automakers, so that meant Don would be gone in June, for the convention was when the president and the rest of the union's International Executive Board were named for the next three years. The dark pallor of uncertainty as to all the ramifications this might entail dimmed the once ever-glowing light at the end of the tunnel to a mere pinpoint.

Don had brought the entire UAW/GM staff (all the reps who served the 136 GM plants and locals) to Tennessee for a twofold purpose: first, to have them strategize what the UAW should look like in the year 2000; and second, to expose the entire staff to the partnership at Saturn and what we were doing under his tutelage to create the labor relations model for the 21st century. He was set to return to Detroit, and with the convention coming in June, this was the opportune time to show our appreciation for his undaunted championship of the *vision*.

On May 18, 1989, we hosted a "very special" Ephlin evening in Nashville, which was trianchored by Skip, Mike, and Hoalcraft. The 100 senior leaders from Saturn, both rep and non-rep, were in attendance as well as videotaped messages from Owen Bieber, Roger Smith, and Bob Stempel. We flew Elphin's family in from Detroit and Boston just to show how special he was to us. It was a magical evening for this humble, soft-spoken, actually quite shy millwright from Framingham, Massachusetts, who had risen to lead the largest unit in the entire UAW. There was no roasting of the guest of honor this evening. Just a tremendous outpouring of love and respect for a man who had the incredible vision to see that there was a better way to manage a car company – man who was willing to put his entire career on the line to protect and promote a dream that he believed into reality. The sadness felt that evening was for ourselves, not for Don. He, in about a month, would be out of the intense pressure cooker of the UAW International Executive Board politics, which were forever being stirred by men who wouldn't listen to a new idea because their only goal was to maintain status quo – as was GM's. The impact of his leaving would be felt long and hard in Spring Hill.

When the evening had finally drawn to conclusion, much too quickly, I remember thinking to myself how meager this homage was to a man who had given another man, Roger, the reasons to launch a daring endeavor that would forever change how automobiles were designed, manufactured, and marketed. Most of the leaders at this "thank you" gathering barely knew Don, and most had no idea until after the evening was over just how important his role had been in the creation and birth of Saturn. Most left that evening having a healthier view of him, but very few knew how incredibly far into the future he could see or knew the integrity, determination, and perseverance he employed to make those futuristic mind journeys come to life. I remember asking him that night, after almost everyone but Mike, Hoalcraft, and I had left, if he thought he would ever get calls from Solidarity House soliciting his wise counsel. I was not really surprised when he said, "No." Sadly, he relayed this identical message to me five years later when he came to the dedication of our magnificent union hall, in 1994. The gridlock of fear is alive and well at the boathouse on Jefferson Avenue.

Spring zoomed into summer and on all fronts progress was being made. The Quality Council and subcouncils were having a significant impact on our development cycle, especially in the critical areas I mentioned at the start of the year. Everyone was getting aligned with the fact that quality would spell victory or defeat, and this helped immensely in gaining support for the training plans that would prepare us to win. July heralded 12 months until SOP and, while our message to the world was one of calm, confidence, decorum, and even a bit of cockiness, internally the anxiety and stress were mounting daily. There was always that nagging little, barely perceptible voice that would whisper precisely at the highest moment of stress, "You're not going to make it!" Only to be crushed with a crescendo of "Yes we are!" after a fleeting instant of panic and nausea. Adherence to the plan had become a disciplined habit, with daily and weekly meetings numbering in the thousands to check and cross-check alignment and make any in-course adjustments. The new structure in the union had greatly enhanced our ability to get real time data on the entire organization, thereby enabling the partnership to grow less encumbered by many isolated decisions being made that, when discovered, adversely affected a different part of the organization than the one in which they were made. The healing of wounds from the consolidation of 12 business units to 3 was taking place slowly, but the political infighting of the union leaders brought about by the four VPs was a grade school fight compared to what was happening in the engineering community. I had always thought union politics were tough but these people were ruthless. A keen eye must be kept on this so that it would not jeopardize our timeline, especially for quality and training. Mike B., Briggs, the three VPs, and their partners ended up handling this threat with the diplomacy of career foreign service professionals, but the handwriting was on the wall – some engineers were not going to make SOP.

Fall raced in like the winds across Lake Superior, fast, furious, and fraught with danger. The processing of the car was still undergoing too many changes. The head count resolution was at a virtual stalemate. Training was dangerously close to taking a backseat to production; and the Body Systems and Vehicle Systems Plants had fallen behind in construction. Even Mike and my fellow VPs seemed to fall victim to the hypnotic hum of manufacturing development and seemed ready to abdicate responsibility for human resource development and totally throw it into the hands of H.R. This was one of those moments when you knew you had to do something – probably bizarre – to break the spell of the activity syndrome. Everyone was still working inhumane hours willingly, but the vision was becoming tunneled more and more each day to each person's own ecosystem. My partner Jim L. in H.R. and I had been discussing this expected phenomena since the spring and had labored behind closed doors with our respective leaders in an attempt to slow down this trend. While we got all the right words spoken to us, accompanied by promised support that it would be addressed, there was no significant change. That was when we decided we would implement our plan to put ownership for people issues back on those who should be responsible for it. We scheduled ourselves onto the next SAC agenda and came prepared not to leave without support and, most important, commitment to our proposal.

The next Monday we stepped in front of the SAC and confidently presented our plan. The first element was simply changing our name from human resources to people systems, something that should have passed without a blink but took 20 minutes to elicit support adequate enough to move on with our proposal. Then we unveiled a tool we had borrowed from engineering, a Go/No-Go review. Just like the reviews done on developmental readiness of the car, we would hold the same reviews on people issues once a month in front of the SAC, and it must be prepared and presented by the joint business team leaders. Not just the union VP and his or her partner but every member of SAC as well.

Finance, sales, service and marketing, product engineering, people systems, corporate communications, and materials management functions were included. Our anticipated resistance to this was even greater than we expected, but our homework had been done. Skip, Hoalcraft, and Mike took all the wind out of the sails of the adversaries, after suitable debate that reinforced our estimate of the points of most resistance. The third element involved the "whats" that would be measured, such as recruitment and selection, orientation and training, relocation, and how each team was dealing with the ever-mounting stress. This and the last element, which dealt with consequences and people system support, passed like a lamb. The date was set for the first people system review at the end of October, three short weeks away, and then we left as graciously as we had entered, partially successful in getting our feet to actually touch the floor on our way out. Back to the people systems area we went, knowing full well that as soon as the SAC took a break our phones would begin lighting up, but we were prepared, confident, and quite frankly, relieved. We had all the support systems in place for quite a while now, but they hadn't been utilized. Now they would be.

Needless to say, the first review was less than smooth. Whining and excuses accompanied the first two presentations when subjected to probing questions by Mike, Skip, Hoalcraft, and me, which lit a fuse under Hoalcraft first and then Skip. They stopped the proceedings, delivered severe verbal invectives to all in attendance, and removed any doubt as to their support for these reviews. Except for finance and people systems, the remaining report outs were sketchy at best, but everyone in attendance left with a much more focused attention span. Once again, I knew our phones would be lighting up. The November and December reviews were very polished and accurate, as accurate as some people could ever be, but more important was what was happening in between that first one and these last two. The three most resistant areas, manufacturing, product engineering, and materials management, had really grasped the importance of the fact that they, not people systems, must be responsible for the people *they* hired. Somehow they had forgotten that a traditional personnel department had not hired the team members in their areas, they had. They individually could not be successful, nor could we be collectively successful, if we failed to prepare our most important asset to win. They finally realized that the old excuse, "You guy's sent us a bunch of duds," was not available anymore. The hat was on the rightful owner.

As more and more represented team members came through the process, it became obvious to us in the local union that we needed to think about elections before the start of production next summer. Supporting us in our viewpoint was Jerry Mills, but Hoalcraft didn't think it needed to be done before SOP. We began serious debate on this in August and, with Brother Mills's excellent mentoring, swayed Hoalcraft to our point of view. Jim Wheatley, while giving lip service support for the appointed Executive Board, had long ago begun grooming others for these roles. He knew we were aware of his intentions but didn't think we knew all the people he was mentoring. Jerry supported the current Executive Board because he knew the potential danger in changing horses in midstream. Jim didn't care. By the end of August things were shaping up for a confrontation with Wheatley, then tragedy struck. Jerry Mills, while home for the weekend, was rushed into the emergency room by his wonderful wife and within days had lapsed into a coma. Having long battled high blood pressure, cholesterol, enormously elevated triglycerides, and his love of any talented chef, his body's resistance exercised its inherent power and his pancreas ceased to function. Initially, there was a glimmer of hope that the pancreas could be surgically removed, but that rapidly faded when it was discovered that the reason it ceased to function was that it had actually exploded, and the resultant damage to neighboring tissue was apparently irreversible. Like he had in all the years I'd known him, Jerry fought valiantly against impossible odds and for weeks would rally and seem, on occasion, to border very close to consciousness. I remember to this very day standing by his bedside, holding his hand and talking to him, gently admonishing him for such lousy timing in getting ill, but always saying how much I believed he would win this fight. I could feel his hand tighten on mine even though his eyes never opened, and I would leave, vowing that when I returned those wonderful blue sky eyes, which danced like only my father's had, would be looking at me.

This was not to be. Returning to Tennessee to perform my duties for the week, the call came from his son, Tony, who was one of my key leaders in people systems. On September 23, my dear friend and trusted mentor passed over Jordan. It had been 10 years since my father died and I had looked at the grim reaper with its reality-filled eyes that glowed with the mortality of us all. I hadn't cried over my father's death until many months after it occurred, but then he had met the Lord by himself. I had never seen him suffer. I found myself crying almost uncontrollably at this stark epiphany, not for Jerry because he had now found peace, but for his devoted wife and sons and for how much I was truly going to miss him. His death cast a shadow over Saturn that can be felt to this very day. No one is irreplaceable, but the politics that evolved when his calming, diplomatic, and when needed, tremendously powerful persuasion was removed from the arena have been a serious hindrance to being all that we had the potential to be.

That fourth quarter of 1989, I felt almost naked. Joe M. had been reassigned, and now Jerry was gone forever. Of the three international reps that started four years ago, only Jim Wheatley remained; and he was bitter and disgruntled to the point that I could barely stand to talk to him anymore. We still had Hoalcraft, but although he was paying his dues, the jury was still out on where he really stood. Joe Malotke's parting words were burned into my memory, "I don't care if Don replaces me, whoever he sends in will find out how hard it is to deal with managing this change process as well as trying to make consensus decisions with career GM bureaucrats on what is good for the business and never losing sight of what's good for people as well." Hoalcraft was seeing it, too, no matter how hard he tried to pretend otherwise.

My return to Flint for the holiday shutdown was a time for sentiment and reflection. Christmas was a somber occasion for many of my friends as well, for we knew that when we returned in January 1990, with only seven months until SOP, the real impact of Jerry's loss would really be felt. This holiday season with my two sons was very special, for we spent the most quality time together we had spent in a long time. They were somewhat dismayed – but not nearly as much as I – at the prospect of me moving 700 miles away, but once they realized that they could come and see me in a different state, quite often, they found that "too cool." Like the four holiday seasons before this one, it passed with the speed of a single weekend. This one also shared the fate of the others, and the new year ushered in – *the year*. This year it must all come together, and come together it truly would. Only seven short months until SOP, and we'll see what all the critics have to say then. I'm sure they will find something negative to say – they always had.

THE LAUNCH

One small step for man,
one giant leap for mankind.

Neil Armstrong

7

The return to work was a slow leisurely drive through those beautiful rolling hills of middle Tennessee. The treacherously slick,
bumper to bumper, dodgem car trauma of Detroit, played in subzero
temperatures, was still too vivid a memory, but having the outside temperature hovering in the 50s would drive those frightful visions to the
back of my subconscious before I reached the site. Focusing on the day
at hand would take a great deal of effort for everyone, because this was
the year. Even though launch was seven months into the future, that
interesting mixture of anticipation and anxiety was coursing through
every vein in my body, and all those I queried that morning felt the
same. Rested and refreshed from nearly two weeks away from the pressure cooker had picked up the spirits of all, and most people were having a difficult time setting priorities on the mountain of tasks that lay
before us. In people systems, we had cut the pie into very eatable slices,
selected very capable leaders and followers, and were trying extremely
hard to stay out of their way and let them do what we hired them to
do. Jim Lewandowski and I had been very busy since September 1988,
working with the leaders of people systems to consolidate the tremen-

dous amount of activity into nonredundant groups that would have the necessary independence to be creative, while recognizing and utilizing the required interdependencies to avoid decisions that would be collectively disruptive at a later date. We also worked diligently to negate the adverse affects of our two locations, Michigan and Tennessee, by alternating sites for our team meetings. The people systems' pie was cut into seven slices, with a rep and non-rep partner leading each in Tennessee and three partners in Michigan. The seven areas of responsibility were recruitment, application, screening and selection, training, reward systems development, human environment group, operations, systems and planning, and Saturn information systems (EDS).

During the previous 15 months, Alan Perrinton and I had been doing very similar work in materials management. We had consolidated many stand-alone groups in each of the business units, including Northfield, into four major blocks of this partnership. Our superordinate goal being the Saturn production system. We sectored the development effort into direct material, indirect material, purchasing, and transportation and established a partnership in each one. The task here was more difficult than in people systems because Alan had not had a formal partner for quite a while, plus this was an area that "management" had traditionally held as its own, so the acceptance level was more difficult to achieve than in people systems, where we had decades of working relationships. This partnership taxed my creativity more than the other three and also reinforced why we created Saturn the way we did. I utilized too many traditional tactics here, but unfortunately, they were necessary until the light went on in some very traditional managers' heads that I wasn't going to go away. More leaders in this group feared me than the other three partnerships combined; so I was constantly assessing my aversion to "the end justifies the means" with the ire generated by finding out about meetings after they were over, unilateral decisions that then had to be revisited, and hostility that was not blatant but could be picked up whenever I walked into a room. This ended up being a very productive and strong partnership in the end, but it caused many of the black hairs on my head to turn white.

Being a partner with Dave Skiven on facilities was truly my most pleasurable relationship of the four. Dave was the kind of leader who, once he understood the tremendous power created by the synergy that literally erupted in a partnership, became the model you would use to compare all other leaders to. Getting him to understand took a considerable amount of patience, but when it hit him, it was smooth sailing from then on. We faced the same opportunities in the other three areas; that is, getting people, who had almost too much autonomy for too long, to work in focused, nonredundant teams that had to rely on each other. One thing that exacerbated this process was that each business team, Northfield, Saturn service parts operations (SSPO), and those in the Michigan sites would be the owners of their respective facilities when they were completed, so we had to make every attempt to give them the individual items they needed. Each of these different facilities' leaders felt that those from our group working in their building belonged to them and must blindly supply whatever they said they wanted. They set the atmospheric climate that the customer is always right – no matter if that customer was functionally ignorant of what was needed versus what was wanted. The leaders could not care less about the interdependencies that we said were jugular, if they chose not to accept them. This could have been as frustrating as in materials management, had it not been for Dave. We sliced this pie up into six slices: internal facilities, external facilities/landscaping, plant floor systems, central utilities, environmental, and maintenance. Partnerships were established in each of these areas, and it was not a big surprise when, in the final tally, we had received over a dozen awards for the planning, building, operation, and maintenance of Spring Hill as a major manufacturing complex.

The last partnership for which I was responsible was with Dan Juliette, who was in charge of manufacturing engineering. As I related earlier, this was the second most difficult partnership to establish and maintain. Geography and tradition were the two main obstacles that would eventually be overcome in the 21 months of my time spent with this group. Almost all of the advanced manufacturing engineers still resided in Michigan and worked with the trades and operating technicians at our 12-mile preproduction facility in Madison Heights. Although a plethora of great ideas were generated within those four walls on how to process the manufacturing build of our product, too many decisions were being made on computer screens by people that would never have to live with those decisions. The UAW technicians were in a different local, Local 1810, and although these decisions were made in partnership, many would have proven unsatisfactory, almost disastrous, if not addressed by this reluctantly forced partnership.

Tradition had very deep roots here, again, for this was also a very "exclusively management" jewel that was trying to be kept that way by a one-sided dominant partnership in Michigan. Even though the rep technicians worked daily with the Michigan engineers, there wasn't any doubt that the ultimate decision really lay with Mr. Juliette. I stopped counting the number of times I heard the question, "Really, what value do trades and op techs really bring to these decisions? They don't have engineering degrees, do they?" This obviously sliver thin view of the world would generally be followed by an equally idiotic statement, " Heck, there is plenty of time to make adjustments, if by the remote chance this doesn't work. That's the way processing is."

Threats and confrontation that bordered dangerously close to physical exchanges of energy were eventually replaced with grudging acceptance, but not until many faces had changed in the engineering ranks. Dan J. ended up being a close associate of mine, once we really understood each other; and we sliced this pie into some more manageable pieces. We settled on five areas: tooling, preproduction build, notice of action change management, new model year management, and advanced product processing engineering. All five areas ended up being tripartite partnerships due to two separate local unions being involved. This necessary arrangement resulted positively in the amount of creativity generated, but it also resulted in a great deal of conflict that was very difficult to manage as well as time consuming. This arena proved to take years to make it fully effective, but we finally got it right. I'll discuss this later as we tantalizingly prepare for the rest of this century.

Mike and the other three VPs had been engrossed in the same partnership development cycle with their respective counterparts. Facilities, sourcing, processing, staffing, training, plant floor systems, and engineering were every bit as critical to them as they were to me. My partners and I were simply resources to them, for they had the responsibility to ultimately deliver the product and understandably were very protective of their turf in all the aforementioned arenas. Our goal was to help them make the right decisions, not make the decisions for them, while at the same time, not let them go off in separate directions. This proved to be quite a challenge for all of us collectively, due to the ever-increasing pressure of Roger's impending retirement and it's very clearly articulated importance to him. He had alluded to the fact that he would delay his retirement day until we were ready, but no one wanted to test his sincerity on that one. We did, however, all agree that we could make the timeline, but it was going to require all of us to keep our eyes unwaveringly tuned to our goal. The redesign was fraught with weekly surprises and continued to tax everyone's creativity, patience, commitment, determination, and perseverance.

The five of us, union local leaders, had also made a commitment among ourselves, and had secured at least verbal support from Hoalcraft, that we would not – I repeat would not – agree to a launch date unless the car was ready from a quality perspective. There wasn't any way we could possibly hit the production ramp figures because this product had so many more parts than the original design, and we would have to debug a significant amount of late arriving machinery and equipment in an extremely small window of time, plus the fact that many of our parts suppliers were faced with the same dilemma, for the same reasons. Even if this were not the case, we in the union were keenly aware that we would have only one opportunity to make a good impression. This was especially true in the Asian-dominated small car segment of the market, for the Asians had firmly established great track records for quality, durability, reliability, and value for the dollar. Even though our clinics had told us that current import owners were still hopeful that a comparable American-made car would be developed and, if so, would eagerly purchase it, they also told us that, if it didn't measure up, that would be the straw that broke the camel's back. For, trying to fool them with wonderful words and promises, and then not deliver, would be met with a backlash of resentment that may never be overcome.

Again, as the saying goes, "Prosperity conceals genius – adversity reveals it." We all faced six months that passed as quickly as six weeks. That nagging little voice raised its decibel level almost daily, "You're not going to make it," and much soul-searching was experienced, but the mind once stretched by a new idea never regains its original dimensions, and we never fell into that decades-proven trap from the Land of the Adversaries of believing that nagging little voice. *Change agents,* one key reason all our partnerships worked was we took the time up front to form a contract with each other on our respective expectations. Most organizations going through the change process make the critical mistake of not doing this. They get caught up in timelines and trying to keep their fingers on every movement in their area of responsibility and vow they will set up these contracts when the time is right, only to find that it is always too late. They are thereby faced with all the scars that result from conflicting expectations not being resolved, unless by accident, and then struggle hopelessly to correct a situation whose cement has hardened beyond change.

We avoided this pitfall by simply being willing to throw in the towel and stop the whole enterprise if our partners tried to do business as usual. Remember when I said that you must come to work each day willing to make it your last if key basic principles are circumvented or ignored. Brother Ephlin had drummed this deep into our cerebral cortex. If you compromise the principles, you lose the undertaking. So by sheer force of determination we would not proceed until our partners sat down and a contract was agreed to. Even though we may have known each other for years, we stated our values – loyalty, honesty, and the rest. We also stated what we expected from this partnership – don't ever lie to me; if you disagree, say it then, don't wait till it has fumed inside you for a week; don't make any unilateral decisions until we establish a healthy degree of trust, and so on. We established what each could expect of the other in the partnership; that is, we asked these questions – How will we establish our communication system? How long will the two of us meet alone every day? How are we going to measure progress in our partnership? What will be the consequences if either partner is not living up to these commitments? By taking this time up front, we did not guarantee the success of any of the partnerships that were established, but we certainly increased the chances of success by at least 50%. Do not avoid this critical step of contracting as you undertake the volatile and unpredictable process of change. The history books are fraught with examples of many who failed and few who succeeded.

Progress was being – literally – hammered out, in all areas of the organization that first quarter of 1990, but we in the union had a separate challenge to manage that our partners could not be a part of, no matter how much they wished they could help. We would have 3,000 rep team members onboard by SOP, and we had to set a date for democratic elections of all the Executive Board positions that had been appointed since September 1988. I must remind you that we had over 500 former union local presidents, shop chairmen, members from the zone, district and alternate committees, benefit, health and safety, employee assistance reps, and some power-hungry team members who had never been involved in their former union locals, but, once here, aspired to lofty heights. Well, as it turned out, 75% of that estimated 500 came in the first year. Over half of those in this category were from plants that had been closed, many due in part to their local union's avid resistance to a less adversarial relationship with the local management. They developed amnesia about this part of their history now that they could run for election among thousands who didn't know them. Buoyed by this situation, they were the most vocal at our monthly union meetings for the many months before the election. Not succumbing to their self-centered pressure tactics, we set the date and time of the election by utilizing the entire membership, not those who simply made the most noise. As you recall, we planned to have this election before the SOP all along. It was simply a matter of timing and working through the politics that were generated by these former local leaders.

We picked the last week of April for the election, to minimize disruption to the launch and also to allow enough time to assimilate anyone who was elected that was not currently appointed. By traditional standards, the politics were very mild compared to what I was used to – a fact that all the former leaders had not counted on. After the date was set, they came out offensively, which was not what the members of this local union wanted. Far too many union members had come here to get away from that, and it was a tactic that backfired explosively for the opposition. We remained focused on the issues facing all of us in the next years and never once fell victim to any of the opposition's attempts to divert the election to a personal level. In the end, the entire Executive Board we put together was elected, and we went on with the development of Saturn Corporation for at least another two years without preparing for the next election in 1993. We made a commitment to ourselves and the membership. If we did what we said, there was nothing to worry about. We let our accomplishments speak for themselves and felt that we would not have to deal with negative politics anymore – so we thought at the time.

The month of January 1990 also brought our Risk and Reward program in front of the GM Management Committee. By keeping Roger and Steve up to speed every step of its development, we had secured their total support, but for political reasons, neither could come out publicly as key promoters. They had to remain in the background ready

135

and willing to privately explain the plan's virtues and garner the necessary support. They tagged Lloyd E. Reuss to make the pitch to the management committee. Although it wasn't certain yet, the inside favorite to replace the current president, Bob Stempel, would be Lloyd. January 24 was the date picked for this presentation, so most of the month of January was spent getting Lloyd prepared. This was the first step in getting our plan implemented, and while no one at Saturn would openly question or challenge Roger, he nonetheless would need everyone's support for the next steps, which would involve approval from the Incentive and Compensation Committee, the GM/Saturn Board of Directors, and the GM Board of Directors.

Utilizing Lloyd was a noble attempt on Roger's part to get support for us, especially after Roger retired. Although Lloyd was always smart enough never to whack us publicly, insiders at the GM building and Don Ephlin continually warned us about where we stood with Mr. Reuss. So, getting him to make all these presentations was a good move both politically and for the long term. Roger's heir apparent, Bob Stempel, was already a staunch ally and was both publicly and privately known for this, thereby making him unacceptable as key support gainer. By using Reuss, it could always be held over his head that Reuss had made all these wonderful presentations to garner approval of what Saturn proposed – so how could he not be supportive, what kind of person was he? Politics, politics, management politics, and they said the union was bad. Roger's plan worked, and worked so well that the recommendation that came for this august group was that it would go to the Incentive and Compensation Committee and the GM/Saturn Board of Directors for review on a "no objection" basis. All the outliers were coming together.

February 5 marked my sixth year of association with Saturn, but only my fifth since it had become an organization. That evening I sat quietly in my apartment and recalled this half-decade and tried to figure out why I had spent the lion's share of this time in human resources. I had spent 19 years in manufacturing and liked it there. That was where the excitement was: the challenge of getting people to work together, a tangible object to measure your work performance against, a place you could see bottom-line results every day – the number of cars built to schedule, scrap produced, rework required, quality level, and so forth. Why had I chosen to work for five years with those I used to call brain-dead, pencil-pushing bureaucrats. Although I had briefly thought about this in the past, I had never really sat down and tried to think it through. Most often the pressures of building this billion dollar corporation didn't allow time for a non-value-added sojourn into the mental machinations of one's choices. But since we put a leadership team together that would be facing the unpredictable wiles of the democratic election process, and we had very seriously discussed moving the VPs around if everyone were elected, I knew that I had to reason this out before any of these plans came to pass. I was very proud of what we had accomplished in the area of people systems over the last five years, but I wasn't sure about the reason why. Anyone who has ever worked with me can attest to the fact that, until the logic of happenings becomes clear to me, I never stop trying to figure them out. This trait has always been a hindrance in personal relationships, but professionally it has helped me immeasurably. Soon it became clear to me, after I had taxed my analytical and memory skills beyond the edge of the envelope, that I chose to work in people systems because I knew from my history what a tremendous hindrance H.R. had been to establishing long-lasting relationships in our plants.

Personnel, as it was known in GM, was where all the policy, practice, and procedure manuals had been generated. It was responsible for the training of everyone. Labor relations resided there and, God forbid, hiring and the rest, with the personnel director reporting to the head of personnel in Detroit, not the plant manager. I had somehow known that we could not succeed if this system were replicated here. I also had deduced that the leaders of manufacturing, marketing, engineering, finance, and other functions were not ready yet to deal with these issues by themselves. It was so vividly clear. This was where the greatest change had to take place first, if we were going to make Saturn a success. Left to business as usual, while the plant was being built, equipment ordered, retailers picked, and so on, this area of our organization would spell certain failure. I felt much better than I had when I undertook this mind search, for now it made sense to me; and if I should rotate to one of the plants, I knew exactly what I would have in place for my replacement in People Systems and, more important, how we could all make the transition so that the moves would be personally and organizationally smooth.

The first quarter of 1990 passed like a week. Construction, for the most part, was completed so I was not spending much time at all with my partner Dave Skiven. We still had considerable work to do in the plant floor systems area, which would continue on after SOP, but most of my time was being necessarily spent with Lewandowski in H.R., Juliette in engineering, and Alan Perriton in materials management. Launch was a mere four months away, and there were far too many changes still taking place on the car. The list of suppliers who were telling us they didn't know if they would be certified by SOP was growing, and team member ramping was not yet up to schedule, which was putting serious strains on the training group to have everyone job-ready. To add to the list of stress inducers, my partner in people systems, Jim L., was under heavy fire from Briggs and company, who were just using him as a diversionary tactic to keep the spotlight off the many areas that were not progressing satisfactorily. Others on the SAC had aligned with Briggs, and they had the ear of Skip and Hoalcraft. So the handwriting that was slowly appearing on the wall pointed to a new partner in this arena. Getting the systems in place, for which we had labored so diligently, before someone new came in, was the highest priority, not just for me, but the other VPs and Mike as well. The rap that forced Jim's demise was one of being "too giving" to the union, that is, "Everything the union wants Jim gives them. This isn't a partnership. Don't anger the union guys or they will threaten you with – something." All this is how they interpreted Jim's relationship with the union. Too many non-rep leaders were still holding onto their personal sacred cows, albeit privately, and the reluctance to really share power with the union was being felt more and more each day.

Jim, meanwhile, did the right things. Although many times he was reluctant to make decisions that would be unfavorably received by other SAC members, in the end, he would do the right thing, knowingly accepting the consequences because that was the kind of man he was. I, along with Jim, was under assault, but Briggs and company knew they could not get to me because Mike, Hoalcraft, and Skip were my avid supporters and, when I won my election, all lobbying against me would be fruitless. Even though Jim didn't always understand why we needed certain things done, he always got out of the way and let us do what was necessary. This is what really angered Briggs and company. So, it was with much vigor that I attacked the remaining unfinished issues in people systems, and I could hardly let anyone outside of our leadership team know I was on to the scheme. Philosophically, I mused, "Didn't I come here for challenges. On with the enterprise."

The next three months were spent grinding out the details to ascertain a clear picture of where we were going to be at the end of July. Many things were happening over these 90 days of challenge and opportunity, trying to put the finishing touches on five years of development. Jim Peters, Joe Rypkowski's partner in Vehicle Systems and the site construction manager, announced he was going to retire. This was met with mixed reviews, because there was no middle ground when it came to Jim. You either liked him or you seriously disliked him. He had done a fantastic job overseeing the construction in Spring Hill and, depending on who you talked to, had done an equally good piece of work in readying Vehicle Systems with Joe for SOP. Having done what he promised Roger he would do, Jim realized that the time to go back to California and play golf every day was a call that he could not refuse. Mike, Joe, Hoalcraft, Briggs, and Skip had been suitably forewarned by Jim and they had his replacement in the wings. Bob Boruff had been picked to replace Jim in Vehicle Systems and came highly recommended by Hoalcraft, having worked with him on the GM/UAW quality network. There was another reason he was picked, which only a handful of people knew. Bob had also run the Ramos Arizpe complex in Sautillo, Mexico, which consisted of both an assembly plant and an engine plant. Bob would be groomed to replace Briggs as VP of manufacturing.

The four of us VPs plus Mike, Hoalcraft, and Don Ephlin had mounted a nonstop campaign from Skip to Roger calling for Briggs to be replaced. We even encouraged that he be promoted, which was what GM always did anyway. Mike's frustration level was about as high as it could go, trying to establish a working partnership with him. Briggs would sing all the right vocal lyrics publicly, but he would meet with those who reported directly to him, alone, and make decisions that were always caught and then reopened with great emotion; and the prognosis was that he had no intention of changing. Mike was the right partner for him, because failing to get Briggs to commit to a workable relationship, Mike – as only he could – unwaveringly parried each thrust and lashed back relentlessly, keeping Briggs constantly on guard. How sad it was to see this relationship.

Early on, I related Briggs's comment when we were trying to get organizational development help early in 1985, "You've got to be careful with those folks. You don't want to lose control." Control was Briggs's driver and release was Mike's. This isn't about good and bad; it's about what is at the core of Saturn. We were designed from our beginnings at the Study Center to be a release organization, one that trusts its team members to do the right things. Unfortunately, Briggs's history never allowed him to accept that. I'm not saying he didn't try, but when things didn't go exactly as planned or someone made a mistake, his first response was to find out who screwed up, not to find out how it could be rectified. The handwriting on the wall, in his case, though very faint, was still beginning to show.

The elections being over and our entire Executive Board winning a landslide victory, we set about looking to the future and who would fit best where among the VPs. Each one of us had a litany of reasons to remain where he or she currently was, but we all knew that in the long term this would not be beneficial to the team as a whole. SOP was only the beginning of what we planned to be a hundred year car company. We would be the model for labor relations across America on into the 21st century. This leadership team needed to be well rounded in all aspects of the organization. We knew very well that our non-rep partners would change over time, and only by understanding all aspects of our enterprise would we be able to overcome the new personalities with their attendant styles and sacred cows. We must guarantee that decisions would continue to be made based on their fit with the mission, philosophy, and values. It didn't matter how many non-reps came and went, we would always be here, for we had nowhere to go.

We and all the other members of Local 1853 had quit GM with no way of going back. With much ado, we sorted through the right placement of each VP and settled on Henry Campbell moving to Powertrain from Body Systems, where he had been ever since he joined back in 1986. Ken Duncan, who likewise had been in Powertrain since 1985, replaced Henry in Body Systems. Joe Rypkowski and I swapped jobs: he came to people systems and I went to Vehicle Systems. We targeted June 1 as the transition date. Much of April and May were spent bringing each other up to speed on our respective organizations. All the while we made sure we didn't skip a beat preparing for the launch. Our ramping and training curves were approaching where they needed to be, thanks to the monthly people system reviews that we initiated. This, along with supplier readiness, was a concern to all of us. We were coming to the conclusion daily that we would not be able to build at the rate we had planned. The redesign had posed some serious quality issues relative to buildability. None of these issues would delay the launch, but they did affect build time on the car; and we were adamant that not a single car would be shipped unless it met our stringent quality targets. This was placing a serious strain on the partnership across all areas of Saturn, just like we knew it would five years earlier.

None of our non-rep partners wanted to be the one pinpointed as having the area that was the bottleneck. It was almost comical, frustration not withstanding, to watch how they behaved at the launch planning meetings – telling Briggs exactly what he wanted to hear and then responding with indignation when we refuted the inaccuracies of what they said, even though we told them ahead of time we were going to do that. I really give Skip credit during these very trying times, for he never once gave the impression that what we faced we could not overcome. His calm and confidant demeanor had a tremendous influence on ordinary people doing very extraordinary things. He and Mike spent great amounts of time together, walking the plant floors and spreading the gospel that we would succeed, don't panic, hold fast to doing the right things, but most important, quality, quality, quality first and foremost. The numbers will come. Too much is at stake to compromise quality.

By the end of June two crews were fully staffed and job certified to the degree that was needed to build to our adjusted line speeds. The recruitment and selection pipeline was full of team members awaiting only a start date when production capability required them, and the orientation and training systems were fully functioning and ready to prepare each new team member for success. Parts for the car, both internally manufactured and supplied externally by our supplier partners, was the major issue in manufacturing. Process capability was the second biggest issue, and fit and finish was the last. Each day both internal and external suppliers brought forth new promises that we knew could not be met, but they were not greeted with hostility, for no one questioned how hard they were working. The redesign had a tremendous domino effect, but we were all betting our futures that it was the right thing to do. The biggest concern we had in people systems was housing for all the new team members relocated to Tennessee.

For over two years we had tried to get Maury County officials to convince the building community that $40,000 to $70,000 houses needed to be built as well as apartments for temporary housing while relocating team members sold their existing homes and then came up with the money to get into a new residence here. Neither we nor the Maury County officials were successful. All the local builders were convinced that this was somehow a plot to rip them off and went ahead with their plans to build homes for $100,000 and up, for everyone knew how rich GM auto workers were, and they were going to be prepared. This decision proved to be very costly for many of them. We had team members with very emotional spouses calling us daily, and the only recourse was to send them to the surrounding counties, who had listened to us, but this meant some significant commutes for a large number of people, and they were not very happy. It ended up costing Maury County a great deal of revenue in lost property taxes, for many team members who eventually bought homes for $100,000 and up did so in the neighboring county north of the plant, Williamson. It didn't take a rocket scientist to figure out that if you were going to spend that kind of money for housing, it would measurably appreciate north of the plant much sooner and to a greater degree than south. Homes in the $40,000–$70,000 range were eventually built, but never to the degree needed and not without easily avoided animosity.

In the beat of a hummingbird's wings it was July 30. Roger and Owen were at Saturn accompanied by every major TV network in the nation plus all the press services and all the major newspapers and magazines. This was the most coverage Spring Hill had received since five years earlier to the very day, when a similar gathering was convened in Nashville to announce Tennessee as the site selected for this noble undertaking. Now, 2,600 team members in Tennessee and 960 in Michigan were poised to present to the world the first salable vehicle produced after five long years of development, perspiration, frustration, adulation, and a great deal of gray hair. Roger and Owen drove that beautiful crimson four-door down Inspiration Point and then across the aisles in the plant, which were simply wall to wall with people. The person who should have been in that first Saturn with Roger wasn't even on site: the single most important person from the UAW who made this day possible, Don Ephlin. Not because *he* felt he should be here, but rather because *we* felt he should be here. Another reason his absence was so sorely felt was that, at his blowout party in February 1985,

Roger told the world that when he drove that first car off the line, Don would be sitting right next to him. The only invitation that came to Don seeking the honor of his presence came from Local 1853 through our president, Mike Bennett. Don, being the man he is, would not just show up without a call from Roger and Skip or Owen, which never came, so he didn't either. Remember I said, organizations don't have loyalty, people do. Many were showing what they thought of loyalty this day, as well as taking credit for something they had ragged on for years.

The entourage ultimately arrived in our audit area, to be totally engulfed by a massive wave of humanity. I will never forget that day as long as I live. I had only a month earlier taken over comanaging Vehicle Systems with Bob Boruff after my five year stint in people systems, but I felt like I had been there from the very beginning, just by the way I had been accepted by the team members. I was totally caught up in the pride and confidence that literally oozed from each one of them. The applause and whistles and laughter and tears at Inspiration Point and down the aisles leading to the audit area were deafening. But I don't think anyone was prepared for the decibel level that was experienced when that car slowly wheeled into audit, with Roger and Owen smiling and waving, followed by every team member in the plant who had previously lined the aisles. When Roger stepped out of that car, raised both of his fists jubilantly into the air and shouted, "We did it!" the house came down. All were on their feet cheering and clapping, and as I looked around, with tears streaming down my face unashamedly, there wasn't a dry eye in the house. Everyone was crying, hugging, laughing, crying again, hugging someone else; and the sound was absolutely deafening. As Roger and Owen ascended the stage, where they were greeted by Skip, Mike, Hoalcraft, and the assistant regional director of UAW Region 8, Bobby Lee Thompson, plus Bob Stempel, and Lloyd Reuss. The standing ovation continued and grew louder. Then Roger turned to all the team members and the press in front of him, pumped his fist repeatedly in the air, blew everyone a great big kiss, and mouthed an unheard "thank you." The noise grew louder yet.

I looked around at the varied venues of the fourth estate and beamed with pride at the absolute awe that was spread across their countenances. They had never been exposed to us Saturnians, where this kind of outpouring of emotion was common, but I think what threw them the most was Roger. In the almost decade he had been chairman of the board, never had he been seen to display this much emotion, for that matter any emotion. They were absolutely amazed at this storiedly stoic man rushing around the stage acting like a poor child who one day awoke in the middle of Macy's toy department with a blank check. Several women team members from the assembly plant rushed up and gave him a big hug and kiss, and his renowned red complexion turned crimson, but you could tell he just loved it. In the aftermath, when all the speeches were done, which took quite a while, for each word met with a thunderous applause, the press wandered around talking to team members. Some asked the ignorant question, "Do you think Roger was just playing up to the news media, the way he acted, or do you think it was sincere?" That question wasn't asked but a few times because the people we hired were not shy at all and visibly proud of what they had accomplished. No interviewer who had any chance at survival asked that question more than once. Festivities over, everyone went back to work smiling and laughing but totally focused on building world-class cars.

In two days, on August 1, 1990, Roger retired and turned the GM helm over to Bob Stempel, as the new chairman, and Lloyd Reuss, as the president. Steve Yokich had his stepping stone to the UAW presidency as director of the GM Department; and we in Spring Hill had that magical moment to remember forever. It was the start of one of the greatest success stories in American history. Don Ephlin went on to lecture at MIT in Cambridge, Massachusetts. He would work with many companies and unions, and he was appointed to numerous government task forces and committees. Our future looked limitless. Later that evening Mike and we VPs were reflecting on the day's events, but we couldn't help but relay to each other our feeling of foreboding that Don and Roger's departure would have a serious impact on us in the next five years. Buoyed by the day's activities, we left each other with hope that our finely tuned instincts were gone awry and committed to determination and perseverance with the mission, philosophy, and values as our guide. Tomorrow would be the first day of the rest of our lives, and we could ill afford to waste time on yesterday. We still had so very much to prove to a deservedly skeptical public that this was not another great GM scam, rather a very noble endeavor with the customer firmly in front of our eyes as people we sincerely cared about.

We started shipping cars that afternoon, July 30, 1990, but we didn't ship the one Roger and Owen drove off the end of the line at Inspiration Point. That crimson four-door went up to Northfield and on display, where it remains to this very day. Inspiration Point was so named by the team members in Vehicle Systems when it was finally designated, during the construction phase, where the cars would exit the plant and go out into the shipping yard. They erected a sign that had written on it, "Inspiration Point – where the world's finest quality cars are shipped." When the assembly building was completed the sign was taken down from its original position, which was outside the wall of the plant, and brought inside, placed right next to the shipping door, and is looked at every time one of our cars comes down the marshaling line.

Production remained relatively slow for the rest of the year, due to the poor fit of some of our supplied parts. Also, each car was water-checked for leaks around the windows and door seals. From August until holiday shutdown, my partner Bob Boruff and I had many, many down and dirty conflicts over quality. I must give him credit – he always ended up doing the right thing, but not without a fight. As I mentioned earlier, the union side of the partnership was firmly committed to quality not quantity. Our non-rep partners were committed to quality, too, but they would always lean toward "Let's build them and put them in the back lot until we get a fix" for whatever the issue of the day was. I could not agree with that because it was how so many bad cars got out to the customer. The bargaining unit team members were counting on me and the leaders I had picked to not let this happen, just as I was counting on them to not put uncertified parts in the car. If an engineer or supplier or module advisor told them to, they knew they could call me. I would be there in a flash and put a stop to that. This was a habit, a bad one at that, and we were not going to develop the habit here.

So, about 10 times between August and December, Bob, Alan Perriton, or Dan Juliette and I went at it about building cars when quality was in question. Each time I had to threaten that I would go out and tell all the rep team members to just sit down. Tempers flared and emotions drove words that weren't meant, but in the end they knew I was right, and we did not build cars. I never had to actually tell the teams to sit down because my partners knew that I would, if that is what it came down to. I never had to go head to head with any of my three partners out on the line because we all knew that would portray a we-they mentality, so all our arguing was done behind closed doors, and then we jointly made the announcement so that any one of my partners would not look like the bad guys and I the good guy but that it was a partnership decision made for the right reasons. This is the win-win that I speak of all the time. If I look like the hero and one of my part-ners looks like the goat, we all lose. It was a tough pill for them to swal-low, having an entire plant at work for 10 hours and no product being built, but gradually they started to understand that by not sending them home, which was always done in the old world, they were building the commitment that was so desperately needed. It was not business as usual.

We truly were a different kind of company building a different kind of car. The failure to get enough design engineers into Design for Manufacturability and Design for Assembly classes back in 1986 and 1987 was really starting to show up at that point. The engineers, of course, blamed it on the redesign, which took up so much of their time that they hadn't had time to go to class. Skip knew that was just a smoke screen, being an engineer himself, so we made sure that these classes were taken before the end of the year, because much work was already under way on the 1992s. Making a mistake is not a crime as long as you don't keep repeating it.

October 3, 4, and 5 were our next festive days. Every Saturn retail partner in North America was invited to Spring Hill for the Saturn Retailer Announcement Activity. Our world-class cars had been slowly but surely filling up their lots across America, and before the first cus-tomer was given the chance to become a proud Saturn owner, we want-ed one last session to finalize our plans, our goals, and our strategies – not only for today, but for the future. To emcee these activities we brought in the former anchor of *CBS This Morning*, Kathleen Sullivan, again to emphasize we were a different kind of company. Many men in the broadcast journalism field wanted this assignment but her unique-ness and upbeat style were exactly what we were looking for. The whole theme was to get everyone focused in the same direction. The message was clear and simple, "After nearly seven years of development, con-struction, and total dedication by people all across the country, it is time to revolutionize the American automobile industry. It's time to show that we can compete with the best that the foreign manufacturers can offer." We wanted to show the retailers just how important they were to our collective success and have them, before and after the business meetings, just wander around the three plants and talk to the team members, to see just how our car was being built differently than any other car in the world. We wanted them to feel the excitement in the plants and take that excitement back to their retail stores.

The bottom line was really clear. It didn't matter how well we built them, if the cars turned the customer off during the buying experience, all was for naught. What a great three days those were! Bonding took place between retailers and teams that have lasted to this day. Everything was falling into place. The rollout strategy was set for October 25, with 30 stores opening on the West Coast, Texas, Florida and Tennessee, followed by the central United States in early November, with 25 store openings, and last, the eastern United States in early 1991, with 45 additional stores. The third quarter of 1990 also started our full blown advertising campaign. Just prior to the launch, we started our ad campaign by teasing the public with exclusive use of advertising focused on how we were a different kind of company and a different kind of car. Primarily we just talked about the people of Saturn and how they were working together to bring a fresh new approach to building and selling a car.

The week of October 10-15, our national TV campaign began. We targeted four programs we felt would get a significant share of the people we had targeted as customers: Monday night football, *Roseanne*, *L.A. Law*, and Arsenio Hall. We had also put a very meaningful videotape together to capture the essence of the first five years of development. Internally we used it extensively from mid-1989 to just before the launch to help the huge numbers of people who came onboard during that large ramp-up period better understand what it was like during the first four years and make them feel a part of the whole experience. We felt we might use it with the public eventually, but with Roger and Owen's drive off the assembly line of our first car, the press had been shown the 22-minute tape called "Spring in Spring Hill" and had fallen in love with it. The telephones of Bruce McDonald and Dora Mack, our partnership leaders in corporate communications and public relations, stayed lit up for months with the idea of showing it on TV in our national ad campaign. We decided to try it but were cautiously reserved in the scope of exposure on national TV. We agreed with CBS to air it in Detroit on November 12; if it met with as favorable a response as expected, we would expand its exposure.

The print media campaign was rolled out in 30 magazines initially, some of which were *Time, Newsweek, Sports Illustrated, Black Enterprise,* and *Rolling Stone.* Different dates were set for various market areas, due to the geographic location and our infant, but rapidly maturing, transportation system. The Detroit and Nashville areas started with *Newsweek* on October 12, *USA Today* on October 15, *U.S. News & World Report* on October 19, and *Time* on December 3. The West Coast and Southeast markets targeted *Time* on November 5 and *Newsweek* on November 12. The East Coast and Middle America were targeted for the last day of December and the first of January 1991. The major newspapers in each area received the same coverage as the magazines, as well as local television, radio, and billboard ads. This was such a gratifying feeling, after seven long years of development, many of which we thought we would never make it through, to see our name and logo appear on the most powerful medium in America, TV, right there with some of the best marketers in their respective fields.

We could open the most popular magazines in America, which were filled with ads for Asian imports, telling every reader how much better they were than the domestic cars, and feel pride and confidence in knowing that, when we were successful, these wonderfully creative and contemporary ads we developed would strike fear in our arrogant competitors. I saved every ad, both print and video. When I or one of my fellow team members would succumb to the human frailty of frustration, I would bring one or more out, and we would watch or read them together and everything would be back in focus. If it were easy, there would be a thousand Saturns, but there weren't. There was just one – and every team member knew that he or she mattered. Without them we would not be successful.

The five months until Christmas shutdown went by swiftly, with the 20-hour workdays being spent on quality, production bottlenecks, teamwork, and honing the partnerships into effective and efficient tools for success. As exasperating as the quality, production, and teamwork opportunities were, none of them could hold a candle to those of the partnership. Even though we were created as a partnership, had spent five years developing as a partnership, the start of salable vehicles seemed to trigger in far too many non-reps the insane notion that it was time for them to take over. "The development work is over, so you guys can stand aside and let us get on with managing." The conflict generated from this throwback thinking was very dangerous and could have been avoided easily – if Briggs and company had embraced empowerment as the key to greatness, rather than hold on to their insecure fear of losing control, which they never had in the first place. Too much time and energy were expended that could have been better spent elsewhere, but as we came to know, this was not an endemic trait to us, just a natural expression of the process of letting go and embracing that which you fear.

By the end of the first quarter, it had become very evident that the tide of discontent surrounding my partner in people systems, Jim Lewandowski, had reached a state where the entire SAC had acquiesced to the wishes of manufacturing. Jim and I talked sincerely every day about how we might stem this flow of discontent and turn it around, but it increasingly looked like he would be replaced. We brought in a consultant that our Local 1853 leadership had used, Dr. Leonard Hirsch, who was a renowned specialist in power, politics, and mounting effective campaigns to change one's image. We spent three days off the site, with all the people systems key result area leaders, building a plan to bolster Jim's effectiveness in the eyes of his peers on the SAC. This was the second time we had utilized Dr. Hirsch, the first being when we decided to establish the people system reviews in fall 1989, and had been very satisfied with his performance in helping us develop the strategy that led to manufacturing accepting its responsibility for hiring and developing its team members.

The partnership between Jim and me had not come under attack for several reasons. First, we had accomplished the goals outlined by the SAC as our responsibility; and second, everyone on the SAC knew I was held in very high esteem by Skip, Hoalcraft, and Mike and had unquestionably the support of our membership. Mounting an attack on me would have been very detrimental to their end in mind. They also knew that we were planning on rotating the VPs and that the final push would be much easier when a new partner for Jim came in. I think all of us in leadership positions knew that Skip had made his decision already, even though Jim kept telling Mike and me that his meetings with Skip had been going well. Mike relayed his feelings to me, and I also knew from my meetings with Skip that timing was the only thing holding back his decision. Shortly after I moved to Vehicle Systems, the announcement was made. On September 1, Jim Lewandowski would be retiring from Saturn and GM and entering into a consulting firm with one of his mentors, Bill McKinnon, the former head of the personnel administration staff at GM.

My emotions ran deep with Jim's retirement, even though we disagreed often. He was a fine man and a good friend, who always did the right things, in the end. I very seldom spoke at testimonials for people who left Saturn, even though I was asked quite often. I felt that to leave was easy but to stay and try to make this new order of things become a viable reality was courageous. I willingly spoke at Jim's retirement dinner, and though I roasted him a little, my main focus was to tell a side of him that most people in Saturn were not privy to. He left as proudly as he came in and justifiably so, for he had accomplished much in five years. I could feel his pain that evening, even through all the smiles and laughter, for it was not his wish to retire. It was someone else's. I would truly miss him. His replacement was R. Timothy Epps, who was brought back from GM's Europe Division, where he had been the personnel director for all European operations. He and Skip were old friends, and although I was not going to have to work with him, I knew his arrival would mean Skip would be the real head of people systems. Make no mistake about it, Tim would shuffle the papers, but the real hand deciding which papers to shuffle and when would be in the office down the hall.

Another reason R. Timothy had been brought in was that we had begun preliminary discussions on executing the paragraph in the memo that called for ratification of the memo when a sufficient number of bargaining unit members were onboard. With our still aggressive ramp schedule for staffing, that number looked like it would be reached around shutdown in July 1991, and Skip and the guys in manufacturing had no intention of having Jim head up those discussions. The timing of this move would allow Epps sufficient time to understand how Saturn worked, who the players were and who were the most powerful, and to build a closer relationship with the GM personnel function. After initially being abandoned by the personnel function, we in the union became very self-sufficient; and when they had tried to make amends we rebuked them. So this would be one of Epps's primary goals.

December 1990 heralded two significant announcements, one of which made many people happy and the other offered a promise of hope. The first announcement was – are you ready? – our current and the only VP of manufacturing we ever had, Guy Briggs, was leaving Saturn. The launch was over and now it was time to move on to bigger and better things. He had been picked to take over the helm of the Truck and Bus Group back in GM. My partner Bob Boruff was picked to replace him and would assume that role in January 1991, when we returned from the holiday shutdown. This was not a surprise to the leadership team, for Briggs's departure had been rumored for some time. Nor was Bob's selection a surprise. We all knew he would assume that position when he was hired. Many were happy, and many were sad. Our rep team members were concerned that, with Lewandowski leaving in August and now Briggs such a short time later, maybe GM was losing its commitment to us. Being assured that this was standard operating procedure in GM, as well as doing what we said in our mission statement concerning transfer of knowledge and technology back to GM, and understanding that the local union felt good about Briggs's replacement, fear quickly dissipated. The Executive Board of Local 1853 had discussed this very issue when we knew it was a done deal and came to the conclusion that was embodied in the Phase II Report and alluded to in our Memo of Agreement – that institutionalizing the process was what was important, not who the leaders were.

The second announcement was the creation of the agreement renewal (or ART) team. The ART team was charged by the corporation and the International Union to work through all the issues in the organization that had not been resolved since the original memo was agreed to in July 1985. This team would bring back to the SAC and the membership of Local 1853 an updated memo to be voted on by all the rep team members in fall 1991. This offered a promise of hope to Mike and us VPs, because many articles in the memo needed to brought in line with the passage of time. One of the most important of these was rep team members' base pay. It had been the same since 1985 and, as the driver of such things as pension and sickness and accident benefits, was long overdue for improvement. On the downside, we knew we would be spending many, many more hours a day at the plant site. No one on the ART team was replaced in his or her normal duties, rep or non-rep, so it wasn't hard to figure out that most of the work would be done after our "normal" 12-hour workday and on weekends. Necessary it was though, and all who were members of this team agreed to work whatever hours were necessary to complete this task.

The team consisted of Mike, Joe, Kenny, Henry, Morris Hayes from Local 1810 in Michigan, and me on the rep side. Epps, Dennis Finn, Greg Hacias, Dennis Richmond and Dan Koenn from people systems, Stan Fox from finance, the three plant leaders – Leon Wieland from Powertrain, Bob Boruff (until his replacement was named) from Vehicle Systems, and Jerry Gibbs from the Body Systems Plant – made up the non-rep side. We also had two process facilitators to work with us, Dick Oddo (a rep) and Barb Grant (a non-rep). These would be very trying times when we returned from holiday shutdown for all of us, but more so for me because my partner Boruff and I would have to agree on a suitable replacement for him and run Vehicle Systems. Boruff would have to make the transition to Briggs's job; and I had 2,600 rep team members in two plants each day who wanted to see me. Even if they didn't need me, they wanted me out on the floor. Having the two crew coordinators that I did, I felt comfortable that what needed to be done could be and willingly went forward on this new quest.

We fondly said good-bye to the launch year and welcomed 1991 joyfully, resplendent with its promise of success. As we Saturnians fanned out to the 50 states of our origin, the product feedback we received over the holidays was guarded but optimistically enthusiastic. Our advertising was heralded as innovative and refreshing. Those who visited our retail partners, just to see how buying a Saturn was different, couldn't believe that they could walk into the showroom and not feel like prey ready to be attacked. More important, someone would just say "Hi," tell them his or her name, and let them know if they had any questions, just ask. If they just looked around and walked out the door, no one chased them to their car begging them to wait and talk to the sales manager. If this was not just a grand opening ploy, boy, were they going to like this. Those who had purchased one of our new offerings were very vocal about how fine an automobile it was, but our exposure, quite naturally, was very limited, for we had product in the retailers hands for only three months. We were very excited by the early reports, and barring a catastrophe, many heads would turn before the next Christmas holiday.

January was a very exasperating month for a multitude of reasons. Many of our supplier partners were having difficulty supplying enough quality parts. Daily, it seemed, I would be called to one of the assembly lines where suspect parts had been identified and supplier partners, who had been living in general assembly (GA) since start of salable vehicles, were trying to tell module advisors, supplier quality engineers, and team members in the work unit that the parts were good. These were very emotional times for the represented technicians, both trades and operators. These moments of truth would demonstrate to them if we were capable of walking the talk. If any leader allowed defective parts to be installed on a car, the five years of work would be lost in a moment. Too often quality issues were identified by the car final team, and that was not acceptable. We were not geared to fix every problem in the car final area.

By design, we were only a third the size of any final repair area in North America, and it wasn't hard to figure out that if bad parts were making it to final repair, then it was just a matter of time before they would make it to the retail showroom. I handled most of these by myself; and only if the non-rep crew coordinator who was on my shift at that time disagreed with me would we call Boruff in from the SAC. Bob and I would disagree on many of these situations, but we would always end up doing the right thing, rejecting a suspect car. This had a very positive impact on the culture that was still emerging in GA, for it had been the last to ramp up and was now going through the growing pains previously experienced by Powertrain and Body Systems, having ramped much sooner. We made it through that first month of the new year with several scares that could have resulted in serious problems in the field, if we had not stuck by our principles of only good cars being sent to the next internal customer. It was a team member's obligation to stop the line if quality was in question, and we constantly reiterated that quality takes priority over quantity.

We were becoming known as true visionaries and practitioners of the mission, philosophy, and values. Our credibility as leaders was rising daily and so was the morale in both of the plants that constituted Vehicle Systems, General Assembly and Vehicle Interior Systems (VIS). Skip, Mike, Bob, and I had agreed on Bob's replacement, the production manager at Lordstown Assembly in Ohio, Bob Sackerman. Bob Boruff had worked with him in Mexico and the report from the Lordstown local union affirmed that he was definitely a team player who would consistently do the right thing. Although he "officially" started on January 1, his transition would take most of the month, and he wouldn't be fully effective for a couple more months, but just the realization that he was on the way was very refreshing.

February poked its head over the horizon and with it came a deadly chill, much harsher than any winter day in Michigan – the frigid word, *recall*. When I first learned from the sales, service, and marketing (SSM) staff that a potential recall was developing, I immediately asked if it was safety related or the much more palatable customer satisfaction arena. Not that the latter was acceptable, but customer satisfaction would be a decision we made internal to Saturn. One that was safety related would involve the National Highway Transportation and Safety Administration. Although we could voluntarily preempt their order of a recall, just having their name associated with a problem with our car could spell disaster in terms of our potential customers. News of this potential eruption on the carefully carved slopes of our emerging mountain was kept to a select few people until it was determined if a recall would be necessary. The problem was identified as being in the front-seat back recliner mechanism; and Sackermen and I heaved a heavy sigh of relief. Not that it was OK to have the problem in the first place, but it wasn't a breakdown in the stringent quality measures we had instituted nor would the heavy weight of this kind of issue have to be borne on the backs of the team members in Vehicle Systems, who were working their hearts out building a car that was, by virtue of the redesign, extremely difficult to build.

This news did, however, signal a breakdown in one of our primary supplier's quality systems. Intense investigation had been going on since we first got word of what the real issue was, to find out both what happened and how many cars were involved. Our supplier partner was very cooperative but understandably defensive. We had worked very well together for several years, and the supplier knew how potentially damaging this could be to us. No one wanted to be the cause of a recall, especially so soon in our build cycle. In the end it came down to the fact that the supplier had changed the specifications on the teeth of the reclining mechanism without consulting Saturn first. The supplier's testing had somehow told them that, by rounding the teeth that locked the seat into position, they could save money and not adversely impact performance. This was a very expensive lesson to learn, for 1,210 cars were afflicted with this malady and every one would have the seat replaced. With the accompanying costs for labor, potential buybacks for those that fell into our 30-day/1,500-mile money back guarantee, loaner cars for those who would not drive them until the repair was made, and the like, this recall was shaping up to cost about $10 million. True to our value of customer enthusiasm, we did not wait until we hashed out the final cost or who was going to pick up the bill before we did the necessary repairs.

We completed the repairs within 90 days, which was unheard of in the auto industry, and we also added a new twist. Every auto manufacturer in the world sent notice to those whose cars were involved in a recall, but we went the extra mile and sent registered letters to every one of our customers and told them not to worry. Every defective mechanism was identified and theirs were not defective, but if they too would like to have their cars checked, they were invited to bring them in. They were assured that nothing was wrong with their world-class quality cars. Again, the synergy resulting from our partnerships was awesome. The SSM staff in concert with their UAW partners and our retail partners had turned what could have been the kiss of death into a tremendous success.

Once we made the announcement, the fourth estate attacked our retail partners and sought out every affected customer, like sharks who had picked up the scent of blood. They smelled a potential controversy, and controversy sells newspapers. They would seek out all disgruntled owners and splash their indignation across the front pages of America. Boy, were they in for a big surprise! Of those they interviewed, 99.44% raved about how they were treated, how friendly, caring, and considerate everyone at their retailers was, but especially the sales consultants from whom they purchased their cars. Usually salespeople get amnesia after the sale is consummated, but these were right in the forefront working hand in hand with the service technicians to make this as pleasant an experience as possible. The journalists found their few sour grapes and splashed their words of venom across the pages for a couple of days, but they too came to see that nothing about our organization was going to resemble the past. Within a week the fourth estate was firmly supporting the excellently professional thing that had been done. We had turned the most feared happening in a marketing environment into an absolute marketing success. Even the naysayers in GM and the International Union begrudgingly paid homage to this marvelous stroke of work.

The ART team had been working late nights, Fridays, and Saturdays for five months now, and we rep members of the team were not at all pleased with the progress that had been made. What was supposed to have been very nontraditional agreement seeking had turned into just the opposite. Epps had gotten the head of GM's industrial relations staff, Dick O'Brien, involved, and whether intentional or not, delaying tactics had become the order of the day. It did not appear that we would have what we needed to take to the membership by shutdown as we had planned. It appeared that Mr. O'Brien was concerned that our agreement in Spring Hill would spill over into GM when negotiations began with the International Union for the 1993 national agreement, and he was seriously endangering what we were trying to do. We still had three months to go until shutdown, but we were getting very anxious as to whether progress would improve. If not, then we would have to face considering a more "traditional" means to get off dead center. By April we had 4,800 team members in Spring Hill and another 980 in Michigan. This offered manufacturing all the engineering support it needed for current model year build and, more important, for the 1992 model build that was just around the corner, during the last two weeks of July.

In the manufacturing area, we had both crews working the same shift, learning the build together, so that when we went to a day shift and night shift, the cars would be built the same. On April 29, we split the two shifts, with each crew working four 10-hour days, Monday through Thursday, and then each week they would rotate, days to nights and vice versa. Our logic in working only four days a week was severely questioned by GM, the press, and industry analysts because we were nowhere near our production plan. We simply told them the truth. Quality would come first, then quantity. No car would be shipped until it was ready. Throwing overtime at our supplier partners who were working feverishly, in most cases, to get us parts that met our high quality standards would not accomplish anything. Many of these partners had been seriously affected by the redesign, so throwing five or six days of production at them would do nothing but guarantee that our standards would not be met.

Methodically, meticulously, and with dogged perseverance, we worked together for our mutual success. We all knew that all the overtime we could endure would come eventually, especially when our

156

product began selling like we knew it would. We had made our team members a solemn oath, that we would not succumb to the external pressures and let quality take a back seat. The real success of Saturn would come only if we kept that oath. To do otherwise would make us no different than the places we left to come here. If we lost the trust of our team members, it would be nearly impossible to regain it, and our dream of a hundred-year car company would vanish as swiftly as the breaking of our oath. The corporation (GM) never understood this and, quite frankly, don't to this very day. Maybe, someday.

Before I go on to our next moment of excitement and anxiety, I would be remiss if I did not relate the tremendous workings of the two crew coordinators, who willingly joined me in the quest to make the partnership a reality in Vehicle Systems. They were Tony Alferio and Jerry Childers. Tony was the former shop chairman of a local union in Sioux City, Iowa, whom Chuck Stridde and I had hired to work on our risk-and-reward program in people systems. He was as good with numbers as any finance manager I have ever met and did an excellent job for us. When I called him after I had taken over Vehicle Systems and asked if he would consider joining me, I did so with a little remorse because of the fine job he was doing in people systems, but more so because I knew what a meat grinder it was going to be in getting Vehicle Systems to where it needed to be now that we had started production. I told him I wouldn't blame him if he declined, but he knew how much confidence I had in him, and I wasn't surprised when he said yes.

Jerry was a former committee member from Cadillac who had gone through the battles of closing two plants and merging the work forces at the new megaplant, Poletown in Hamtramck. He had also worked in the Q.W.L. program at Cadillac and was a skilled facilitator in team building. Joe Rypkowski, our first VP, had been on the committee with him and had already placed him in a coordinator's job before I arrived. The biggest issue we faced in Vehicle Systems was that we had over half the population of manufacturing working here. Powertrain and Body Systems were more equipment focused, but Vehicle Systems was almost exclusively labor intensive. Half of the self-managed teams were looking to us for direction, and it would have been impossible for me to institutionalize the partnership with just myself, module advisors, and charter team members, all of whom were still learning their roles. The dedication and brilliance Tony and Jerry exhibited toward the partnership and toward me will always be remembered as one of the high points of my career at Saturn. Their job was frantic, trying to help teams solve production bottlenecks, meet the hiring ramp, focus on quality, be a priest and psychologist in team member confrontations, make sure that communication was working both upward and downward, and in their spare time, help their partners understand what a partner really was. What was accomplished in the two years I spent in Vehicle Systems could never have been accomplished without them and the excellent job they did helping their partners Greg Gloss and Earl Ice, respectively, understand the tremendous power that was embodied in letting people be involved in decisions that affect them.

All three plants were making progress in both quality and quantity. Our retail partners were doing their part to develop enthusiastic customers. The reports from the field showed the cars produced in the first six months of this year were much better than those made in the six months following launch. In another two months, the increasingly important J. D. Power report on customer satisfaction and sales satisfaction would reach the press, and generally speaking, our development was going well. May 1, however, that dreaded *frigid* word, made its chilling reentry into our midst – *recall again*! All of the Saturn leaders, both rep and non-rep, were desperately fighting to avoid lapsing into a coma. How in the world could this have happened and so soon after the reclining mechanism just three short months ago? Again, the mind once stretched by a new idea never regains its original dimensions held true. There was no wholesale panic and especially no witch hunt for the guilty party, although certain members of the manufacturing leadership initially espoused that concept. This, too, had to be handled with cool heads and imaginative minds, free of the swirling clouds of emotion.

The first thing we ascertained was how many were involved, then how we were going to make it right. Was it safety or satisfaction related? How were we going to announce it? And, last, what was the cause and corrective action to be taken to ensure it never happened again? The overnight warranty data we received daily from the field, as well as the quality-control measures we had established to capture the status of all supplied parts, both internally and externally, enabled us to identify every car that was affected. They were all built between March 25 and April 4 and totaled a whopping 1,836. The field data also told us that this was not going to be a simple replacement of parts because it was a progressive problem. It was not safety related, whereby someone could be injured or killed, thank God, but it would cause a car to stop running altogether; that definitely made it a serious customer satisfaction issue. How we were going to announce it did not have a simple solution and had to wait for the decision on making it right.

We did find the cause relatively easily. Our supplier partner, Texaco, who supplied us with the coolant for our engine, had misformulated a batch we had received on March 25. We do not conduct incoming inspections. It is our partners' responsibility to ensure that what they send us is good. Their quality control measures had broken down, and the coolant they had batched and pumped into our feeder tanks on March 25 did not cool, it ate. It ate the hoses from the radiator to the water pump, the water pump, the hoses from the water pump to the engine, and then it ate the engine. Although our supplier was in serious denial initially, Texaco quickly joined in to resolve this very serious problem that we must collectively turn into an opportunity. We had to make this an opportunity for this fledgling car manufacturer to show its creativity and dedication to having more than satisfied customers. How the bill for this as yet unknown solution would be paid was turned over to both our attorneys to resolve.

We had to focus on our two remaining opportunities: What was the fix and how were we going to announce our *second* recall only 10 months into production? Our field service technicians and our product engineers, in concert with Texaco's chemists, relayed the news that every engine and transmission must be replaced. What glad tidings to hear when we were barely able to produce enough powertrains to keep up with production and supply our service operations the minimum requirements for replacement parts. This was getting more complicated by the hour. Where there is a will, there is a way; and that so misunderstood entity called synergy again proved that our potential lie in our imagination. Rep and non-rep Saturn leaders in partnership with our retailers came up with the wonderfully brilliant idea to buy back all 1,836 cars. Much diplomacy had to be employed at the GM Building to reach this end, but there really was no other viable solution that would suffice if we really cared about our customers.

So for the first time in the history of the automobile industry, we sent a letter to approximately 25,000 owners by registered mail, just as we had done in February, informing them that their cars were among the 1,836 with defects or categorically were not. Those whose cars were being eaten from within were all offered a brand new car, identical to the one they now owned, or the full purchase price would be returned to them – it was their choice. The only option that was unavailable to them was to keep their car. It would only be a matter of time before their engine would be scarred beyond repair, and we could not take the chance that they would change their mind about keeping it and sell it to someone else. Our public relations and corporate communications team worked around the clock, once the decision was made, to contact all the national TV broadcasting entities. Every newspaper in our market areas and all the popular magazines that carried our advertising heralded the news as courageous, which it was. Saturn is truly a "Different Kind of Company, a Different Kind of Car." The bashers and doomsayers were quickly spreading their gospel of deception and skepticism, as we knew they would, but they didn't matter to us. The people who chose to listen to their all-too-familiar rhetoric of negativism would do so, no matter what we had done.

What we really cared about was the people who had purchased our fine car, showing them how we cared for them and anxiously waiting their judgment. Once again our honesty, predictability, and consistency, not to mention our creativity, turned the tide from one of gloom to one of another marketing milestone. A very few asked for their money back, but 98% said they had never been treated like this and willingly accepted our offer of a brand new car. We then did one more thing that set the auto industry abuzz. We told the world, and then crushed all but 90 of the 1,836 cars. These 90 had not been damaged, as far as we could ascertain, beyond the water pump, but not being absolutely sure, we donated them to vocational schools and universities to be used for alternative fuel research and tear-down and build-up vehicles for aspiring young mechanics. There was only one condition to receive a car and that was signing an agreement *never* to sell the vehicle or face sure litigation. The remaining cars were stripped of all recyclable material. All fluids were environmentally captured and disposed of properly. Then we rented a car crusher and, one by one, supervised the cars' destruction. Our fear of having a negative response in our retail partners' showrooms proved to be 180 degrees from what happened.

The American customer, long searching for a company with integrity, flooded our showrooms eager to buy from a company that cared about its owners that much. The credible press, also pleased with the way they were informed, quickly rallied in support of this obvious display of commitment to those who had taken a gamble on this upstart auto company and had not had their trust thrown away. In due time, the lawyers hashed the cost sharing, and Texaco willingly paid the lion's share of the awesome $23 million bill. They, too, were overwhelmed with our integrity in not waging a media war attacking their character as a lousy supplier partner or taking steps to have them replaced. We worked hand in hand to make sure this could never happen again and cemented our relationship as we wanted them to be a hundred-year supplier to our hundred-year car company.

Change agents, this probably won't be the last time I bring this up but here it goes anyway. Developing a corporate culture that will stand the tests of adversity, external influence, and slow deviation from its established mission, philosophy, and values can be achieved only if it is founded on principles. All the decisions of the organization, be they small or large or steeped in controversy, must adhere to its principles. If you really care about the people who pay for the product or service you supply, the principles can never be violated. They, first, cannot be violated with the team members in your organization, for they are the ones who supply the ultimate product or service. Violating your principles to them will result in your external customer being violated. Remember, principles are like lighthouses. You cannot break them, you can only break yourself upon them. Internal and external customers don't listen to what you say, if what you do is clearly opposite of the wonderful words that emanate from the technique polished tongues of self-centered individuals solely out for their own agenda. Customers have never been fooled for very long. Just ask all the companies that went out of business or were relegated to a minimal share of their markets. When the perception of integrity is lost, sadly, it will be too late. You must constantly measure how you adhere to the principles you have established if you want to stay in the game. Live by them or change them and have the courage to tell all that this is what you really are. If they find out on their own, you will be among the unforgiven.

The second point to be made is how partnerships are so powerful in helping an organization remain principle centered. From 1984 on, we in the union have helped our non-rep partners better understand the importance and power in satisfying the customer. Slowly, but surely, they were beginning to understand and received a much needed boost of comprehension from our retail partners, all of whom were very successful in this arena prior to becoming one of our partners. That is why they were chosen. Anytime a partner wants to take the easy way, it is not that the partner doesn't care. It is really just the result of lapsing into old comfortable habits when faced with serious controversy. Utilizing the equal decision making power of each partner in the consensus process to promote managed conflict and adhering to the organization's principles mean the organization will not suffer the fate it once suffered when principles did not drive decisions, that fate being total vulnerability in the reality of power corrupts and absolute power corrupts absolutely.

Buoyed by our owners' loyalty and the great satisfaction of doing the right thing, the plants were ever increasingly improving. July broke over the trees of our beautifully landscaped site, and J. D. Power made its surveys of the car purchasing public. We were far from being satisfied at where we were ranked in problems per 100 vehicles, 16th out of 34, but we also knew that these figures contained a large number of the early build cars. While they were totally salable, they were less than we would have liked in fit and finish. The mechanical was fine. Our powertrains received very good marks. Most of the complaints were on door seam gaps and window molding trim. These were corrected through a joint effort with our suppliers. What was gratifying was how our retail partners were rated, fourth in customer satisfaction in relation to the buying experience. Very impressive for the market niche we were in, which was so laden with imports that had spent years building a customer satisfaction rating. We were not measured on many of the factors yet but would be the next year. All in all we were cheered and became even more determined that, when the report was published next year, we would significantly rise in all of the rankings.

One thing that was not encouraging was the progress of the ART team. Mike, Morris, and we VPs were now convinced that Epps fully intended to listen to Mr. O'Brien in Detroit and not put any credence in what we were telling him our membership would accept. Mike had all too many meetings with Skip requesting that he set Epps straight. He would then meet with Epps and assure Mike that everything would work out, but it never did. Here it was, nearly shutdown, and we were still far apart on base pay, pension, and the risk-and-reward formulas we planned to implement in 1992. I think Mr. O'Brien had them lulled into the belief that, given how we were doing as an organization and how much the partnership was being heralded in the press as being one of the best things about Saturn, the members of Locals 1853 and 1810 would accept whatever they were offered. This was a tragic mistake. They underestimated our commitment to what we told our membership we would work for. After doing our first member-to-member survey, we understood where their energy lay. Mr. O'Brien and Mr. Epps were banking their careers on the false notion that these two locals would not ask their members to authorize "serious action" to be taken to resolve this impasse. This false premise would leave long and lasting scars on our infant organization. I don't think I will ever forget the effect it had, and our membership won't either. We had scheduled ART meetings for the entire two week shutdown, but the six of us (reps) seriously leaned toward canceling them and telling our non-rep team members to use the time to think about what we told them would happen if we didn't make significant progress in the next two weeks. We would call a general membership meeting in each local union and request a serious action vote. Emotions were rising and it all could have been so easily avoided. It really didn't appear that they took this last warning seriously. We were almost backed into a corner with the only viable option left to come out swinging.

The last two weeks of July were scheduled for our first summer shutdown. The time would be used to purge our systems of all the 1991 model year parts and fill the system with 1992 parts, which had some significant improvements made to them and the vehicle component systems. This was the first test of our ability to change over and have all the systems up and ready in two short weeks and build to a very aggressive production schedule. The final tally of our first year of production was in, with 50,069 cars produced and 37,398 cars sold. These numbers were not what we had planned, but neither were the two recalls. As a whole, we looked back to learn what had gone right and what had gone wrong. Then it was time to get on with building the 1992s while steadily improving on our first year of production. Some of the improvements of our second year car included more flexible torque-axis engine mounts than those used during our first year. This would allow the natural vibration of a four-cylinder engine to be diffused more easily, resulting in less cumulative noise heard in the passenger compartment. Our fuel economy was raised 1 mile per gallon to 28 mpg city and 38 mpg highway. We also added many new colors and more expressive trim and styling options.

Official production commenced on August 8, and the new year of production began with great morale, spirit, and dedication to make this year enormously more successful than our first. I remember the first day back from the two-week shutdown. Bob and I assembled everyone in Vehicle Systems in our final audit area, 1,400 team members, and talked to them about what we had done from July 1990 to July 1991. We discussed how we had proven all the doomsayers wrong. We emphasized the awards we had received for our revolutionary thermoplastic exterior panels. We reminded them of our outstanding achievements in community relations and internal communications efforts. In defects per 100 vehicles, we had finished 16 out of 34 in our industry our first year of production. That meant that 18 established firms were below us. We made spectacular successes out of two recalls that could have been disasters. All that was now history. No matter what we would like to have done differently, it didn't matter because yesterday's events were frozen in time, never to be changed. Today is where we had to focus all our collective energy because we had discovered only the tip of our potential and our unbounded potential resides in our imaginations. We had to dare to believe that which we believed: we could be. (My oldest son Sean had moved down with me over the summer shutdown. Having turned 14, he was able to decide which parent he wanted to live with, and I remembered I had given him this same thought a few days earlier. He must believe in himself or no one else would.)

August also brought us our first real look at our owners' profile from our first year of sales. We had set specific goals for the buyer segment we were in, as well as getting additional business for GM; that is, putting people in Saturns who had owned non-GM or foreign cars. This is a look at our first year:

CUSTOMER SATISFACTION:
69% were owners of non-GM or foreign cars
45% would have bought a foreign car if not purchasing a Saturn
97% would recommend buying a Saturn to others
95% would recommend their salesperson
Saturn was second to Lexus on a retailer satisfaction index

DEMOGRAPHICS:
38 years, median age of Saturn buyer
Three out of four were college educated
48% were women
52% were men
35% were single
65% were married
50% had annual incomes of over $50,000

Every target we had set had been exceeded by 2-10%. Our marketing team members were beside themselves, for they like the rest of us had been laughed at and scorned when sharing our goals. Didn't they know that foreign owners were totally loyal? People who earn over $50,000 a year don't buy $10,000 cars. Get real! After this impressive data was shared in Detroit, the auto industry finally knew we were real, even if it wouldn't publicly admit that. Another aspect of believing in ourselves was the confidence it instilled in us not to listen to the so-called industry experts and media automotive analysts, but to put our trust in our customers. We had to believe that they would, on seeing the value of their purchase and our genuine commitment to their enthusiasm, in both the buying experience and ownership, help us overcome the effects of the skeptics, naysayers, and negative industry "experts." Just listening to them speak, in person, through the letters they sent us, and in both the print and electronic media, after only 50,000 of our cars had been purchased, the feeling grew that the seedlings of a cultlike loyalty had sprouted. Wherever I went in my Saturn – Tennessee, Kentucky, Alabama, Georgia, Florida, Mississippi, Louisiana, Indiana, or Michigan – whenever I was spotted by other Saturn owners, they would honk their horn repeatedly, smile and wave. This was the start of something big. Star Trekkies, watch out.

The ART team met the first week of shutdown, but progress had almost transformed to regression. So the second week was scrapped, and those who chose to do so went on holiday, with the rest staying and working on the start-up of the 1992 model year production. Mike, Morris, Joe, Kenny, Henry, and I started pulling all of our crew coordinators together in weekly meetings to come up with a strategy to move us forward. We also used these sessions to keep track of the energy in the membership about the lack of progress in modifying the memo as they had been promised. Our main purpose was to utilize the synergy of this larger group to help us look at options that the six of us could not see by virtue of being so close to the situation. We also had ever-increasing emotion around the blatant attack on our credibility, questioning our level of knowledge about what our membership really wanted. We requested that the non-rep members of the ART team meet with random groups of rep team members from each of the plants to get firsthand the energy we received every time we set foot on the floor. When these were described as unnecessary by our non-rep team members of the ART, and they sang the same old tune, that what we wanted was not realistically possible, we knew for sure that Epps and O'Brien were convinced that our membership would not support any "serious action" measures. They believed that, if they waited long enough, they would get exactly what they wanted. Seeing this callous disregard for our members needs, not wants, and their total disdain for what they were doing to us politically, these two men left us no alternative.

We knew long ago that our membership would support even the ultimately drastic measure of authorizing a "strike vote." Almost embittered and with great frustration, we did what they didn't think we would do and called emergency general membership meetings at each local union to get the support to draw the saber that we had been rattling for four months now. The meetings were conducted in September, quickly, efficiently, and with the much forewarned result, unanimous support for us to do "whatever was necessary" to get GM to "bargain in good faith" as we, sadly, now called it. We videotaped these sessions, just as we had always done for our regular membership monthly meetings, and a copy was available for the non-reps to view, as always. They could see for themselves, firsthand, what rekindling of the memories from the adversarial wars had done. It was not pleasant viewing. The fourth estate, who had its usual "sources" within, had a field day. Headlines flashed bright across the country with statements like "We knew it wouldn't work" or "They have been enemies for too long, and it was just a matter of time." National and local TV and radio reporters were parked all around the site, trying to get a scoop on controversy, and generally the whole situation sucked. Skip suddenly took a new interest in what was going on and got with Mike; Stempel called O'Brien; Skip met with Epps; and they all called each other. The next meeting was opened with loud expressions of surprise at what we had done, which fell on deaf ears. Then came a much more urgent focus on wrapping up the three major issues and several minor ones whose impasse had led to this tragic and avoidable moment. We explained very calmly and coldly that they had one month to bring these "negotiations" to an acceptable end, or we would deliver to Epps a five-day letter of intent to strike. If we did not reach agreement, they must understand very clearly, we would walk everyone off this site and set up picket lines at both entrances. That is not what we wanted to do, but do it we would if the same kind of stalling and delaying is what they intended. Point very keenly understood, we set about doing what we could have done months earlier. For the first time since Epps joined Saturn, I felt we could make progress.

The plants were running better in both quality and quantity, but we were still losing too much production time to supplied parts, both internally and externally, in General Assembly. October 3 was here and our next milestone event was upon us. On this day, 70 Saturn-Saab-Isuzu retailers in Canada began selling our beautiful new 1992 model year cars. Canada was the only place in North America where we allowed more than just Saturns to be sold in the same store. Given its low population, in comparison with the United States, and its wide dispersal, stand-alone retail stores could not survive in that economic climate. Nonetheless, we had 70 new stores to ship cars to and were really struggling to meet the demand of the stores we had opened. We had started production on August 8 and in only two months we had already sold almost 11,000 of the 1992s.

We accepted this challenge in earnest, as we had all those before it, and kept our focus on having nothing but enthusiastic customers. We now had 70 new stores to generate them from. Our team members in the plants, both rep and non-rep, were able to separate the disturbance of the ART process from the value of customer enthusiasm, in part because we did not conduct our business in the press after the warning shot across the bow of Epps' boat. We became incommunicado and worked on our differences behind closed doors. Primarily our young Saturnians could fall back on the time, money, and effort we had expended in giving them a clear understanding of our mission, philosophy, and values. They knew the ART endeavor would pass, although it would not be easily forgotten, but they really understood that our customers would not forget poor quality or workmanship. Their spiritual bond, as customers in their own right, with the customers who would buy our product and place their trust in them to build it right was deeply ingrained in their minds and hearts. By nature of our excellent communication systems, we could supply our team members with real-time data on anything they needed or wanted, and they truly felt they were owners of this great enterprise.

The improvements they developed in the build of the car around quantity, quality, and cost were just short of miraculous. It rubbed off on everyone who came in contact with them. We labored almost 20 hours a day between the ART and the plants, but it never seemed like we were there that long. The time spent on the floor watching the op technicians, trades technicians, engineers, suppliers, and leaders work the magic of consensus and synergy made every day worthwhile.

We were dangerously approaching the deadline for agreement in the ART process and had resolved all of the issues but two. Of course, the most emotional ones were wages and pensions. Rapidly closing in on the witching hour of 12 midnight, after most of us had been in the plants since 5:30 A.M., it appeared that the thing we didn't want to happen most was going to happen. Epps left the trailer we had been working in for the last 10 months, with its walls lined with chart paper full of proposals and counterproposals, the long rectangular table covered with reams and reams of data as well as remnants of dinner and post dinner. He went next door to our other trailer, where we housed the phones we occasionally used when paged for an emergency in one of the plants. Upon returning, he announced almost gleefully that we were going to reach agreement, that he was not going to have us walk out, for we really weren't that far apart. We had seen him on the phone next door and didn't know for sure who he was talking to. He wasn't saying much other than "Yes" – quite often. We pieced it together the next day for certain, but that night we were pretty sure it was Skip. Skip had had his talk with Mr. O'Brien (who was not supportive of Saturn at all) and then he talked with Tim.

What could have been the death knoll for the partnership was averted. The rest of the month of October and the first two weeks of November were spent dotting *i*s and crossing *t*s. We had enough drafts printed of the amended memo and then called roll-out meetings with the membership to explain what they would vote on November 14. The proposed changes to the memo were ratified by almost three to one with 95% of our members voting, an unheard of number in local unions. We had agreed early on in the ART process for this team to stay together after the changes had been agreed to and meet once a month, at least, to resolve any conflicts that might arise. It had been 11 months since we began this process, and all of us were physically and emotionally drained. The corporation and all its partnerships still needed tending though, as well as all the issues we had not been able to satisfactorily resolve the last several months in the plants. As my eighth Christmas holiday with Saturn approached, it was the first time I didn't want to stay and work. I was ready for some serious R&R.

In our first model year, by the nature of our July launch, we were not heavily involved in the 126 auto shows that are done worldwide. In the 1992 model year though, we had a continuous presence. All through the last six months of 1991 we had teased about the wagon we were going to produce in model year 1993, but it wasn't ready until the Los Angeles Auto Show. On January 3, 1992, we unveiled it with much pomp and circumstance. The initial reviews were good, but California writers had become so negative over the years with the domestic automakers, we were encouraged by their guarded optimism. We continued to expose it at the remaining shows and then formulate our opinion. The response from the public was very warm, and that was what mattered the most. January also brought the sales figures for both the 1991 model year and the first five months of 1992. Our retail partners had sold every one of the 1991 models we had sent them and so far had sold 58,000 of the 1992s. We were on track to more than double our sales and had not even approached our production targets yet. The spirit in the plants and the entire organization was as high as I had ever seen it.

Every team member in Saturn optimized the synergy of our teams, and we made improvements steadily. We looked at the impact we had had in 1991 on the economy in Tennessee, and it was impressive. A total of $309 million in payroll was spent in the tricounty area, $201 million in Tennessee supplier purchases, and $469,000 in donations to the United Way of Middle Tennessee. For calendar year 1991 we had garnered 1.32% market share in the auto industry, and we accounted for 1.39% of GM's total market share. Team members at Saturn had been awarded 25 patents with 28 more patents pending. Our awards began mounting in 1991, and we received the *Popular Mechanics'*

1991 design and engineering award for our manufacturing process; *Motorweek*/PBS's 1991 Drivers' Choice Award for the best small car, as well as AAA's 1992 Auto Test Award for our sports coupe, as the best new car model. The last bright news we shared in January was that we were going to have a driver-side air bag in the spring of this year, as well as a full frontal air bag system within 18 months. February 6 we told the world that we would begin exporting cars to GM of Taiwan later in the year.

While our ultimate goal was to ship cars into Tokyo Bay, we knew we had to get firsthand experience in selling in the Asian market before we attempted to assault that bastion of unfair trade. Taiwan offered us a good learning opportunity to that end but stirred reservations in having to deal with GM Asia. The chance for the learning experience outweighed the other concern, and we knew that if we ever wanted to be successful in Japan we could not turn this opportunity down. Taiwan also offered the luxury of left-hand drive so we would be spared the development costs of right-hand drive until we were more solid financially. Barely a month later, the rankings for new car sales per facility in 1991 were released, and Saturn was number 1 with 776 units. This marked the first time in 15 years that a domestic name topped the list. Many tried to pass this off as insignificant because of having only about 125 retail stores open, but they could not attack the success of our market area approach. We countered the naysayers, that it indeed was a big deal, by reminding them that every other manufacturer in our industry had more cars, many more models than our two, and also had trucks and vans. March also brought us the Grass Roots Motor Sports – Editors Choice Award based on our sport coupe's performance in Autocross tests and value for the money. Our supply of cars in the field was stuck at about 45 days, with the optimum being about 60, so we knew we were losing sales. We could sell more if we could make more. The planning we had been doing for the last six months aligned with timing so we went through the process of getting total buy-in from the team members in the plants and added another day's production. We now ran two crews, two shifts, five days a week, and every week our teams rotated. This was hard on people because weekly rotation should only occur on four day work weeks or less. The circadian rhythms specialists we had used told us that, so we took the time to get the buy-in to the extra day.

Of the three main partnerships we had in Saturn, two were progressing marvelously, with the third, which had actually been the first created, was weakened and struggling from the wounds of the ART process. We five members of the Local 1853 bargaining team had developed serious mistrust of R. Timothy Epps. Regardless of whether he knew what he was doing or not, a wedge had been inserted in our membership that would widen over time. Prior to taking our "serious action" vote, we had been able to keep the politics within our local very clean and focused on the issues that faced us, rather than the politics from the old world, which were totally based on personal attacks and discrediting any candidate's character. Since those emotional general membership meetings, the 500 plus former shop chairmen, presidents, and zone and district committee members saw the emotions unleashed that would give them an avenue for political gain. Ever since Steve had removed Hoalcraft as our international rep on the SAC and appointed, by this time, his second replacement, a covert mood had been generated with help from Detroit to bring Saturn back closer to the GM/UAW relationship.

Exacerbating this situation even more, Skip hired Hoalcraft as a non-rep eighth-level manager in people systems, which really blew Yokich's hair back. This process was also being helped by a person on our Executive Board who had his own personal agenda. Mike received a call from one of the crew coordinators in Body Systems, requesting a meeting with the five of us on the bargaining team. The meeting was set up by Henry Campbell, and at the agreed-to time, four people came in and sat down. Three of them were from Body Systems and the fourth from Vehicle Systems. The group included the crew coordinator who had made the call, Tony Kemplin, two module advisors, Bob Hoskins and Cliff Goff, who hailed from Body Systems, and Greg Tackett, an op tech from the chassis module in Vehicle Systems. The conversation initially focused on how Epps and LeFauve couldn't be trusted anymore and that the membership was being worked too hard, for too many hours, and so forth. When we countered that Epps finally understood the resolve of this membership and Skip, although lax in keeping his eye close enough to what was going on, really wasn't a threat.

The real issue finally surfaced. Cliff Goff, who was the real force behind this meeting, had been bypassed for a crew coordinator's job and told Kenny Duncan he was not going to sit still for that. The op tech, Greg Tackett from Vehicle Systems, had been passed on several times for module advisor openings, and he was of the same mindset as Goff. All four of these people were from the same plant in Ohio, just outside Cincinnati, called Norwood. It had been closed and torn down, with its product sent to Van Nuys, California. Hoskins was a shop chairman there and Kemplin was elected district committee member the final year of production. Goff had never held a union position until he came to Saturn and had actually been a per-diem supervisor at Norwood. Tackett had never been elected either but had come in second to Kemplin in the election for district committee member. The diplomacy stopped and Goff presented a proposal that would change the structure of the local union and would add four new spots for – guess who – these four. Four of the five of us questioned the value this would add to the membership. The fifth, who had set up the meeting, remained mysteriously quiet. After discussing this considerably to understand its merit and finding none, we rejected the offer for what it really was, pure unadulterated self-service. This was countered with a promise that, if accepted, there would be no opposition to any of the current Executive Board in the upcoming 1993 elections.

Four of us sat there in wonderment when Henry broke the silence and said, "What do you think, Mike?" Mike spoke for Joe, Kenny, and me when he told them if they wanted to tear this local apart for their own self-serving purposes, that would be a choice they would have to make and live with. Their proposal was not acceptable. They sat back in wonder, the silence growing ever louder, and then got up and left with a parting shot about how we had made a big mistake. Once alone, we questioned Henry's resolve with our position and received the lip service we expected – he supported us – but he didn't fool anyone in the room. When election time came in April 1993, Henry was not with us. This meeting was hardly a surprise to any of us, for Kenny had counseled all three of these "upstanding leaders" from Body Systems on their performance during the last year.

Their partnership responsibilities had taken a back seat to their politicking; and Kenny had called them on the carpet for it. I had not had any unpleasant dealings with Tackett in Vehicle Systems, but he had always talked about "management" – how screwed up they were, how you couldn't trust them – all the old world stuff. On questioning the module advisors in his area about his work ethic, after this meeting, I learned that he had an attendance problem that the team had been trying to help him handle and were getting very tired of doing so, as well as counseling him numerous times about stirring the team up on issues that were very easy to handle. Four stellar team members they were, who just wanted to serve the membership in a larger capacity. Funny, when you consider they couldn't do their current jobs. The gauntlet had been dropped, however, and the next year would be rife with politics.

April also brought us our second consecutive *Motor Week*/PBS television, Drivers Choice Award for the best small car. Judging how our cars were being received in the marketplace, we felt confident that this would not be the last award we would get this year. On April 28, our first shipment of cars left port in California headed for Taiwan, with sales expected to begin in June. It was time to rotate the VPs again, for we were long overdue. Our plan originally called for a yearly rotation, but due to the ART process and trying to maintain some level of continuity in getting production bottlenecks, quality, and cost in order, we had spent 22 months in our current assignments. Wow! Had it been almost two years? Where had the time gone. It seemed like yesterday when I came to Vehicle Systems. I went to Powertrain; Kenny went to People Systems; Joe went to Body Systems, which really ticked Henry off because he went to Vehicle Systems. The four of us were not about to let him team up with the trio from Norwood, not yet anyway. We had new partners, new opportunities, and were rapidly approaching our second shutdown for model change, where we would introduce our new line of wagons, to keep on expanding our market share and get people out of foreign and into domestic vehicles.

June 13, we began marketing two models of our sedan, the SL1 and SL2, and our sports coupe the SC in Taiwan. We were a legitimate exporter outside of North America. We learned a great deal in this market that would prove invaluable down the road toward our goal as a world exporter. Sales remained very strong and our day's supply in the field had not increased much even with the two extra shifts of production we had added. This was a good position to be in, when you consider the alternative, but we were still losing sales because many people would not wait the three to five weeks it took to get a special order delivered. We had implemented our risk-and-reward system earlier in the year, but for calendar year 1992 there were only rewards because our non-rep partners were still under the GM system and the merit increases would not allow them to put the minimal 5% of their pay at risk. We were not going to implement the risk part until everyone in the organization had the same percent in the game. The reward system would have only two goals this year, building to schedule and hitting agreed-to quality targets. The amount that could be earned by each team member was $6,000 tops but realistically about $2,500 if we performed to our potential. So a new incentive was added to the pot with the hope it would spur even higher performance than we had already achieved. Only time would tell. We knew the introduction of the wagon into the build process would slow down our start-up, but factored that into our production and quality targets and remained ever confident in our team members to exceed those targets.

July brought the long awaited J. D. Power survey results from new car buyers. We knew we had gotten better, but how much? The initial quality study said we were:

- Sixth among all makes, up from 16th in 1991
- First among all domestic makes
- Problems per 100 vehicles improved 27 points to 108, down from 137 in 1991
- Fourth in sales satisfaction
- Third in customer satisfaction, behind Lexus and Infiniti

The results were met with unbridled enthusiasm in all corners of our upstart corporation. People everywhere were walking proud and feeling really good about their accomplishments and themselves. The end of the 1992 model year was almost here; our ratings were tremendous; sales were really gaining steam; and after making about $600 in the first quarter in reward payments, the second quarter looked even better than that. Our shutdown for changeover to the 1993 model year, for those who didn't have to or didn't volunteer to work, was spent in joy, rest, and relaxation, knowing that, when we returned, a check for $900 was waiting for our second quarter reward payment.

We started our production of 1993 Saturns on August 5, 1992. It wasn't as smooth as we had hoped, for several reasons. The two models of wagons and all three lines had a driver's-side air bag and refinements to the exhaust system, fuel pump design, and structural changes to address engine noise. The wagons were giving us fits with the rear tailgates (a debate that was lost on product engineering, which had designed it). The product engineers from Michigan were living with the technicians and helping them build and finesse the tailgates they had told us not to worry about. That was one thing about us that was really different from GM, which so significantly helped change to take place faster. Here, the engineers not only could work on the line with op and trades technicians, we required them to. After two or three days of 10-hour shifts of engineers building their mistakes, the CAD tubes hummed when they got back to Michigan and changes flowed to Spring Hill like a flash flood. The other bottlenecks were not as serious as this, but they were bothersome. A minute here, a minute there, and at the end of 20 hours of production, all those minutes really added up.

August 20 brought in our sales figures since SOP:

Through August 20, U.S. sales	200,766
Through July 30, Taiwan sales	515
August 20, Canadian sales	10,409
Total	211,690

In slightly over 24 months we had sold almost 212,000 cars. Given that we sold only 50,000 for the entire 1991 model year, in the previous 12 months we had tripled our sales and still wound up higher in the rankings than any other domestic-made car in the United States. Again, we were behind only two foreign brands, in the *luxury* category, whose base price was almost $5,000 above our top of the line model. You would think that our parent company, the press, and the industry analysts would say, "Way to go, guys and gals!" You might even think they would ask the question, "Where are Mercedes, Cadillac, BMW, Volvo, Saab, Buick, Jaguar, Lincoln Towncar and Continental, Ford Taurus, and the like?" Ah, but no. We still heard the same endless diatribe, "The engine is too noisy; they haven't yet reached full production; they are still losing money; it's too early to tell if the public has really accepted them; and if they don't make a profit soon GM may get tired of supporting them." Again, how much money had all the other divisions of GM in North America made over the previous 24 months? Given that we had tripled our sales in one year, why was GM still losing its market share? These questions were never asked. September brought another award, this time from the U.S. Labor Department. We received the Exemplary Voluntary Efforts (EVE) Award, for our unparalleled recruitment of women and minorities. Along with this award came a nice letter from GM. You had better make money next calendar year – or else. I guess that is why the roses smell so sweet. They are always accompanied by thorns.

I really missed Vehicle Systems since I had rotated to Powertrain. As frantic as it was at times, I could always walk back to Inspiration Point and watch those beautiful cars drive out the door, knowing that very soon a customer would take ownership of them and what we had set out to do would be repeated again and again, enthusiasm. I could then walk back toward the front of the plant. It took me an hour, minimum, to reach my office, and it was only a couple of hundred yards from the back door. All those team members who had relocated from the four corners of America, would say "Hey, Jack! How are you?" They would put out their hands and shake mine vigorously and say "What about this...or this...or this?" It wasn't important at all 99% of the time...They just liked to see me, and I really liked to see them. I would much rather spend all my time out on the floor with these people who care so much, but if I did that, the past had shown me that decisions would be made without me and a good share of them would not be in their best interest.

Powertrain was a different kind of plant. The people were great, but they had been led far too long by one of Briggs's right-hand men, who felt teams should build engines, and if they had time, do that soft and fuzzy other stuff. I was appalled that my two predecessors had not sufficiently neutralized this behavior because the mood in Powertrain was very different from Vehicle Systems. This was in part due to the nature of the building. It was very capital intensive, heavy with machinery and automation and not a large number of people, but I remembered when the lion's share of Powertrain's team members had come in, in 1988, 1989, and 1990. At that time I was doing a piece of the orientation for every group, and they were so upbeat and positive. Their mood now was much more subdued. The business team leader, Leon Wieland, was set to be announced as Boruff's assistant in coordinating production across all three plants, and I would have a new partner very soon. But I knew that some drastic changes had to be made now. Leon and I did battle for several weeks and then my new partner came on the scene, Jim Munsil. Jim was the leader of one of the three areas in Body

Systems, but he had never in his career managed an entire plant. After doing our "expectation contracting" with each other, during which we had come to the agreement that our first priority had to be turning the attitude in the plant around, we set out to do just that.

The last quarter of the year also hailed major changes in GM. Lloyd Reuss had been replaced as president by Jack Smith and assigned to the chairman, Bob Stempel. Smith had been the head of GM Europe and was highly regarded for the turnaround that happened there, putting that operation handsomely back in the black. The pressure from the board was heating up on Stempel, in lieu of the ruling that board directors could be held liable for sitting idly by while the stockholder's interest, in their opinion, was not being optimized. Bob was a good man and really understood the industry, but he wore the coat for Roger's spending spree and the handwriting on the wall said he was next. A member of the board for quite some time, John Smale, had become very vocal, which was interesting after the recent ruling. Being the former head of Procter & Gamble, he felt qualified to chair the board and had become the most aggressive of Stempel's detractors. Corporate politics were in high bloom at the General and everyone in the industry knew changes would be made. They didn't take long either.

December was greeted with Jack Smith being named president and chief executive officer. Stempel remained chairman until a replacement could be picked, and the world knows the rest, the last person in GM's top leadership who was a Saturn fan, would soon be gone. This truly was the harbinger of things to come for Saturn. This time of year was also the political season in Local 1853. With the general elections about six months away, the four former Norwood boys had come out of covert politics and into overt politics and were mounting a run at all the Executive Board positions, but primarily they were after Mike. Their strategy was very simple. Capture the president's spot, and the rest don't really matter. It would be a long, dirty, and bitter battle, perpetrated by self-seekers, that would rip our membership apart. That's what the democratic process does sometimes, albeit unnecessarily. We determined to hang our hats on our track record and let the chips fall where they may. Our principles wouldn't be violated.

Production and quality were making steady improvements in all three plants but still couldn't keep up with sales. Our plan had always been to get to three crews with two shifts six days a week when demand called for it, so we had been hiring ever since we split the crews, back in April. Slowly at first, but now with our sales not leveling off just going higher and higher, it began to look like we would have to add the last crew about model change in July 1993. So the Recruitment Assessment, Screening, and Selection team (R.A.S.S. team) in people systems geared up for another massive hiring push and the three plants got ready to receive them. All signs indicated that 1993 would be another challenging and exciting year. December also brought a plethora of awards our way that wouldn't stop until well into the new year. The National Automotive Dealers Association, in its annual report, rated a Saturn dealership the Most Valuable Automobile Franchise, the first time a domestic make had ever won that honor outright. *Motortrend* magazine named the Saturn SL the Domestic Econocar of the Year, for 1993. Kiplinger's *Personal Finance* magazine picked the 1993 Saturn SL sedan as its Best Choice for Best in Class for cars in the under $10,000 category. *Motorworld* magazine named our 1993 SL sedan, Number 1 in the Economy Car Class; and, last, *Consumer's Digest* named our 1993 sedans and wagons as Best Buys in the compact segment.

One could get a big head if one didn't understand that these accolades were given by organizations that could in their next printing whack us unmercifully. It was still rewarding, especially considering we had two more customer satisfaction campaigns. One was on our automatic transmission for 1992 model cars and a second for a trunk lock assembly, both supplier partner deficiencies, on 43,000 sport coupes. They both had been handled in a way that was now being referred to as the "Saturn difference." As disturbing as they were to us, by handling them the way we did, our sales only increased. We had 162 retail stores in 42 states, which were handling their "moments of truth" with each customer before and, most important, after the sale. Our future couldn't have looked any brighter. We had over 6,000 team members in Tennessee and another 900 in Michigan when our annual holiday shutdown came to call. The team members were happy; our retail partners were happy; most of our supplier partners were happy (all but two); but we leaders of Saturn, both rep and non-rep, really felt the change in the wind, both at the General and the Boathouse on Jefferson. The coming year would be pivotal in holding onto the vision, so our brief hiatus was ambivalent with both cheer and anxiety for our eighth year in existence.

Back from holiday, the first issue we faced was one generated by the boys from Norwood. They had stacked the last union meetings with their fellow former Norwood workers, hundreds of whom we had hired. They secured a referendum on changing the current joint selection process for module advisors and crew coordinators to strictly an election process. (Remember Goff's pet peeve at being bypassed for crew coordinator.) The date picked was January 13. This was a crucial issue to the partnership at Saturn. If module advisors and crew coordinators were elected, codetermination at two critical decision making levels of Saturn would cease to exist. Saturn Corporation was not about to have politics determine how decisions were made. The fiduciary responsibility that these two groups currently had would be precluded by law from existing. Of our membership, 90% voted. The tally was that 71% voted to stay the way we were and 21% voted for change. A setback for them, yes; but we knew they would keep stirring the rift they had created in our membership. The general elections had been set at this same meeting for March 25 and 26. Thank God, at least the membership wouldn't be exposed to this ever-increasing old world campaign for another six months. Although we didn't yet have definitive proof, the International Union was heavy into the upcoming elections. Defeating the current Executive Board was right on track for their long-term plans for Saturn.

The plants were working well, despite the political distractions, and putting out record numbers of world-class quality cars. Buoyed by another $600+ reward payment on their January 30 paycheck for the fourth quarter of 1992, the outlook for the next two quarters looked very positive as well in this regard. On January 22, we received the prestigious Washington Automotive Press Association's 1993 Golden Gear Award for Saturn as an organization, "In recognition of outstanding contributions to the automotive industry." February brought two notable happenings. The first, the sale of our 300,000th car. In 11 months we had tripled our sales. The second was not as auspicious. The politics in the local union had generated enough noise from the vocal minority, which the silent majority sheepishly had not countered, that the VPs were not available enough on the floor, especially to the late crew. Conditions being what they were and our current Executive Board changing some faces for the upcoming election, moving the VPs around became the order of the day. Kenny and Joe, who had swapped jobs earlier in 1992, and Henry would go to the plants. I did not run for VP again in March for personal reasons, so I rotated back to people systems with Joe going to Body Systems and Kenny to Powertrain, with Henry remaining in Vehicle Systems. Henry had dramatically announced at the November union meeting that he was no longer a member of the team that made up our current Executive Board (hardly a surprise). The lesser of two evils was to leave him where he was. The other member of our Executive Board not running for reelection, also for personal reasons, was my friend Tony Alferio. He remained a crew coordinator at least until after the elections but my move was immediate.

The first week in March also brought the results of new car sales per retailer for 1992, with Saturn consecutively winning that honor with an industry setting number, a whopping 1,072 cars per store. Honda, which prior to our advent on the scene, had been the perennial leader, came in second again with 654 per store. What made it really valuable to us was that Honda had three times the choice of models we had, and Toyota and Nissan also sold vans and trucks. March 9 brought our next award, presented to our VP of engineering, J. Jay Wetzel, the *Design News* magazine's 1993 Engineering Quality Award, in recognition of excellence in the design, engineering, and manufacture of the Saturn line of vehicles. Externally, we could not be in a better position. Sales were up, awards were flowing in, and our name recognition in the marketplace was spreading like a wildfire. Internally, however, there was considerable discord. Our non-rep partners were getting the heat from Detroit to build more cars. Our reward program had a profitability element we added this year because the General told us flat out that we had to break even, at least. The politics around the general elections had gotten, as we knew they would, in the press, and our retail partners pleaded with us to tone it down. We would have, if it were under our control. All of these factors had a great number of people confused and concerned. March 25 and 26 came and the votes were tallied, with 10 of the 12 positions ending up in runoffs. The runoffs were held, and every candidate the current Executive Board ran won. Replacing me as a VP was David Holman, who had been a trustee. Replacing Henry as VP was Clay Corder. While not on the original Executive Board, he had been our coordinator of benefits and compensation. Lastly, replacing Tony Alferio as trustee was Jesse Rivera, who also was not on the original Executive Board but had been our coordinator of quality. Elections finally over for another three years, the new Executive Board tried to bring our local union back together and go on with the comanagement of our rising star. The losers said they wanted the same thing, but that would never happen. They had a different agenda from serving the membership, they were only concerned about their own plate.

April brought the tripling of our Saturn service parts organization (SSPO) warehouse from 100,000 to 300,000 square feet. The more cars we sold, the more replacement parts we needed; and we replaced them better than anyone in the industry. In the recent GM competitive dealer satisfaction survey, our SSPO was rated as number 1. Sales were incredibly strong, and it looked like we would sell 100,000 cars in just over a three month period. The third crew was coming onboard on schedule, receiving their orientation and training and being divided equally among the existing two crews to get certified to build our product. The emotion surrounding the elections had calmed down and then a Scud hit. On May 6, Epps received a letter from Yokich stating his intent to modify our Memorandum of Agreement. This was the dastardly result of a letter Mike had sent to Yokich's administrative assistant, Cal Rapson, at Rapson's request. Through the monthly ART meetings, we had come to a stalemate on five issues that, by all indications, Epps couldn't or wouldn't address. Three of the five were in the original memo from back in 1985, and two were the result of the 1990 GM/UAW National Agreement. Nowhere in Mike's letter did it ask for the memo to be modified. Yokich's letter ended with the statement "These negotiations are considered a function of the International Union, UAW and not the local union." After numerous phone calls to Solidarity House for several days with no replies, we informed the membership, and over 900 appeals were sent to Detroit challenging this action on the grounds that, since we had ratified the memo as a local in 1991, the International Union did not have the right to renegotiate it without us asking them to. This dilemma would go on until Christmas 1994, because the GM and the International Union powers had a different end in mind for Saturn than we in Spring Hill did. Amid the pallor cast upon us by this infamous letter, there was some very good news also. May ushered in our 400,000th car produced, but much more important, we made a profit for the month.

For the first time since we began production in July 1990, we made money. June 30 would find an extra $1,000 in every team member's pay. Now we had to focus on the next seven months to break even or, we hoped, make a profit. Many thought this an exorbitant amount to pay out for one month of profit, but it was an emotional barrier we had finally broken through, very much like running the first four-minute mile. You always feel like you can do it, but until you do, you really don't know if it's achievable or just an unrealistic dream. We knew we could do it now, so even if we lost money from January through April, we had seven months left to make a profit that would offset those four months and propel us to a profit for the year, at which time we would all receive $2,000 in reward plus a percentage of the amount over break-even, not to exceed $1,000. The money was nice to have but the emotional charge accompanying *finally* making money, after hearing for eight years that it would never happen, was so, so sweet.

We had now done all the things that we were told we would never do. The list was very long on the doubter's walls. For example, we would never build world-class quality cars; we could never make a plant work without foremen; people will not buy cars if they couldn't bargain with the seller; people won't buy a plastic car; they have too many unproven processes to ever hope to run at rate; they can't let the union block decisions, none will ever get made; and last, they will *never* make a profit. These "never wills" were all checked off now, but we knew a new list was already being generated. We didn't care. Our opponents could make a dozen lists, and we would check off every item on those, too. We were not alone anymore, our owners were with us every day. Not just with the thousands of cards and letters they sent to us each week, but they were with us in spirit. It didn't matter what anyone else said. We could feel their trust every day, and that has the power to change the face of things.

On June 14, 1993, we went to our long awaited capacity utilization schedule. C crew was split off from A and B, and we began three crews with two shifts, six days a week. We decided not to wait until after shutdown to make the split, because this way all three crews could settle into building the last of the 1993 models and also prepare to build the 1994s solely with the people they would be working with. You'll recall, C crew had been equally split between A and B during ramp-up and had never worked with just the team members who would live with them for the next year or two. Also, not everyone recently hired would be going to C crew, for we had asked all those on the other two crews if they wanted to go first; if they did, they would have priority. As it turned out, C crew ended up being about one third of each, which is what we hoped it would be. Our shutdown for model change was almost here, and I had reacclimated myself in people systems after having been in the plants for two years. There are no trains home as the saying goes. It wasn't the same and never would be. I caught myself too many times saying, "What if I had stayed? What if...What if...?" Maybe Epps wouldn't have turned out the way he had. I knew this was wasted thought and stopped it because it was frozen in time. The loss of all our champions had left us very vulnerable, and the predators had struck like they have always done and will do in the future. Focus, Jack! Focus on things you can do something about, like people systems today. GM and the International Union were bargaining a new National Agreement that would have a large impact on us in the fall, so prepare for its announcement and get your own house in order.

The 1994 start-up began smoothly the first week of August, with our new model sporting a full frontal air bag system. There were no structural changes, just some new colors and interiors, improvements to further restrict the sound of our engine, which only the press seemed to dislike, and significant refinement of our already impressive audio system. The announcement came that week of a recall on a problem we had been investigating for the preceding several months. We had, in the last three years, 36 minor engine fires from a short circuit occurring in the generator. The number of incidents was in about 0.001% of the cars we had sold. It was another case of not being forced by the National Highway Transportation and Safety Administration to do anything, but rather just doing the right thing. We contacted every single owner of every car built prior to April 14, 1993 (352,767 customers) and voluntarily replaced the generator wiring harness with a fusible link design that would forever eliminate this potential for a fire. Our target goal was to have 95% of the affected cars done in 90 days. About 5% would take longer than that due to multiple resales or vehicles that had been scrapped due to damage. The press made a big deal of this again and promptly stuck their feet in their mouths, as usual. Our owners ho-hummed that this is what they would expect from us and had always received, and our sales went up again. Adding to our woes, during the last week of August, the International Union finally showed its hand as to what its feelings were about us.

We were now at 7,500 team members in Spring Hill, with 6,300 of them being represented. The International Union claimed that it was getting 20 to 25 calls a week complaining of civil rights violations by our Executive Board and was sending down four members of the Civil Rights Department to have open meetings with the membership to find out just how deeply our local officers were involved in this unacceptable situation. It was really clear now and out on the table. Since the International's covert support of our opposition in the general elections had failed, it would attempt to discredit the local union's Executive Board for the purpose of achieving the ultimate goal of bringing Spring Hill back under the National Agreement. Our membership saw through this lame ruse as well as the follow-up meeting in November. In the end it proved to be the same 10 or 15 people making all the calls; and they had been represented to the letter of the law. They just didn't get the answer they wanted. Our membership knew them all, very well, for they had the dubious pleasure of working with them every day. Mike and Yokich had met in Detroit on August 3, and Yokich had assured Mike that he supported Saturn and our local union and wanted us to succeed. Boy, he sure had an odd way of showing support. On the nonrep side, August 1 brought the replacement of another of the original SAC members, J. Jay Wetzel, our VP of engineering, was promoted back to the corporation in the North American operations engineering group. Jay had tried to do the right things while at Saturn but faced a huge uphill battle with many years of tradition. He would serve GM well. He was replaced by Ron Rogers, who had been his chief engineer and who had replaced my old partner Bob Sackerman in Vehicle Systems. Ron had gotten a crash course as head of the plant for seven months and had a much sharper understanding of the impact engineering had on manufacturing.

Sales were still very hot, but our day's supply of cars in the field was climbing. Marketing was passing it off as a result of adding the third crew, but that quiet little voice in the back or our brains kept saying, "Warning! Warning!" Maybe it just hadn't been heard for a while and was reminding us it was still there. Nevertheless, we closely watched this trend for the next several months. September 16 we hit our next milestone, 500,000 cars produced. In two years and two months we had produced half a million cars. Our retail partners, who had all done very well for themselves with our franchises, cohosted a celebration in Spring Hill with Saturn, honoring the fine men and women who achieved this significant accomplishment. The car, a black/gold sport coupe, had already been sold, and everyone in the organization was encouraged to sign a great big thank-you card to be delivered with the car to the person who had ordered it. The media came. Our retailers bought everyone in Spring Hill free drinks in the cafeterias all day, with cake for lunch and free *USA Today* newspapers that contained a full-page color ad thanking our team members for being so great and achieving such a significant milestone.

This was just another example of how powerful our partnerships were. In my entire career in the auto industry, I never thought I'd see the day when retailers would compliment car builders for a good job in the national media. Anything is possible, if you believe. September also brought a call from Mike to me, requesting my help. A crew coordinator in the Powertrain Plant was going to resign or be removed, and he asked me if I would fill the role until a permanent replacement could be named. This is the kind of man Michael Bennett is. Being my leader he could have simply told me that he needed me there and to go, but contrary to the dictator label that was erroneously given him by his detractors, he never acted in that manner. I told him I would gladly go and would stay as long as he wanted me there. So October 1, I was back in Powertrain after only eight months away. A new role, a new opportunity for creativity and away from Epps. Who could ask for anything more?

October 14 and 15 brought to resolution the vote on building our Local 1853 Union Hall, after a year of politics that cost our membership over $500,000 in escalated building costs. Being the most visible local union in the auto industry, we wanted a facility that would complement our status of being so progressive. The membership finally saw through the smoke screen that had been thrown up by some self-seekers and opted for building a world-class facility, complete with gymnasium and Olympic size swimming pool. The cost originally figured was $3.2 million. As I said, it had risen to $3.7 million by the time of approval, but we could still pay for it ourselves without having to borrow any money from anyone. On top of that, our general fund never fell below $190,000 at any time. At last a fitting tribute to the men and women who had worked so hard and long to make Saturn the showplace that it was. They would now have a facility of their own to showcase.

October 25 brought the start of discussions on the economic package from the recently negotiated National Agreement. This was done every three years, years after the Big Three automakers had settled on their pattern agreement, and usually just involved compensation and benefits to keep us at parity with the rest of the industry. These never took very long. They were completed in five weeks and rolled out to the membership. The last quarter of 1993 was disturbing, as I mentioned earlier, because cars were piling up in the field. Sales were still going well but every week the day's supply inched up. Sales, service and marketing kept saying that everything was OK and the whole industry was slowing down, but there was more to it than that. Just before the Thanksgiving holiday, Skip, Mike, and Don Hudler called all the leaders together, and we discussed how and why everything was not OK. In an effort to help us achieve our break-even goal for the calendar year, SSM had decided in the latter part of the third quarter to cut back on advertising in all venues. The rationale was that we were selling so well that we could sustain our momentum on word of mouth referrals and regional advertising by our retailers. It didn't count on our retailers doing the same thing, on their own. So here we were, a month before Christmas shutdown, with retailers' inventories swelling and orders for the first quarter of 1994 nowhere near what our capacity to build was – now what do we do? Many organizations would panic in this situation, but we calmly and collaboratively and with determination decided that we would not build cars the first week of January 1994.

Every team member would come to work, we just wouldn't build any product. Instead we would train, do maintenance, build teams, accelerate any areas we could for the 1995 model year changes, and kick off 1995 with a very accelerated ad campaign. We also developed contingency plans in the event that the situation became worse, such as building fewer units per day but still working 20 hours 6 days a week, not building at all one day a week, and even the possibility of not building for a full week, if it got that serious. Another effect of slowing sales could be attributed to an article published November 1 in *Automotive News*, one of the print media that our customers and potential customers frequently read. The article alluded to what we in the union had been saying for quite a while. It speculated that we were being left to ourselves to do battle with the imports, spurred by the recent national agreement contract announcement of a union negotiated feasibility study for a new small car to be built in the United States and not by Saturn. It alleged that this announcement signaled that we no longer had a monopoly on GM's small car future, as well as going on to attest that every new model we had proposed to GM had been rejected, as well as the exterior facelift to the sedan and wagon we asked for on the 1995 model, which was being pushed back to 1996, due to money woes at the corporation. It ended by saying that, without new models, GM would allow us to lose our allure. One could see where this might stretch concern into caution in the marketplace. The lack of champions had reared its ugly head over the horizon again. The resistance to change was becoming more overt without champions, to the point that we were no longer the only ones to see it. Comfortable with our planning, as well as one could be having no direct control of the marketplace, we once again set out to the places we lived before coming to Saturn. We unwound from another pressure cooker year, fully confident that, when the final numbers were tallied for 1993, we would not just break even, we would make a profit.

My thought process over the holidays focused heavily on the 10 years I would have at Saturn in the approaching new year. I thoroughly analyzed the striking difference between 1985 and 1990 and 1990 and 1994. During the first five years, we were expected to fail. Very few people took us seriously, rather, they sat back smugly waiting for the day when they could say, "I told you so!" The predators had always been there, sporadically making forays in, to deliver a sharp bite, and scurrying back to their holes when the shadows of our champions would darken their horizon. They would remind us they were there, not really concerned that there was a chance of our being successful, more to let us know that when we *did* flop, their bite would be much harder, to the jugular. Then from 1990 to now, the ferocious anxiety felt by our "miraculous" success had metamorphosed into a very covert but doggedly determined strategy, by these same predators, to try to discredit every single accomplishment we achieved, to keep the spotlight from turning on them and their blatant inadequacies in the very same arenas.

This was when our champions could have served us so very well in GM and the UAW, in focusing on why they were not performing and perhaps pointing up what could be learned from Saturn. Not to make them a clone, but rather, to look at what we were doing and pick things one by one that would work for them. That's why GM and the UAW created Saturn in the first place. But, alas, to no avail. Change was not what they had in mind for themselves, but merely renaming what they were currently doing and insanely hoping for different results. I wrestled mentally with Saturn and all our team members' different perceptions about why they were taking this journey, at first with exhilaration and exuberance to a person, and then "arriving" and, in some cases, comfortably settling into an auto plant's inherent characteristics of routine and repetitiveness, forgetting why we were here. This pervasive thought process butted heads with an oppositely strong feeling of many, perhaps most, toward the cradle to grave satisfaction of involvement in system design, development, and implementation. Did these powerful mental and behavioral characteristics have to clash or could there be peaceful coexistence, centered on collaboration for the welfare of us all? How much did what we meticulously researched, the role of corporate formational leadership and willingness to transition positive collaboration to steady state leadership, or refusal to do so, have to do with the daily enactment of our corporate culture? How much of the problem concerned the fluxes of an ever-growing organization and its effect on the dilution of genesis visioning of what we could become and what we were? As the numbers grow, is the vision harder to see? How were we going to manage the external entities, relentless charges to exert control over a tail that had become very adroit at wagging the dog?

These were some of my questions. Unfortunately, I had more questions than answers. But I knew the answers to these questions resided within Saturn, within our partnerships, within our team members' tremendous imaginations and the synergy that was bursting from synapse to synapse in our collective brains, desperately yearning for the catalyst that could unleash this cosmic potential and rescue us from ourselves and our detractors. It was very clear, the only thing that was clear. GM was slowly distancing itself from us, for internal reasons and fear of taking on Solidarity House in our behalf. Hardly anyone in the upper echelons of GM understood what Saturn was all about and had very little commitment to it. This would be an interesting year, to say the least, this ninth year of corporate existence and my tenth anniversary in the orbit of Saturn.

The first week back seemed so odd. I was accustomed to the soothing whine of automation springing into action and team members reenergized from two weeks of sorely needed R&R. The atmosphere that these two forces birthed with their blending was invigorating. For the first time in our history, this wasn't to be. The machinery was here, the people were here, but there would be no blending this first week of 1994, for we had too many cars in the field and this week of idleness in production, we hoped, would stop its escalation. The news we were relatively assured would come did come. We announced an operating profit for calendar year 1993! We had generated sufficient profit for the months of May through December, with the exception of July, to exceed our target of 1993 being a break-even year. Our shutdown for model changeover being in July, there was never enough production days to turn in black numbers. Everyone's reward payment on the last day of the month would show $2,000 for breaking even and another $225 per person share of our profit.

Coupled with the money earned for quality and schedule, our risk-and-reward program for 1993 totaled over $5,200 for each team member. This exemplified once and for all that our hardworking team members would get a fair share of the success they had helped so much to create. One could hear the gnashing of teeth across the industry at such a handsome payoff, but not a word about, "Why can't we get on that system?" Too many were much too much engrossed in maintaining the status quo. This was great news within our respective halls and walls, but it could not sufficiently overcome the anxiety of this idle week, or the thoughts of what might transpire if our field stock didn't stabilize, then start to go down.

Our voluntary customer satisfaction campaign was over 94% complete. This meant that 331,405 cars had been fixed to date, which was firmly on track to achieve our goal of 95% in 90 days. On January 14, Saturn received its second letter from the International Union, requesting a meeting to address its intent to modify the memo. Evidently, at least Skip wasn't in a hurry to jump at their beck and call, but this would not sit well at the Boathouse on Jefferson. January 19 was the day picked for a profitability celebration in Spring Hill. No matter how much the analysts and so-called experts were trying to downplay its significance, we were very proud of our collective effort of hard work and cooperation that netted these excellent results. Steve Yokich was invited and expected to come and also to meet with our local Executive Board to discuss a variety of issues. We also expected the GM executive VP and former Saturn president, Bill Hoglund. The morning of the January 19 came, but the plane only carried Bill Hoglund. Yokich had fallen victim to bad weather in Detroit, the same city Hoglund had just left. Bill was stellar, as usual, and left all feeling worthy of the pride they felt, as well as the pride he felt. For although he was our president for only a year, he had been watching and rooting for us ever since he had left. A point that was not endearing him in the eyes of the 14th floor at *the* building on West Grand Boulevard.

Little did we know that the storm that hit Detroit, raced across Lakes Erie and Ontario, gorged itself on the expanse of open water until it was a raging monster, and headed straight for the eastern seaboard was the precursor of the winter yet to come this year of 1994. Before April's showers could bring May's flowers, Mother Nature's often harsh hand slapped a striking blow to not just our sales, but industry sales as a whole. January 28 saw Mike Bennett and Steve Yokich meeting in Detroit a second time, with the – too predictable – results being the same as the last meeting. Promised words of support were belied by behaviors of antagonism before Mike touched down in Nashville. We had been building cars at rate for the last three weeks, but our field stock was still rising, with the effect of our blitzkrieg ad campaign not showing its expected results yet.

February was spent building to our 1994 production plan between vicious attacks of freezing rain in Tennessee and huge dumpings of snow north and east of us that brought production to a halt, mercifully, on several occasions. Our field stock had now neared 100 days and March brought a decision on adjustment of that plan, for we could no longer go on with what we were doing. Field stock being what it was and orders trickling in, we had every open space on our site full of brand new world-class quality Saturns. This new month also brought us our fourth International Union rep since Hoalcraft had been yanked by Yokich. Bob Farley was his name and he had been assigned to us once before, when Joe Malotke and Jerry Mills (rest their souls) were still here. He had been very supportive then, with Ephlin at the helm, but clearly came this time with marching orders from the current king of the UAW/GM Department. March also saw the arrival of a letter from the UAW president, Owen Bieber, with his response to the 900 plus appeals sent North, which had never been acknowledged until this letter. He totally supported (surprise, surprise) the director of the UAW/GM Department as being constitutionally empowered to open our memo in the manner that he had. Not only denying our appeal for him to overrule what we had shown in the constitution as being out of the director's authority, but he also denied our appeal to have this matter turned over to the Public Review Board, outlined in the constitution, in an unprecedented manner by empowering himself with the authority to do so. Their plan, as we had guessed, was to take control of the memo and write Locals 1810 and 1853 out of having the ability to ever modify it themselves, without the International's permission. The not-well-kept secret desire to stop expansion from happening in Spring Hill was crystal clear, and GM and the self-seekers in our midst had played right into the International Union's hands. With lack of vision and intestinal fortitude horribly occluded by their personal goals, the 30 pieces of silver had been accepted. On March 15, we courageously adjusted our production plan with 106 days' supply of cars in the field. Instead of building 1,100 cars a day, we went immediately to 800 cars a day. The anxiety in our organization was as thick as the fog that rolled across the lochs of Scotland. Now, more than ever, the leader's role had to rise to the occasion with principles and values determinedly consistent with our mission, philosophy, and values to drive this lecherous anxiety back into the filthy caves of skepticism it had snaked its way out of.

Communication, visibility, confidence, and patience to listen would be the clothes of battle they must wear. The events of the last 18 months, most visibly led by those who were supposed to support us and not thwart us at every turn, had worn heavily on our partnership. How we would handle this external bombardment, internally, would greatly determine the direction our partnership would take. Which path we took would be critical. Would we choose to stay on the path less traveled, take the well-worn one, or daringly go where there was no path and leave a trail? We chose the last and brought, at least, temporary remission to this disease of self-service. This battle we secured, but the war was dangerously looking like it could not be won, at least not now. In January we announced the Saturn homecoming to be held on June 24 and 25, with all the Saturn owners being invited to Spring Hill to tour the birthplace of their fine cars, meet the team members who built them, meet other owners, and enjoy a wide variety of family events. If we were not successful in restimulating sales, there would be no room at the inn, amidst all of our parked cars.

The last half of April and the first half of May saw our collective efforts turn the tide, and our field stock began to steadily go down. All of our attempts to solicit approval for new models and expanded capacity were being sucked into a mysterious black hole. Instead of becoming defensive, Mike once again startled not only the Saturn leadership with his brilliance, but GM and the International Union as well. He had, on his own, studied employee stock ownership plans (ESOPs) and their benefits to the team member owners of organizations who had daringly undertook this approach. He had also thoroughly studied the advantages afforded ESOPs in securing alternate funding external to the parent company. The only mistake he made was securing a referendum at the monthly union meeting for June 16 and 17 to let the membership approve the proposal. Hindsight always being crystal clear, he could have, under the union bylaws and the UAW constitution, made all the necessary overtures to GM and then reported back to the membership to secure a referendum seeking their desire to actively pursue this option. This bold move did, however, stir GM and the chairman of the board out of the incommunicado stance they had chosen and scared them into the press with forked tongued words of total support for Saturn and a plethora of money to fund new models and capacity expansion. They were just waiting for "a concrete business case" from us outlining our needs. Throw a rock into a pack of wolves, and the one you hit yelps! Things heated up in the weeks leading up to the vote. Now we just had to educate the membership properly, so they could make an informed choice, not an emotional one.

The end of May brought three other significant events to bear. First, even with cutting back on our schedule, we kept track with a pattern of producing 200,000 cars every seven months. This month we produced our 700,000th. Sales were rising so rapidly, in the next couple of months new records would be set. The second event was so very gratifying it almost precluded words. GM in reciprocating an unprecedented tour of Toyota's facilities in Japan, were hosting Mr. Toyoda himself and the top 13 managers reporting directly to him. When asked which facilities they wished to see, Mr. Toyoda responded instantly without blinking an eye and said, "Only Saturn!" I cannot begin to express my feelings when I learned of this. Here was one of the biggest doubters, from 1985 to 1992, of our ever being any competition to their fierce juggernaut of sales in the United States. Toyota took us seriously now. I also laughed, at the total disdain for GM, fearing it so little the visitors didn't care to see any of its operations. Toyota had become like the rest of the world, loyal followers of the J. D. Power's report and its impact on the marketplace. The General wasn't threatening Toyota in any of its markets but we sure were. It was also the Japanese way of acknowledging a worthy opponent who did battle with them well. I'll never forget Toyoda's tour of the plants; how the visitors had the roofs of the tram taken off, and unlike every tour group before and after it, which sat down for the hour and a half ride, the Japanese stood, straight up, in respectful salute the entire tour, to all the men and women who had done what Toyota never felt was possible to do, take them on and win. The third event that occurred June 1 started off a roller-coaster month with the announcement that we had gone "on-line" with an interactive marketing program on the Prodigy computer service. Prodigy subscribers were able to access information on Saturn products, request full line brochures, and locate their nearest Saturn retailer. The service also included an electronic bulletin board that allows Saturn owners, prospects, and team members to talk to one another. Another first in our market segment.

The politics leading up to the ESOP vote on the June 16 and 17 had no relationship to the "let's work together" theme after the full slate victory in the General Elections. This was the first real issue to test the other political group's commitment to pulling the membership together, and they did exactly what we expected them to do, those oh-so predictable folks from Norwood. They mounted a campaign to defeat the ESOP, totally based on unadulterated lies; that is, Mike had already secured financing with a major Japanese firm, and if we passed the proposal he would take over control of the company. We have the most educated work force in the industry, with over 30% of our members having some type of accredited degree and the other 70% with over 1,000 hours of internal training, yet too many believed these obviously false statements. I wasn't really surprised because I had seen it many times, both in and out of Saturn, over the previous 20 years. It's involves individual high-mentality transgressing temporarily into collective cretin mentality. Nevertheless, the proposal was defeated by 58% to 42%, and the self-serving men and women cheered wildly at what they had done. What they had really done was to throw the last real opportunity to get new models and expansion of capacity in Spring Hill out the window, not to mention the ability to more than triple their individual savings accounts for anyone who worked 15 or more years for the company.

The bottom line is that the mere threat of independent action was the only weapon of influence we had to force GM into a decisive commitment to Saturn's future in Spring Hill or otherwise. Several days after the vote, GM North American Operations (NAO) president Rick Wagoner made a trip to Spring Hill. He very quietly and unceremoniously announced that there really were money problems back at the General, and it looked like an existing plant would get any new Saturn models. Strangely, outside of the folks from Norwood, I couldn't find anyone who voted against the ESOP after Wagoner left. It wasn't solely the fault of individual team members. For over two years, they had been subjected to the worst kind of politics there is. Every day, no matter how trivial the issue, the self-servers stirred the pot with half-truths and outright lies. The individual fault, however, lay in the fact that four years of prosperity had pushed them back toward the "what's in it for me" mentality, but far worse than that, they remained the silent majority and would not take the persistently loud "anti-everything's" on.

On the upbeat side of this roller-coaster month came homecoming from June 23–25. Over 44,000 owners and their families came from all 50 states, Canada, and Taiwan to spend the weekend with us in Spring Hill. It really hit the spot and gave everyone a real boost, just before model changeover the first two weeks of July. Without this emotional release, many of our hardworking folks would have left for shutdown and replayed the turmoil of the last six months over and over in their heads and would have come back unrested, weary, and more confused than ever. What a weekend it was! The entertainment was great, as was the food, our retailers, every public official and politician within five states, but the real purpose of these 44,000 owners and their families was to meet the men and women who built the cars they liked so much. They stood in lines for up to four hours in 90 degree heat and 80% humidity just to walk through the plants, take pictures of the technicians, talk with them, and sign every inch of white space in every facility, in memory and thanks. Throughout this weekend and the next two months, our retailers also held regional homecoming events, attracting over 130,000 more owners. In all, one of every six Saturn owners participated in the homecoming. The first two weeks of July, our 9,400 team members, except those who worked on the model change, roared across America, spirits high and wallets fat with vacation stash.

When vacation was over, back they came with their stories, pictures, and tokens of visits made, to a brand new interior on the 1995 models to build. The biggest change was a completely restyled instrument panel, meticulously fashioned from four years of suggestions from our loyal owners and sporting driver-side and passenger-side air bags. New colors were sporting the exterior as well as new colors and fabrics on the interior. The passenger compartment was quieter and more solid, almost taking on the appearance of a luxury car costing thousands more. The big change didn't come until July 1995, but this was a good challenge at handling significant change while maintaining our stringent quality standards. July also marked the opening of our 300th retail store. Not bad for a company that wasn't supposed to compete and had been laughed at for even thinking it could ever support our original estimate of 250 stores maximum. July 30 brought an angry Steve Yokich to Saturn's Troy, Michigan, headquarters to meet with Skip and address the lack of progress in the ongoing negotiations to modify the memo. He also let it be known that Module II was on his agenda to discuss and where he thought it should go. (Spring Hill? Nah!)

It is interesting that three issues surfaced germane to our plea for expansion during that last week of July. *Autoweek* magazine, in an unscientific fax poll, asked its readers if GM should invest more in Saturn. The result was that 88% said yes, GM should invest whatever money was necessary to develop an expanded product line. In general, the comments were best summed up with this statement: "GM seems to have settled into a pattern of making the wrong decision at every opportunity for the past two decades. Saturn – as a division – appears to be the only real possibility GM has at this time. It seems obvious that GM should invest in its only real star." The second was an announcement from *Automotive News*: More than 14 Asian car companies would introduce an aggressive product plan in the United States over the next five years, with 40 makes of cars and trucks to capture more of the 15 million car market. A third of these 40 models would be in our market segment. Last, the *Wall Street Journal* said,

Following an employee buyout of United Airlines last week, the Airline Pilots' Association is proposing the buyout of the financially troubled US Air Corp to save the company and union jobs.

Last week, the flight attendants and machinists agreed to join ALPA if needed. The union's proposal would cut $1 billion in operating expenses in exchange for a majority ownership.

What is wrong with this picture?

The 1995 model build was going well in August, but the last three months were really stellar for sales. On August 29, our sales for the month was announced, and we had sold a record 31,814 cars. September 12, we were informed by the General that our right-hand drive export program was indefinitely put on hold due to lack of development money. In the same breath we were quietly told that Chevrolet Cavalier and Pontiac Sunfire's export programs were not on hold. How could they eat with the same mouth this garbage was coming from?

October 1 brought the enactment of the American Automotive Labeling Act for North American content, where all producers or sellers of cars had to put in print on their customer information label what percent of the car was North American content. We proudly put in print our North American content 95%. No one in the industry could exceed that number, not even one GM brand. Three days later, GM announced its organizational change of the day, "In an effort to enhance its competitiveness throughout the small car market, GM's NAO announces the formation of the Small Car Group, formalizing a strategic relationship between Saturn and the Lansing Automotive Division. Skip LeFauve is named Executive in charge of the new group, while retaining his position as Saturn president." Well, well, well – the dog would start wagging the tail. Unfortunately, it would be in a room full of expensive small vases, on very low tables. Sales had been setting record levels each month, and we saw the opportunity to make up the lost units from the first quarter, so we proposed to our team members working two Sundays a month until the end of the year. This met with their approval, but in the process, one of the teams suggested we look at asking if we could suspend team meetings for the rest of the year. Two crews each Friday shut down for an hour for team meetings, resulting in 125 cars not being built. This would help supply the ever-increasing demand and would also have a significant impact on making a profit for the 1994 calendar year. Duly proposed, a referendum was put to a vote on October 21, and 71% to 29% voted to suspend them until January 1995.

The last big news of the month came on October 28, when GM and the International Union announced they had worked out all the details and Saturn rep team members, all of whom were required to quit GM with no recall rights, would be allowed to go back to GM. All the team members who were unhappy here or whose families were unhappy here, actually for any reason, could now return. They could pick any plant and the corporation would try to get them it, but they had a list of about nine plants that really needed people, and the transferring worker might end up at one of them. The first moves wouldn't take place until after the first of the year. How many would go? When it came down to signing one's name, how many? I don't care how many would say they were going, I'd bet anyone a paycheck it wouldn't be over 200. Many laughed at my estimate, but I could wait.

November 4 saw Saturn and Yokich coming to an agreement on modifications to the memo. What a personally sad day it was for me, not unexpected but sad nevertheless. The major changes in the proposed memo were that teams would no longer hire their own members; all transfers in manufacturing would no longer be based on skills, experience, and ability but strictly by Saturn start date (seniority); the crew coordinators, three in Powertrain and Body Systems, six in Vehicle Systems, and two more in the trades area would no longer be jointly selected but now elected; our three crew/two shift/six day operation would be changed to three eight-hour shifts five days a week; and the icing on the cake, what this whole thing was really about, Locals 1810 and 1853 could no longer issue a letter of intent to modify the memo. That would be the exclusive domain of the International Union. November 11 was picked as the date for the membership to ratify this travesty. Informational meetings conducted by the International Union were held for all crews, and seven days later the vote took place. The silent majority finally spoke, albeit after the horse was out of the barn, but the vote came in 75% "No" to 25% "Yes." The International Union was shocked. We thought this was what you wanted...it whined. Data-gathering meetings were scheduled and held. Farley and Epps clustered again to make changes based on this data gathering, but the only thing that came back different was that, in certain key areas, skill and ability would take precedence over Saturn start date.

The next ratification vote was scheduled for December 2, and as expected the personal interests had come to bear. This time the tally was

60% "No" to 40% "Yes." The International Union was fit to be tied now. "What in the devil do you people want?" was its icy response. "For four years all we have heard from you is how hiring is messed up; transfers are messed up; crew coordinator selection/deselection is messed up; you hate to rotate, and so on." They wouldn't admit that the hundreds of phone calls and letters they had received had come from about 200 people. They would never show them to the membership, so we members had no way to respond. Finally, it brought Mike, the four VPs, and the trades rep into the process with Farley and Epps. "What is it going to take for ratification?" the International Union asked. Not liking the answer they received, they countered with, "Steve, if push comes to shove, will enact these changes without your approval." The retort was, "Fine. Go ahead, and let's see if he can stand up to the heat from that brilliant move." The response was, "Steve doesn't really want to do that, so what is the answer?" Mike told them both, very clearly, "This membership does not want three eight-hour fixed shifts, or to be written out of the memo. Make those changes and let them mull it over during Christmas shutdown and hold a vote when they return." Well, the international reps couldn't make those calls. Farley had to check with Yokich, and Epps with LeFauve; they said they would get back to Mike.

A week passed and back they came with a new proposal for ratification. For shift rotation, they would have the Manufacturing Action Council (MAC) develop various scenarios of both fixed and rotating shifts and have the team members do an elimination process to come up with the one that would be implemented, but the local union not being able to modify the memo was not going to be changed. This was agreed on. But the International Union wanted another vote before the shutdown on the December 23, and the local union wanted to wait until January, when all the team members would have a chance to vote. This evoked extended discussion, until Farley got the word from Yokich, that he wanted the vote to happen before the holidays, not after.

The days they wanted it held, of course, were December 20 and 21, when a third of the membership would be on holiday – one whole crew by virtue of their rotational five days off butting up to the shutdown. Our arguments fell on deaf ears, with the reply being, "If it's important enough, they won't start their holiday until after they vote." It was evident when they picked the dates this was their plan – the vocal minority would make it important enough – and a letter was sent authorizing the vote to take place on December 20 and 21. Only 70% voted. This third version was the charm, and it passed by 54% "Yes" to 46% "No." As Yogi Berra once said, "It ain't over 'til it's over." Well, now it was over. The silent majority, as we feared they would, had run out of gas and succumbed to erroneous thinking that the International Union would get what it wanted anyway. Besides we put up a good fight, they told themselves, rationalizing that we could try these changes – let the International Union run things for awhile – and if it doesn't work out, fix it. Sadly, they would learn, change will always be constant, but there are no trains home.

The last two days of production being done, the rest of Saturn headed out for parts unknown, with two weeks to do whatever they wanted, and on everyone's return we started our 10th year as a corporation. Almost the entire 700-mile drive up to Michigan, I pondered the impact these changes would have on our partnership: the work we had done to show the world that codetermination not only could work but did work, the future of not only Saturn, into the 21st century, but this codetermination model as well. January 1995 would begin the interpretation of what had been agreed to and what had not been, like our reward formula for calendar year 1995; how the crew coordinators would be elected; and how long it would take to develop the different shifting scenarios. Softer winds also blew coolly across the hills and valleys of my cerebrum, at the great fortune I had had being involved in Saturn all these, soon to be, 11 years. I pondered how my feelings of discomfort were good, because when you are comfortable, you are stagnating. My two boys had grown into fine young men, one off to university study in eight short months and the other taking driver's training in the summer. I had learned much in the last 11 years. I had the good fortune to be around brilliant minds, and like a sponge, I sucked up the knowledge that flowed from their very beings like water. I would return in a couple of weeks and accept the situations I could not change, aggressively assault those I could, and continue to believe in what we could be for we just weren't there yet.

THE FUTURE

> We cannot use the template of the past
> as the predictor of the future. We must
> imagine what we want it to be, and then
> form our future.
>
> Jack O'Toole

8

M an is the only animal that both laughs and weeps. For man is the only animal that is struck with the difference between the way things are and the way they might have been.
— William Hazlett

This quotation has very significant meaning to us at Saturn, but it should also have meaning for every organization in America. If every organization focused on what could be, it could laugh with the double pleasure of exhilaration from going where there is no path and leaving a trail, and in the process achieve success and lead its marketplace. Unfortunately, too many weep at the way things are and spend untold hours agonizing over what might have been when they should spend their time bringing their hopes and dreams to fruition.

Saturn's 10th year as a corporation dawned on January 7, 1995, a decade of existence and half decade of manufacturing and marketing our world-class cars. All of us rested and ripe with the opportunity to show our creativity in yet another year on the way to being a hundred-year car company, the general spirit in the organization was high. There were pockets of doom and gloom for sure, both rep and non-rep shared equally in this human weakness. Many were never going to change. Many would change after squandering irretrievably precious time. The advocates of skepticism were actively recruiting as were the proponents of integrity, on each of the issues we would solve during this year of our Lord 1995. We had "help," 99% of it unsolicited, but nonetheless it was given. Leaders had to stay focused on the "vision," which was what we could and should be. We must live it, not talk about who is or who isn't. We must model and not preach, teach not lecture, listen not talk, manage conflict not avoid it. This 10th year of our existence would truly be an exciting one.

On January 4, our 1994 calendar year sales figures and profitability were announced to our team members, first, as always, and then to the world. The final count was 286,003 vehicles sold, a 25% increase over 1993. Our operating profit was more than 10 times what we generated the previous year. We had set new records in each of the goals we had jointly developed for the year. We had too little time to celebrate this sweep, but it would not soon vanish from our mind's eye. Sales were strong the entire month, and February brought us our 900,000th car produced. Just 100,000 more, and we would join the millionaire club. The crew coordinator election took place at the start of the second quarter, and of the 12 production and 2 trades positions in contention, 9 production and 1 trades positions were won by those whose mind-sets were adversarial. They campaigned strongly on a single issue, they would write grievances. That was what they did for several months, until they really got involved in the daily issues, and now had to solve them, not just sit back and accuse someone else of doing it wrong, or different than they would have done it.

With all the crew coordinators elected, I had fulfilled my promise to Mike and left Powertrain with fond memories and a sad heart. There are so many good, hardworking people in each of the plants, but Powertrain had been the first to come on-line, first to staff up, and it had suffered from Leon Wieland-itis for too long, for too many years. While always being a feisty bunch, these workers were going through a rebellious period that I was confident they would come out of, but many of the hardest working team members in all of Saturn were very disillusioned and angry. We did some really good things together in the preceding year and a half around safety, quality, bottlenecks, and especially team building, but now two out of the three crews were left to the guile of self-seekers. The fires burning and the cauldrons bubbling intensified before they were quenched. May 1, I joined the Saturn Outside Services (SOS) team full-time. I had taken part in workshops delivered to the 12 to 14 outside companies that came in each week to learn about us. I also went on the road and spoke at conferences, seminars, corporate gatherings, and to companies that wanted a personal touch. I have been making speeches for Saturn since 1985 and have worked part-time for SOS since its inception in 1992, so it is not a "new" role I was assuming. I have spent four out of the last five years in the plants, and being in Northfield full-time feels like a vacation. It lacks the intense urgency in almost every situation that arises in manufacturing involving one of our team members. I plan to keep on teaching and team building in manufacturing, so I will maintain association, albeit, I will become a "visitor" to them now. It doesn't matter how long you have worked in the plants, once you no longer work there every day, you are an outsider.

The wait for our millionth car was a short one. On June 1, a dark green SC2 sports coupe came out of roll test onto the marshaling line at Inspiration Point, and the 1 millionth Saturn produced was greeted by the Spring Hill High School Marching Band, Skip LeFauve, international rep Bob Farley (filling in for Yokich, the weather must have gotten to him again), Mike Bennett, several hundred cheering Saturn team members, and the governor of Tennessee, Don Sunquist. Governor Sunquist got behind the wheel and was joined by Skip, Mike, and Farley. Following the Spring Hill Marching Band, they drove down the aisles lined with cheering team members to the audit area in the middle of the plant. Awaiting their arrival was an assemblage of local and state dignitaries, team members, and the press. Thunderous applause intermixed with eloquent hyperbole ruled for an hour, then it was back to work on the next million, as the sleek dark green coupe was driven up to Northfield and parked next to the first one produced, which Roger Smith had driven off Inspiration Point on July 30, 1990.

June 30 brought our sales figures for the five years of our existence to 1,035,156 world-class quality cars on the roads of the United States, Canada, Taiwan, and the many other countries where our zealous owners had taken them. Given that we only sold a little over 50,000 our first year, we had done quite well. Our next million sales would come much sooner based on projections from our 1994 and 1995 performance. We would probably cut 18 months off that time frame. The first two weeks of July was our usual model changeover, and normally only a few operating technicians worked to support the mass of trades technicians and engineers who readied the machinery and equipment for the new model. This year was different. Our new sedan and wagon looked like none that had preceded them. We had been building these 1996 models since January and had built over 600 by now.

The industry norm was a build of about 60 for a new model, with interim engineering work being done during the three to six months following its release for sale. We, however, couldn't ever let that happen. We had to bring them our best at a very aggressive pace, for our retail partners were anxiously waiting to deliver them to customers whose appetite had been whetted by our unique and personable advertising and the unceasing recommendations of our loyal owners. This year, more than half of the operating technicians worked over shutdown. In a mere three weeks, we had to get from 500 cars a day to 1,150. An aggressive schedule, yes, but not impossible, as most of our detractors were saying. Our Saturn team rose to the occasion so well, that our supplier partners could not keep up with the rhythmic hum for the first couple of weeks. With our help, they too rose to the occasion, and we were at our scheduled production level early. Our third quarter reward goals were very lucrative, but it only matched our aggressive schedule targets. Money, however, was not the great motivator in our latest achievement. It was our irrepressible spirit that swirled unseen like the wind, but was felt nonetheless, as time after time in the last six years we gelled our individual creativity into an awesome team. A team can change the face of things, where integrity triumphs over skepticism again and again. This trait is what Saturn is really all about.

On August 7, Don Hudler, our vice president of sales, service and marketing, was named the fourth president of Saturn, replacing Skip LeFauve. Don was also made a vice president of General Motors. Skip was named chairman of Saturn while keeping his other role as head of the Lansing Automotive Division (LAD), the General Motors Small Car Group, of which Saturn was – sort of – a part. Mike had been very vocal about how little time Skip was spending at Saturn since he had been made head of LAD. He had repeatedly pointed out how Skip was only making it to Spring Hill about every six weeks, and the SAC was very reluctant to make decisions without him. Mike was not criticizing Skip, but merely pointing out that we needed someone at the helm, on the company side, full-time. The partnership was suffering from long-distance leadership and this appointment would help.

Well, this is where our sojourn through the first decade of Saturn must end. I hope that these 11 years and seven months of Saturn and my life – learning, feelings, and emotions have been portrayed in a manner that allows you to empathize with the joy, laughter, sorrow, tears, elation, and frustration of building a multibillion dollar corporation from an "idea whose time has come" into a very successful enterprise. Writing this book has been the most difficult undertaking I have ever chosen to take on. I have discussed writing this book with several successful authors and have been duly warned, "Just sit down at your P.C. and open a vein!" I thought I understood this, but I was truly mistaken. I have always been a good speaker and made the erroneous assumption that I could simply talk my way through this endeavor. Wow, not so! It has all been worthwhile in the end. Anemic from two years of vein openings but satisfied that I have told a real-life story, in need of telling, to people who can relate to something as basic as this pioneer spirit come to life.

Before I go, I would like to present some final thoughts for you to consider until we meet again. It seems the automobile writers, industry analysts, and investment analysts will continue to spread the tripe that the only success of Saturn is our marketing strategy. I know you can see through this myopic viewpoint now, but please think about why this viewpoint persists. Why isn't any credit given to the courageous team members who build this product so well that our marketing plan can work? Why have outsiders repeatedly criticized our product for being too noisy and too outdated when, year after year, we keep setting sales records and our owners keep denying these criticisms? Why is there an unending tirade about our not making huge profits in the least profitable segment in the entire industry, especially in lieu of the dismal performances of the other players in this market? Why is there a deaf ear and sad tales of lack of funds coming from Detroit in response to the pleas of our retail partners, and especially our owners' pleas, for new product offerings? What is behind the International Union's unending assault on our progressive new model for a labor relations agreement that is flexible and vague or nonspecific enough to allow us to meet the constant force of change and not be overwhelmed with specific rules and guidelines that would stifle our ability to meet the challenges of the 1990s and beyond? Last, why was there investment in another plant, under the GM/UAW National Agreement, that, from a capital investment point of view, is a wash when Spring Hill has demonstrated by our performance that having control of the key quality elements of our product, by being produced in our own factories, could better serve everyone's long-term interests? Could it be that their refusal to change – GM, UAW, writers, analysts, and self-ordained experts – runs so very deep that they are willing to risk losing a market base that successfully brought people back to a General Motors brand, after virtually giving up the hope there would ever be an offering worthy of their purchase again? Maybe they so enjoy the battles, those that are engaged in them and those who write about them, like the seven UAW strikes against key General Motors plants that cost the corporation untold millions of dollars and market points, which they can ill afford to lose. The historic victories of the past, respectively, whirl in their heads and incessantly urge behavior such as when the head of the former automotive components group, Delphi, stated in the media that the International Union of Electricians (I.U.E.) have much lower labor costs than the UAW and are more productive.

Oh, by the way, the new plant that Delphi is building in the deep South will be paying $8.50 per hour, about two-thirds less than the UAW plants. Now if that isn't a cannon ball amidships, I don't know what is! It could be as simple as having many groups of men and women who need a severe hormonal dump, to clear the occluded arteries leading to the cortex of the narcotics of power and ego. I think they understand all too well what this external, blistering barrage is doing to the team members of Saturn. I think they know full well it is ever slowly driving them, methodically, toward that which they came here to get away from. Maybe GM and the International Union are so arrogant that they are blinded to the data that the rest of the world sees so clearly. Only one of the products manufactured under their system is anywhere near us in the rankings. I have only my view of this bewildering behavior, as do you, but here we are less than three model years from when a new version of product needs to come out, and where is it? It is still being talked about, talked about, I might add, to be built somewhere other than Spring Hill.

We stand less than four years from the dawn of a new century, which should be primed and ready for this new labor/management model of codetermination, win-win abundance perspective, and collaboration (not confrontation) as the keys to survival in an ever-increasing competitive global economy. Yet, we are not prepared for it. America is not prepared for it. The prevailing attitude of most leaders in labor, management, academia, government, and the media is akin to filibustering. If we talk about it long enough and do nothing, it will go away and status quo will survive and prosper in this composting brew of adversarialism. This trait is far from being endemic to the good old United States. The former communist bloc nations of Eastern Europe, Indonesia, and even China have embraced the charms of capitalism. Who are they, and from whom have they learned it?

Our academic system, our labor and management leaders, our venture capitalists, our media, and even the immigrants from their countries, who now reside here yet return on visits, relay how things really are in America. Is there any optimism to be squeezed from a horizon girded in yesterday? I believe there is, but I question the understanding of the severity of the situation by industry (labor and management), government, and academia. The theorem that the only constant in the universe is change will prove true once again. Change will happen for sure, most likely in a crisis, but how many more crises will it take? How many more people will lose their $12 to $20 per hour jobs and replace them with $5 to $7 per hour jobs before we realize that our manufacturing base is so deep in the vortex that our standard of living may be doomed? Time, for the moment, is still with us. Many organizations in America are looking at ways to cooperate, not enough yet, but at least they are looking. We host 12 to 14 companies a week, 48 weeks a year, but that is hardly enough. Several MIT professors have spent considerable time and money on the work *The Machine That Changed the World*, and many others support the collaborative approach to conducting a business. We have our partnership with the University of Tennessee, jointly exploring and discovering new ground in industry/academia collaboration on competitiveness. They in turn work with many organizations to share our collective learning. Vice president Al Gore has visited us several times in his quest to make government more responsive to the people it serves.

I believe the greatest opportunity we have lies in the hardworking men and women of America. They know in their hearts, if not yet clearly in their minds, that what we are currently doing isn't going to fit the bill, not only for themselves, but especially for their children. They hold little hope that government will come up with viable options to speed the needed transformation, so they look elsewhere for the champion that will pull them together, and "look" is what they are doing. Employee stock purchase programs are on the rise, where more and more of these folks are out of patience with a system that continually seeks concessions from the many, both rep and non-rep, to obscenely reward the few. The working men and women believe in the beauty of their dreams and understand more clearly than those who are supposed to be leading them, that their minds are being stretched and will never regain their original dimensions.

Yes, change will come! So I leave you with one of my favorite Irish sayings, one that offers hope for the future:

When the shamrocks flood the meadow,
And the heather's on the hills,
'Tis the time when hearts are singing,
And the world is standing still.

Au revoir, for now. There is more to come, before the Century of 21!